CIVIL SOCIETY REGIONALIZATION IN SOUTHERN AFRICA

This book investigates civil society regionalization in Southern Africa. The point of departure is the study of 'new regionalism', which refers to the wave of regional integration globally since the 1980s. However, whilst the current regionalism studies undoubtedly contributes to a deeper understanding of regional processes, important gaps remain, in particular the relatively scant emphasis given to civil society. This particularly relates to regions in the global South, including Southern Africa. The overarching aim of this book is therefore to analyse the dynamics of civil society regionalization in Southern Africa, both empirically and from a theoretical perspective, through analysing the cases of trade and HIV/AIDS. The study finds that CSOs can be more active in regional governance than has previously been conceptualized and are also highly active in terms of constructing regionalization through framing issues and, to a less extent, making identities 'regional'. Furthermore, the book enhances knowledge of the heterogeneous nature of civil society regionalization. Lastly, it is demonstrated that 'going regional' is only partly an autonomous process and also has to be understood as under the influence of the deeper statist and capitalist social structures marking the regional order in Southern Africa.

Andréas Godsäter is a Senior Lecturer at the School of Global Studies at University of Gothenburg, teaching International Relations. He is also an Associate Fellow at the Center for the Study of Governance Innovation, University of Pretoria where he coordinates Work Package 8 on Interregionalism and Regionalism within the Atlantic Future project. His main research interests are regionalism, governance, civil society, democracy, development co-operation and environmental issues with a special geographical focus on Africa.

'This book is a much needed empirical account of how civil society contributes to shaping regional governance in Africa. New forms of regionalism and the involvement of non-state actors are critical to make regional governance work for the people, not only for states and markets. This book investigates a critical case and provides valuable information to all scholars and students interested in forms of regionalization from below.'

Lorenzo Fioramonti,
University of Pretoria, South Africa

'Regional dimensions of civil society engagement of contemporary governance are understudied. Andréas Godsäter does a great service by providing a rare detailed analysis of both the potentials and the limitations of collective citizen action in regional spaces.'

Jan Aart Scholte,
University of Gothenburg, Sweden

The International Political Economy of New Regionalisms Series

Series Editor: Timothy M. Shaw

The International Political Economy of New Regionalisms Series presents innovative analyses of a range of novel regional relations and institutions. Going beyond established, formal, interstate economic organizations, this essential series provides informed interdisciplinary and international research and debate about myriad heterogeneous intermediate-level interactions. Reflective of its cosmopolitan and creative orientation, this series is developed by an international editorial team of established and emerging scholars in both the South and North. It reinforces ongoing networks of analysts in both academia and think-tanks as well as international agencies concerned with micro-, meso- and macro-level regionalisms.

Most recent titles:

1. Crisis and Promise in the Caribbean: Politics and Convergence
   Winston Dookeran

2. Contemporary Regional Development in Africa
   Edited by Kobena T. Hanson

3. Eurasian Regionalisms and Russian Foreign Policy
   Mikhail A. Molchanov

4. Africa in the Age of Globalisation: Perceptions, Misperceptions and Realities
   Edited by Edward Shizha and Lamine Diallo

5. Governing Natural Resources for Africa's Development
   Edited by Hany Gamil Besada

Civil Society Regionalization in Southern Africa
The Cases of Trade and HIV/AIDS

ANDRÉAS GODSÄTER
School of Global Studies, University of Gothenburg

LONDON AND NEW YORK

First published 2016
by Routledge
2 Park Square, Milton Park, Abingdon, Oxon OX14 4RN

and by Routledge
711 Third Avenue, New York, NY 10017

Routledge is an imprint of the Taylor & Francis Group, an informa business

© 2016 Andréas Godsäter

The right of Andréas Godsäter to be identified as author of this work has been asserted by him in accordance with sections 77 and 78 of the Copyright, Designs and Patents Act 1988.

All rights reserved. No part of this book may be reprinted or reproduced or utilised in any form or by any electronic, mechanical, or other means, now known or hereafter invented, including photocopying and recording, or in any information storage or retrieval system, without permission in writing from the publishers.

Trademark notice: Product or corporate names may be trademarks or registered trademarks, and are used only for identification and explanation without intent to infringe.

British Library Cataloguing in Publication Data
A catalogue record for this book is available from the British Library

Library of Congress Cataloging-in-Publication Data
Names: Godsäter, Andréas, author. Andréas Godsäter
Title: Civil society regionalization in Southern Africa : the cases of trade and HIV/AIDS / by Andréas Godsäter.
Description: Farnham, Surrey, UK ; Burlington, VT : Ashgate, [2016] | Series: The international political economy of new regionalisms series | Includes bibliographical references and index.
Identifiers: LCCN 2015034278 | ISBN 9781472452375 (hardback)
Subjects: LCSH: Regionalism—Africa, Southern. | Civil society—Africa, Southern. | AIDS (Disease)—Africa, Southern. | Africa, Southern—Commerce.
Classification: LCC JQ2720.A38 R4346 2016 | DDC 300.968—dc23

ISBN: 978-1-472-45237-5 (hbk)
ISBN: 978-1-315-57227-7 (ebk)

Typeset in Times New Roman
by Apex CoVantage, LLC

Printed in the United Kingdom
by Henry Ling Limited

Contents

Notes on author   ix
Abbreviations   xi

1   Introduction   1
    Studying civil society regionalization 4
    Key concepts 11
    Methodology 17
        Case selection 17
        Research techniques and material 19
    Outline of the book 20

2   Theoretical considerations   23
    The importance of social structure and agency for the study of civil society 23
    The statist-capitalist world order 28
    Relations between RIGOs and CSOs 31
        RIGO issue preferences 32
        RIGO focal point creation for CSOs 33
        CSO Inclusion and exclusion in RIGOs 33
    Relations between donors and CSOs 34
        CSO Dependency on regional donor funds 34
        Donor influence on the CSO agenda 35
    Relations between CSOs 36
    CSOs and issue-framing 36
        Regional issue-framing 36
        Construction of regional target groups 38
    CSOs and identity-making 38

3   The statist-capitalist regional order in Southern Africa   43
    Implications of the statist social structure 43
        The authoritarian state 43
        State domination of civil society 45
        The SADC and sovereignty-boosting regional governance 46
    Implications of the capitalist social structure 50
        The neo-liberal project 50
        Problem-solving civil society 53
        The SADC and neo-liberal regional governance 56

4	Civil society regionalization in the trade sector in Southern Africa	61

    Key RCSOs 61
    Relations between the SADC and CSOs 63
        SADC issue preferences 64
        SADC focal point creation 67
        CSO inclusion in the SADC 69
        CSO exclusion in the SADC 73
    Relations between donors and CSOs 78
        The funding rationale for donors 78
        Key donors 79
        CSO dependency on donor funds 80
        Donor influence on the CSO agenda 82
    Relations between CSOs 83
    CSOs and issue-framing 86
        Regional issue-framing 86
        Construction of regional target groups 88
    CSOs and identity-making 91

5	Civil society regionalization in the HIV/AIDS sector in Southern Africa	99

    Key RCSOs 99
    Relations between the SADC and CSOs 100
        SADC issue preferences 100
        SADC focal point creation 104
        CSO inclusion in the SADC 106
        CSO exclusion in the SADC 110
    Relations between donors and CSOs 113
        Key donors 113
        Dependency on donor funds 114
        Donor influence on the CSO agenda 117
    Relations between CSOs 119
    CSOs and issue-framing 119
        Regional issue-framing 120
        Construction of regional target groups 122
    CSOs and identity-making 124

6	Conclusion	129

    Dynamics of civil society regionalization 129
        Relations between RIGOs and CSOs 129
        Relations between donors and CSOs 132
        Relations between CSOs 134
        CSOs and issue-framing 138
        CSOs and identity-making 140

How 'regional' is civil society in Southern Africa? 141
Problematizing civil society regionalization 144
Future research areas 150

References *155*
Index *181*

Notes on author

Andréas Godsäter is senior lecturer at the School of Global Studies at University of Gothenburg, teaching international relations. He is also an associate fellow at the Center for the Study of Governance Innovation, University of Pretoria. His main research interests are regionalism, governance, civil society, democracy, development co-operation and environmental issues, with a special geographical focus on Africa.

Abbreviations

AA	Action Aid
ACA	Africa Capacity Alliance
AFRICASO	African Council of Aids Service Organizations
AFRODAD	African Forum and Network on Debt and Development
AFS	Africa Social Forum
AGS	Africa Groups of Sweden
AIDC	Alternative Information and Development Centre
ANGOC	Asian NGO Coalition for Agrarian Reform and Rural Development
ANSA	Alternatives to Neo-liberalism in Southern Africa
APF	Anti-Privatization Forum
ARASA	AIDS and Rights Alliance for Southern Africa
ASCCI	Association of SADC Chambers of Commerce and Industry
ASEAN	South-East Asian Nations
ASEM	Asia-Europe Meeting
AU	African Union
BOCONGO	Botswana Council of Non-Governmental Organizations
CAF	Charities Aid Foundation
CARICOM	Caribbean Community
CBO	community-based organization
CBTA	Cross-Border Traders Association
CCM	Conselho Cristão de Moçambique
CCS	Centre for Civil Society
CCT	Coxian Critical Theory
CIDA	Canadian International Development Agency
COM	Council of Ministers
COMESA	Common Market for Eastern and Southern Africa
COSATU	Congress of South African Trade Unions
CSO	civil society organizations
DFID	Department for International Development
DHAT	Disability HIV and AIDS Trust
DRC	Democratic Republic of Congo
EAC	East African Community
EC	European Commission
ECOWAS	Economic Community of West African States
EJN	Economic Justice Network
ELS	Employment and Labour Sector
EMG	Environmental Monitoring Group
EPA	Economic Partnership Agreement

ESA	Eastern-Southern Africa
EU	European Union
FANR	Food, Agriculture and Natural Resources
FOCCISA	Fellowship of Christian Councils in Southern Africa
FTA	free trade area
FTAA	Free Trade Area of the Americas
GEAR	Growth, Employment and Redistribution Programme
GIZ	German Agency for International Cooperation
GTZ	German Technical Cooperation
HAS	Hemispheric Social Alliance
HIVOS	Humanist Institute for Development Cooperation
HR	human rights
ICBT	informal cross-border trade
ICM	Integrated Committee of Ministers
ICT	information and communications technology
IGD	Institute for Global Dialogue
IESE	Instituto de Estudos Sociais e Económicos
IFI	international financial institution
IDEA	International Institute for Democracy and Electoral Assistance
IGO	inter-governmental organization
ILO	International Labour Organization
ILRIG	International Labour Resource and Information Group
IMF	International Monetary Fund
INGO	international non-governmental organization
IOM	International Organization for Migration
IR	international relations
IS	infrastructure and services
LGBT	lesbian, gay, bisexual and transgender
MEJN	Malawi Economic Justice Network
MCLI	Maputo Corridor Logistics Initiative
MDC	Maputo Development Corridor
MDG	Mozambican Debt Group
MERCOSUR	Mercado Común del Sur
MoU	memorandum of understanding
NAFTA	North American Free Trade Agreement
NAPSAR	Network of African People Living with HIV for Southern African Region
NCA	Norwegian Church Aid
NEPAD	New Partnership for Africa's Development
NEPRU	Namibian Economy Policy Research Unit
NGO	non-governmental organizations
NGDO	non-governmental development organization
NRA	New Regionalism Approach
OAU	Organization for African Unity

OIC	Organization of the Islamic Conference
ORIT	Inter-American Regional Labour Organization
OSISA	Open Society Initiative for Southern Africa
PAAR	People's Agenda for Alternative Regionalisms
PATAM	Pan African Treatment Access Movement
PF	Partnership Forum
PLWHA	people living with HIV and AIDS
PPP	public–private partnership
PRSP	Poverty Reduction Strategy Paper
QCA	qualitative comparative analysis
RAANGO	Regional African AIDS NGOs
RATN	Regional Aids Training Network
RBA	Rights-Based Approach
RCSO	regional civil society organization
REC	Regional Economic Community
RIGO	regional inter-governmental organization
RISDP	Regional Indicative Strategic Development Plan
RMT	Resource Mobilization Theory
RNE	Royal Netherland Embassy
RPO	Regional Poverty Observatory
RPRF	Regional Poverty Reduction Framework
SACBTA	Southern African Cross Border Traders Association
SACU	Southern African Customs Union
SADC	Southern African Development Community
SADC-CNGO	SADC Council of Non-Governmental Organizations
SADC-PF	SADC Parliamentary Forum
SAfAIDS	Southern Africa HIV and AIDS Information Dissemination Service
SAFCEI	South African Faith Communities' Environment Institute
SANASO	Southern African Network of AIDS Service Organizations
SANGONET	Southern African NGO Network
SAP	Structural Adjustment Programme
SAPA	Solidarity for Asian People's Advocacy
SAPP	Southern African Power Pool
SAPSN	Southern African People's Solidarity Network
SARDC	Southern African Research and Development Centre
SASF	Southern African Social Forum
SAT	Southern African Aids Trust
SATAWU	South African Transport and Allied Workers Union
SATUCC	Southern Africa Trade Union Coordination Council
SEATINI	Southern and Eastern African Trade Information and Negotiations Institute
SECC	Soweto Electricity Crisis Committee
SPSF	SADC Employers Group

SHDSP	Social and Human Development and Special Programmes
SIDA	Swedish International Development Co-operation Agency
SMO	social movement organization
SPSF	SADC Private Sector Forum
TAC	Technical Advisory Committee
TAC	Treatment Action Campaign
TAN	transnational advocacy network
TEIA	Forum Nacional das Organizações Não Governamentais em Moçambique
TIFI	Trade, Industry, Finance, Mining and Investment
TUCA	Trade Union Confederation of the Americas
UNAC	União Nacional de Camponeses
WSF	World Social Forum
WTO	World Trade Organization
ZCC	Zionist Christian Church
ZIMCODD	Zimbabwe Coalition on Debt and Development

Chapter 1
Introduction

Since the late 1980s processes of regionalism have intensified across the globe. This new wave of regional integration is often referred to as 'new regionalism', to distinguish it from the 'old regionalism' of the 1950s and 1960s (e.g. Fawcett and Hurrell 1995; Hettne 1999, 2005; Söderbaum 2004a; Fawcett 2005). Many parts of the world are today involved in regionalist schemes in which states but also non-state actors reach out from their local and national domains and 'go regional' to solve common problems related to, for example, trade, security, the environment and development. The number of regional inter-governmental organizations (RIGOs) is multiplying, and they are enjoying increasing prominence in international relations. The expansion and transformation of existing regional organizations such as the European Union (EU) and the Association of South-East Asian Nations (ASEAN) and emergence of new regional groupings, for example the North American Free Trade Agreement (NAFTA) and the African Union (AU), has led to a revival of the study of regionalism in the academic community (O'Brien and Williams 2010: 46).

Africa is no exception. In line with the 'new regionalism', African countries have also been keen to foster formal, institutionalized regional co-operation in order to enhance regional integration and development (Farrell 2005). Following the historical trend of regionalism, African countries have experienced two waves of regionalism, with important differences (Bøås 2001: 29). The first wave emerged in the 1960s and was associated with decolonization and Pan Africanism, manifested in the establishment of the Organisation for African Unity (OAU) in 1963 (Bøås 2001: 29). In this period, a range of regional schemes was established in order to combat on-going European exploitation of the continent's resources and to achieve political unity. Since most of these regional arrangements largely concerned economic co-operation, they were and still are often referred to as regional economic communities (RECs). The earliest of these were the East African Community (EAC), which dates from 1967, and the Economic Community of West African States (ECOWAS), formed in 1975 (Ajulu 2005). Another significant attribute of the first wave was the strong focus on state actors (Grant and Söderbaum 2003).

The second wave of African regionalism started in the early 1990s, partly as a counterforce to the uncertainties of economic globalization (Bøås 2001). One important concrete incentive was the Abuja Treaty in 1991, which was adopted at the 27th summit of the OAU and called for a strengthening of the existing and establishment of new RIGOs on the continent (Ajulu 2005: 20). Hence, the Southern African Development Community (SADC) was formed in 1992, and the EAC was revived in 1999 after lying fallow for more than two decades. The regional integration process gained further momentum after 2001, when the Treaty of the African Union was signed and the New Partnership for Africa's Development (NEPAD) was launched (Farrell 2005). In addition, many RIGOs such as the SADC underwent major organizational restructuring. One important novelty about the new regionalism in Africa is that the institutional agendas and strategies assigned to sub-regional institutions have broadened to include social, politico-strategic and other concerns besides traditional economic integration (Bach 2005: 179). Although trade still dominates the regional agendas, some new issues have caught the attention of African regional policy-makers, such as the environment, security, poverty reduction and HIV/AIDS.

Most importantly, the 'new regionalism' in Africa involves a broader range of actors when compared with the state-centric first wave of regionalism. Hence, besides states, market actors and civil society organizations (CSOs) also play important roles in regional integration. According to two scholars, the new regionalism in Africa is marked by 'intense and multi-dimensional processes of regionalization' (Grant and Söderbaum 2003: 1), where multiple state and non-state actors are linked together in multifaceted networks and coalitions, together creating complex regionalization patterns (Grant and Söderbaum 2003: 1). Hence, CSOs have engaged in various regionalization processes independently of state-driven regionalism, and they play different roles in so-called regional governance, with different objectives, work strategies and relationships with state actors.

In Southern Africa, this trend is particularly pronounced. There are clear signs of spontaneous cross-border activities by groups within civil society, and various regional civil society networks are emerging (Odén 2001: 86, 95). One major stakeholder in civil society regionalization notes that 'recent [. . .] experiences have demonstrated and confirmed increasing links within regional civil society organizations and a growing awareness of the need to build regional solidarity to address common interests' (SADC-CNGO 2005). Similarly, according to Trust Africa, a major African donor, there is an 'exponential growth of non-state actors and the emergence of transnational civil society in Africa', including at the sub-regional level in Southern Africa (Trust Africa 2008: 16). These observations are backed up by a quantitative study of the regional engagement of CSOs listed in South African and Zimbabwean civil society directories, which was carried out within this research project, explained further in the methodology section below. According to the study, a large number of CSOs show regional interest. In the economic development sector, 24% of South African CSOs claim to be regionally active. The corresponding figures for the HIV/AIDS, environment and community development sectors are 15%, 25% and 18% respectively. In Zimbabwe, the figures for CSO regional engagement in the HIV/AIDS sector are 22%, 17% for the education sector and 34% for the human rights sector. Furthermore, in a SADC-wide survey conducted by the Namibian Economy Policy Research Unit (NEPRU) on the perceptions of non-state actors from various countries in the region about regional integration, 69% of all responding CSOs claim that they have internal discussions about regional integration within their organizations, and 48% say that they have attended workshops and conferences on regional integration (Deen-Swarray and Schade 2006: 4–5). One form of regional engagement is interaction with the SADC. In a major study by the Southern African Trust, assessing the state of CSOs from various countries doing regional policy work, about 90% of the involved research organizations, 70% of the faith-based organizations (FBOs)[1] and almost 60% of the NGOs across issue-areas reported linkages with various SADC institutions (Southern Africa Trust 2009: 14). Some important examples of CSOs engaged on the regional level are the SADC Council of Non-Governmental Organizations (SADC-CNGO), the Southern African People's Solidarity Network (SAPSN), the Southern and Eastern African Trade Information and Negotiations Institute (SEATINI), the Southern Africa HIV and AIDS Information Dissemination Service (SAfAIDS) and the AIDS and Rights Alliance for Southern Africa (ARASA).

The research community is not ignorant of the regional processes sweeping the world, including Africa. In fact, regionalism has become an academic growth industry in many social science specialisms. Most global regions are covered in the plethora of studies dealing with this topic, which come from a wide range of theoretical and disciplinary viewpoints. Indeed, the volume of regionalism studies is overwhelming, and even if the majority of those studies concern (inter-) regionalism projects in the global North, for example the EU and NAFTA (Söderbaum 2004a; Ruland 2014), more and more scholars are devoting themselves to regional processes in the global South, including Africa. Whilst the current literature undoubtedly contributes to a deeper understanding of regional processes, important gaps remain. In particular, the relatively scant emphasis given to civil society in studies dealing with regionalism would, unfortunately, seem to suggest the low relevance of civil society in this context. When civil society is raised in such studies, if at all, it is mainly in the context of state-led regional frameworks and regional organizations. This is regrettable because, as this book elaborates, civil society can be a dynamic and relatively independent force at the regional level and deserves analysis in its own right.

In Southern Africa in particular there is a lack of understanding of the dynamics of civil society regionalization and of what forces and circumstances have driven CSOs to 'go regional'. In fact, most of the time scholars dismiss the role of civil society in regional integration as insignificant or even non-existent (e.g. Matlosa and Lotshwao 2010; Peters-Berries 2010; Pressend 2010; Landsberg 2012), contrary to the many empirical signs of this process described above. A recent authoritative book on region-building in Southern Africa, for example, devotes only a few paragraphs to the role of CSOs. When CSOs are mentioned they are either lumped together and ruled out as weak and fundamentally marginalized in regional processes, superficially described without any further analysis or in a wishful manner or called upon to participate in conflict resolution, improvement of human security and democratization in the region in some distant future (Saunders et al. 2012). There is hardly any research about the ways in which civil society has regionalized, including the types of co-operation strategies being built, the dynamics within regional civil society, the internal motivations of CSOs to engage regionally, that is the agency of CSOs on the regional level, or the external relationships between CSOs and other actors, such as states and donors. It is argued here that the general neglect of civil society in regionalism is at least partly a theoretical and methodological problem. There is therefore also a need to develop the ways we theorize and study civil society at the regional level. In particular, it is important to link civil society to regionalism theory, as well as to recognize that civil society logics are intimately dependent upon the socio-economic and political-structural contexts within which they are played out.

The overarching aim of this book is to analyze the dynamics of civil society regionalization in Southern Africa, both empirically and from a theoretical perspective. This is done by building on existing research on civil society regionalization in Africa and elsewhere and through the collection of new empirical data. The focus is on the regional agency of CSOs and how this is influenced by their interaction with external actors such as the SADC and donors. The main research question is: *What dynamics have marked the regionalization of civil society in Southern Africa?* This implies analyzing what forces have shaped the nature of civil society regionalization. 'Dynamics' refers to the process whereby CSOs create and shape regionalization while at the same time being influenced by social structures. Hence, 'dynamics' involve both agency and structure, which are considered intimately related in the process of civil society regionalization. Interchangeably with forces, the book sometimes uses the concept of dimensions of civil society regionalization. The particular forces/ dimensions behind/of civil society regionalization studied in this book will be discussed at length in the next chapter. Apart from the stated primary, empirical, aim, this book also contributes to the larger theoretical debate on regionalism and international relations in general and to the discussion on civil society regionalization in particular.

Studying civil society regionalization

The literature on regionalism in Africa and elsewhere places considerably less emphasis on civil society than it does on state-led and market-led regionalization. Generally, the role of civil society in regional processes receives little systemic analysis and is in fact often neglected when studying regionalism (Van Langenhove 2011: 89). Mainstream and rationalist schools of regionalism, such as neo-realism, neo-liberal institutionalism and regional economic integration, have had a profound impact on the research field. For example, neo-realists analyze the formation of regions as 'miniature anarchies', that is the international anarchical system manifested on a regional level (Buzan and Wæver 2003), in a process solely driven by states. Regionalism occurs when the distribution of power (according to the 'balance of power logic') opens up for alliance formation in order to counter the power of another state or group of states within or outside the region (Söderbaum 2004a). Neo-liberal institutionalists study the creation of regional, supra-national state institutions as a response to increasing economic regional interdependence. The process of formal regional co-operation creates more and more institutions in more and more sectors, weaving an institutional net in the region which is expected to spill over onto more politically sensitive areas such as security. As with the neo-realist understanding, states are seen as the most prominent actors in this process and are induced to co-operate and solve common problems only if this increases the level of national prosperity (Hurrell 1995: 59–62). Last, another important version of regionalism deals with regional economic integration in terms of so-called open regionalism. Here, regionalism is seen as an economic project whose primary objective is to promote the consolidation of global free trade between states (Odén 1999: 174–175).

It is without doubt that neo-realist and neo-liberal studies of regionalism have generated important insights into regionalization processes around the world. However, in the mainstream rationalist versions of regionalism states are considered the principal agents, and only limited attention is given to non-state actors such as civil society organizations. The recognition of civil society at the regional level as either superficial or non-existent is ontologically related to the fact that many regionalism studies, particularly in Africa, depart from a state-centric worldview (Söderbaum and Taylor 2008; Godsäter and Söderbaum 2011). This is both an empirical and a theoretical problem, and more empirical data are needed, as are new theoretical tools.

At the same time, regardless of whether the focus is on states or civil society in regionalization processes, another problem with most research output is the lack of interest in agency in region-building. In fact, this has been a blank spot in most regionalism studies. Hence, knowledge of the 'who' in regional integration is rather incomplete (Neumann 2003). One important exception is Lorenz-Carl and Rempe (2013).

The New Regionalism Approach (NRA), which is a reflectivist and critical perspective towards the study of regionalism,[2] takes these criticisms seriously. It conceptualizes regional integration as a multi-dimensional process which embraces economic and political as well as cultural and social aspects, going beyond free trade arrangements and security regimes and as driven by a variety of region-building actors: state as well as non-state (Söderbaum 2004a: 28–29; Farrell 2005: 8). The NRA, then, focuses on the dynamics that shape the regionalization processes. Regions are not considered homogenous and unitary entities but are constantly reconstructed in the process of regionalization by all the actors involved, state as well as non-state (Reuter 2007: 83). The NRA is based on a triangle of regionalizing actors, broadly grouped in terms of states (governments), markets (business) and civil society (Söderbaum 2004a), and the latter is given a prominent role in regionalization processes. In fact, even though states can be seen as the main actors in the process of building regions, civil society actors such as business networks, churches, unions and non-governmental organizations (NGOs) are highly important in developing regional projects and visions (Van Langenhove 2011: 92). One of the most prominent architects of the NRA, Björn Hettne, even claims that 'cultural and social networks are developing more quickly than the formal political co-operation at the regional level' (1999: 10), which implies that regionalism presupposes the growth of a regional civil society (1999: 10). Regionalism, then, is considered more comprehensive and dynamic than inter-state action and is not reduced or limited to the dynamics of intergovernmental regional organizations. Referring to the new regionalism in Africa and elsewhere as qualitatively different when compared with earlier regional processes, one commentator concludes that '[b]orrowing from the jargon [of] Internet users, one may say that regions are transitioning from a 1.0 phase dominated by technocrats to a 2.0 stage characterized by horizontal networks, alternative models and citizens' contestations' (Fioramonti 2012: 159).

However, as for regionalism studies in general, there are important gaps in the study of the proclaimed multi-dimensionality and diversity of the new regionalism (Söderbaum 2004a: 35), particularly with regard to the involvement of civil society. With the words of Hettne, 'civil societies are still generally neglected in the description and explanation of new regionalism' (2005: 555). When studying regionalization processes it is important to emphasize agency and actors more, as well as to bring in ideational forces such as identity and ideology, hence shedding light on the 'sociology of regionalism' (Söderbaum 2004a).

Scholars have recently begun to study civil society regionalization in different parts of the world more systematically (e.g. Acharya 2003, Curley 2007, Gilson 2011a, Igarashi 2011, and Kim and Fiori 2014 on East/Southeast Asia; Korzeniewicz and Smith 2005, Grugel 2006, Ruiz 2007, Saguier 2007, 2011 and Botto 2014 on Latin America; Hinds 2008 and Anyanwu 2014 on the Caribbean; Reuter 2007 on the Baltic region; Landsberg 2006, 2012 and Söderbaum 2007 on Southern Africa; Kimani 2007 and Godsäter 2013 on East Africa; Iheduru 2014 on West Africa; Godsäter and Söderbaum 2011 on East and Southern Africa; Schulz 2011 and Pinfari 2014 on the Middle East; and Olivet and Brennan 2010 on Latin America, Southern Africa and Southeast Asia). This especially relates to reflectivist and critical scholarship and often somehow related to the NRA, though the number of such studies remains limited. Yet despite contributing important insights into civil society regionalization, the research output suffers from several shortcomings which, on an overall level, relate to the fact that most research on civil society regionalization is affected by the state-centrism inherent in regionalism studies, including the NRA. Civil society regionalization is generally discussed in the context of state-led regional frameworks, with arguments that this process is ultimately determined by the behaviour of external actors such as RIGOs. When the regional dimension of civil society is studied, it is often understood in terms of the marginalization of CSOs in regional governance. Consequently, most studies dealing with civil society regionalization focus on how civil society actors (lack) influence and (fail to) make their voices heard within state-led regional organizations. This tendency is most pronounced in the African context but applies elsewhere.

Kimani, for example, paints a dark picture when studying environmental governance in East Africa. He claims that the nature of regional collaboration within the EAC is inherently state centric and concludes that environmental NGOs had limited success in connecting regionally (2007). Furthermore, Kimani argues that in those instances when CSOs do try to interact with states in regional environmental governance, there is a tendency for domination and subordination by the state, and constructive two-way engagement is not taking place (Kimani 2007: 135). Landsberg is equally pessimistic about civil society involvement in regionalism in Southern Africa and deems it marginal at best. He claims that civil society actors have not seriously influenced the regional agenda, concluding that '[r]egional civil society remains for all practical purposes demobilized and highly ineffective' (2012: 74). Similarly, Grugel (2006) and Ruiz (2007) discuss the formation of regional coalitions and networks around inter-state regional governance frameworks in Latin America, such as the Free Trade Area of the Americas (FTAA), the Summit of the Americas and Mercado Común del Sur (MERCOSUR) and the different strategies used for influencing regional policy-making. They argue that institutional obstacles within these frameworks and the exclusion of most CSOs in trade and economic development negatively affect the regionalization of civil society. In the same vein, Anyanwu argues that structural challenges, such as state domination, impede the ability of CSOs to influence regional policy in the Caribbean Community (CARICOM) (2014). Last, in terms of East Asia, Kim and Fiori concludes that '[t]he role of civil society in East Asian regionalism has not been significant so far. Most existing initiatives . . . have been designed, initiated, led, and managed by governments and their loose inter-governmental groupings' (2014: 87).

RIGOs and their member states can also play a role in facilitating civil society regionalization, both indirectly and directly, even though such support is still marked by domination and control. Curley (2007), for example, argues that the emergence of regional civil society in East Asia is partly generated by the provision of region-wide focal points by regional economic and security institutions such as the ASEAN Regional Forum and the East Asia Summit, where CSOs consolidate regionally and direct their advocacy and campaign activities in parallel sessions. States in the region have also more directly facilitated civil society regionalization by, for example, creating and supporting the ASEAN People's Assembly, a regional forum for both government officials and NGOs (Acharya 2003). Similarly, Igarashi analyzes the inclusion and exclusion of CSOs in ASEAN-led regional governance in Southeast Asia and concludes that the creation of the ASEAN Charter, where the role of civil society in regional integration is acknowledged, has greatly facilitated CSO involvement (2011). Last, in the Caribbean, even though civil society access to the regional trade-related policy-making space within the CARICOM is heavily managed by states, which use the expertise of (some) technically oriented CSOs for strategic reasons, nevertheless state-led regional governance has opened up avenues for regional CSO activism (Hinds 2008).

Moreover, in terms of external state actors influencing civil society regionalization, some studies specifically bring up the role of foreign donors. It is argued that financial support from foreign donors is important for developing regional civil society co-operation, for example in the Caribbean and East Asia, considering the financial resources that are needed for CSOs to 'go regional' (Curley 2007; Hinds 2008). However, writing from a Latin American perspective, Korzeniewicz and Smith (2005) warn that regional networks can easily become dependent on donors, who tend to shape development agendas. Additionally, regional activities are more difficult to sustain. In a similar vein, Anyanwu, writing from a Caribbean perspective, argues that '[t]he sustainability and longevity of several civil society organizations are severely constrained due to the unwillingness of donors to fund administrative costs and other overheads' (2014: 72).

All of these observations are important research contributions, which this book will build on, but they also need to be challenged. The current literature on civil society regionalization suffers from three shortcomings. First, it is indeed crucial to highlight the role of external state actors when studying civil society regionalization and to increase awareness of the ways in which RIGOs and donors affect the propensity of CSOs to 'go regional', for example in terms of creating platforms for regional mobilization and deploying funds for regional activities, but also in potentially dominating and obstructing regional civil society co-operation. Many of these studies have contributed important insights in this regard, and this book will certainly develop this knowledge further. However, most studies fail to make explicit the underlying social structures that affect civil society regionalization, and its relation to RIGOs and donors is discussed in a rather vague and non-theoretical fashion. This is related to the fact that most studies on civil society regionalization fail to link understanding of this process to a particular theoretical framework. This book tries to pin down the deeper social structures from which the domination of state actors in civil society regionalization originates. In fact, it is argued that RIGOs and donors are as much affected by these deeper structures as CSOs themselves. The notion of 'deeper social structures' refers to the underlying principles of social order which shape all relations of people on a global scale.[3] These systemic patterns, for example, open up or constrain the possibility of CSO participation in global governance schemes (Scholte 2011: 335). Statist and capitalist social structures are specifically important here, having a great bearing on global and regional governance processes (Scholte 2011). This book aims to deepen knowledge about the relationship between, on the one hand, CSOs and RIGOs and, on the other hand, CSOs and donors in the regionalization process, and more specifically how RIGOs and donors affect civil society on a regional level. This involves linking these relationships to the deeper social structures of statism and capitalism.

Second, what also unites much of the research output related to civil society regionalization to date is a narrow focus on the nature of a few specific regional civil society actors. Many of these studies are fairly descriptive, focusing on the organization and advocacy strategies of regional networks and coalitions. For example, Gilson examines the nature of transnational advocacy networks in East Asia and the means and targets of regional advocacy through the examples of

Forum-Asia and the Asian NGO Coalition for Agrarian Reform and Rural Development (ANGOC) (2011a). In the same vein, Saguier (2011) analyzes the dynamics of the mobilization and rights-demanding practices of the labour movement in the Americas, focusing on the Inter-American Regional Labour Organization (ORIT), which later transformed into the Trade Union Confederation of the Americas (TUCA). Many studies also tend to focus on one aspect of the regionalization of civil society: namely the more 'radical' regional CSOs, referred to as 'counter-hegemonic forces' (Olivet and Brennan 2010: 112), 'counter-hegemonic resistance' (Saguier 2007: 252) or 'alternative regionalism from below' (Igarashi 2011: 2), such as the Hemispheric Social Alliance (HSA) in the Americas, Solidarity for Asian People's Advocacy (SAPA) in Southeast Asia and SAPSN in Southern Africa. These studies neglect the heterogeneity of regional civil society co-operation. According to one commentator, this results in generalization eventually clouding the complexities of regional civil society (Söderbaum 2007). Two important exceptions are Korzeniewicz and Smith (2005), who show the divergence between so-called 'insider' and 'outsider' regional networks in regional governance in Latin America, and Iheduru (2014), who challenges generalization of regional civil society in West Africa by showing that CSOs can be both partners and legitimisers, as well as counter-hegemonic, in relation to ECOWAS. In line with this thinking, this book argues that CSOs play many different roles in regionalization in general and regional governance in particular. Some are more active and successful than others, and different strategies are deployed for different ends. The more radical orientation is but one of many different civil society approaches to regional governance. The often conflictual relations between CSOs on a regional level fundamentally affect the process of civil society regionalization. This book, then, assumes that civil society is inherently complex and, regardless of which level of collective action is focused upon, cannot be generalized or reduced to a specific type of actor. The book aims to account for and understand the complexity and heterogeneity of civil society regionalization, including regional intra-civil society relations. This also includes analyzing the different roles that CSOs play in regional governance.

Third, equally important to a structural perspective is the study of CSOs as conscious actors in regionalization. This implies taking into account the emergence of shared norms and cultural meanings that underpin networking in regional integration processes (Keck and Sikkink 1999: 100). In fact, in the wider field of international relations (IR) ideational forces such as issue-framing, knowledge production and identity-making are widely acknowledged as important to understanding how and why transnational/international state and non-state actors are formed, how they take certain kinds of action and how efficient they are (e.g. Wendt 1994; Melucci 1995; Keck and Sikkink 1998). Reuter (2007), for example, studies in depth the motivations behind CSO participation in regional networks and coalitions in the Baltic region. She accounts for 'the image of the developing regional civil society as seen through the eyes of the actors directly involved in it' (Reuter 2007: 21). Furthermore, Gilson (2011a) discusses the influence of the perception of an East

Asian 'region' and 'Asian' identity and values in the formation of regional networks such as Forum-Asia and ANGOC. However, research on CSO agency in regional processes is generally weak. This implies that studying CSOs as conscious actors in regional processes, the motivations behind their regionalizing, and how they use ideational resources to consolidate regional formations is on the whole under-researched so far, and those studies, such as Gilson (2011a), that do touch on this important aspect fail to reach a deeper level. In contrast to most studies on civil society regionalization, which often view CSOs as passive objects, this book treats CSOs as subjects consciously and actively involved in constructing regionalization, albeit within existing deeper social structures. Hence, the relation of civil society to formal regionalism and donors will be studied partly from the point of view of CSOs themselves. This book, therefore, aims to enhance understanding of the agency of CSOs in terms of the motivations for 'going regional'.

Before moving on to the conceptual and methodological sections, a few words will be said about the general contributions of this book to the understanding of civil society regionalization. This book shows that when analyzing civil society regionalization it is important to take CSO agency seriously into account, even if it is true that regionalism tends to be state centric. In this regard, the book provides important input into the understanding of the active role played by (some) CSOs in regional governance. Contrary to many previous studies, CSOs can be more active in regional processes than has previously been conceptualized, and they contribute to regional policy-making and service provision. Additionally, one major contribution of this book is to show that CSOs are highly active in constructing regionalization in terms of framing issues and making identities 'regional' in scope and should therefore be taken more seriously in regionalism studies as actors in their own right. Regional civil society gatherings are especially important for regional issue-framing and identity-making. In fact, there are indications that CSOs play a more significant role in constructing regions and creating a regional awareness than states involved in regional integration.

Another major contribution of this book is to show that CSO participation in regional governance, regional issue-framing and the construction of identities is greatly influenced by deeper statist and capitalist social structures, of which regional governance and donor funding are two manifestations. Hence, CSO regional engagement is only partly an autonomous process and also has to be understood as under the influence of these structures. In this vein, first, this book contributes to enhanced understanding of the power dynamics inherent in CSO participation in regional governance. The decision of states to include certain CSOs and exclude others ultimately stems from the dominant neo-liberal discourse. Second, the book contributes to deepened knowledge about the effect of donor funding on civil society regionalization. Regional donor funds indeed facilitate this process, but through their market orientation and volatile funding preferences, influenced by the neo-liberal discourse, donors can also create a very vulnerable financial situation for CSOs, as well as shaping their development agendas. Third, the book shows that CSO regional issue-framing and identity-making often centre around RIGOs as perceived 'regional' actors, which in turn spurs 'going regional'. RIGOs, then, help to foster civil society regionalization and are not necessarily 'weak' in terms of supporting regional integration, as is often perceived in regionalism studies. On the other hand, influenced by statism, some CSOs tend to adopt a national discourse that plays against strengthening regional awareness. In fact, the book shows that regional identity-making is not as important for civil society regionalization as originally expected. Through these three points, this book contributes to the understanding of the interplay between structure and agency inherent in civil society regionalization.

Last, the book makes an important contribution to enhancing knowledge of the heterogeneous nature of civil society regionalization. CSO engagement with regional governance is more multi-faceted than commonly perceived in regionalism studies. The roles played by CSOs in regional governance are often reduced to 'insider' and 'outsider' strategies in the literature, but, in fact, civil society on the regional level is more diverse than that. The book also contributes to an often overlooked aspect of civil society regionalization: the relations between CSOs involved in this process, which should be understood as conflictual and based on ideological rivalry and resource-based competition.

Key concepts

In a broad sense, a 'region' is frequently understood in terms of a macro or world region that is a territorial unit between the national and global levels. Yet regions can also be referred to as micro-regions existing between the national and the local level and are either sub-national or cross-border. In mainstream rationalist thinking, regions are taken for granted and are often seen as inter-state regional frameworks (Söderbaum 2005). Hence, the perception of the region by state and non-state actors involved in regionalization is often linked to the geographical area covered by the main RIGO in the region. This has to do with the general tendency to talk about the region using states as a point of reference (Van Langenhove 2011: 66).

However, if regionalism is understood as a multi-dimensional process and it is argued that patterns of regionalization do not necessarily coincide with the borders of states, then the rationalist understanding of region is a little blunt. Regions cannot merely be seen as formal regional organizations and pre-given entities 'out there' but are rather understood as socially constructed by different regional players in the process of regional and global transformation (Farrell 2005: 8). In the words of one commentator, 'there are no "natural" regions, just as there are no "natural" nations' (Reuter 2007: 84). This implies that the region is constantly contested and renegotiated by different types of actors in a dynamic process of change. Therefore, regions are heterogeneous, with unclear geographical delimitations. In fact, it is the *idea* of the region which is most important, constructed by various types of actors and driven by certain interests or forces (Van Langenhove 2011: 88). Therefore 'it is because they [regions] are being talked about that they start existing' (Van Langenhove 2011: 65).

Hence, a region is always constructed through discourse, and building regions should, in consequence, be seen as discursive practices allowing regions to come into existence as institutionalized facts, which is sometimes labelled 'regionification' (e.g. Van Langenhove 2011). Hence, regions only exist or come into being if they are recognized as 'regions' by people, often through states, organizations or other regions. Therefore, in order to understand the making of regions it is important to study the people who speak about regions, for example in terms of why and when references to regions are made (Van Langenhove 2011: 65–78). This presumption is taken seriously by this book, giving importance to how state actors, donors and CSOs understand regionalization and the meaning they give to it in the construction of 'Southern Africa'.

'Regionalism' is an ambiguous term, and the debate on its definition has not reached consensus. There are some common denominators, however. First of all, geographical proximity and contiguity distinguish regionalism from other forms of organization and integration below the global level (Hurrell 1995: 38). Second, on a broad level, regionalism can be conceptualized as a general phenomenon of regional integration in a specific world region (Söderbaum 2004a). Third, more specifically, regionalism can be referred to as specific formal regional projects driven by state, civil society and/or market actors. Related to this is the important separation between regionalism as description and as prescription. Where the former empirically accounts for a certain regional project, the latter implies some kind of moral position regarding how international relations are best organized that is advocated by policy-makers, CSOs and/or researchers. Here, the states in a specific region *should* put aside their national agendas and embark on regional co-operation for the sake of development, security, trade or some higher good (Hurrell 1995). This implies that regionalism can be an ideological regional project of constructing a regionalist order in a particular part of the world for a higher good (Farrell 2005).

Related to the concept of regionalism is 'regionalization', which in a general sense refers to the process of growing social and economic integration within a region. According to many scholars, the process of regionalization has an economic flavour and is understood in terms of increased intra-regional trade (Farrell 2005). However, this is only one of many aspects of the process in which a certain geographical area acquires a distinctive regional character. In this vein, Hettne (1999) describes regionalization in terms of five levels of 'regioness', which implies that a region can be more or less of a 'region' due to the depth and breadth of the regionalization process. At the first level, the region is seen as a geographical unit delimited by natural barriers and marked by certain ecological characteristics. At level two, the region as social system implies increased social contact and trade transactions between human groups. Level three implies organized co-operation in the cultural, economic, political and/or military fields and the region is defined by membership of a regional organization. Region as civil society, level four, takes shape when the organizational framework in place at the regional level promotes social communication and convergence of values and ideas across the region, creating multi-dimensional regional co-operation. Last, at the fifth level of regioness the region has become an acting subject in its own right, with a distinct regional identity, legitimacy and structure of decision-making; hence the creation of a new political entity on the regional level. These five levels of regioness can be understood as five phases in the process of regionalization in which a region 'becomes' a region (Van Langenhove 2011: 81).

Hence, one important new dimension of regionalization, at least in terms of the fourth and fifth levels of regioness, relates to increasing flows of people, the development of complex social networks in which ideas and identities are diffused across the region and the creation of a transnational regional civil society (Hurrell 1995: 40). This is commonly conceptualized as 'from below' and implies a regional process where people engage in co-operation within diverse types of regionalist civil society frameworks, partly beyond the conscious regional policies of groups of states (Farrell 2005: 8). In this book regionalization is primarily referred to as the process of formation of a regional civil society.

In line with Reuter (2007), civil society regionalization is not referred to as an absolute process whereby national civil societies in their entirety are structurally transformed and become 'regional' but rather a process creating additional, regional structures in which CSOs participate alongside the 'national'. This implies that the regional is interwoven and closely related to other levels and scales, not least to the national level. Although it is often possible to identify a distinct 'regional' arena, activities on the 'national' and 'regional' levels are intimately interconnected. As will be shown in the empirical chapters, even if CSOs engage regionally, they are still often active within a national context. The focus in this book is on those CSOs that strongly orient themselves towards the region and the means of doing that. These CSOs are referred to as 'regional' CSOs, or RCSOs, which will be discussed in the section on civil society.

As in the case of globalization, regionalization cannot take place without governance arrangements that promote the process (Scholte 2005: 140). On a general level, 'governance' refers to 'a process whereby people formulate, implement, enforce and review rules to guide their common affairs' (Scholte 2005: 140). It denotes rules, structures and processes providing some measure of regulation, by various actors, over specific areas of activity and working towards certain objectives (Armstrong and Gilson 2011a: 1). Governance is normally used in three broad contexts. First, international governance relates to a process where the prime actors are states and the objectives relate to the regulation of inter-state relations. Second, global governance involves state and inter-governmental as well as non-state actors, since it is concerned with the regulation of broad areas of interaction and has more complex objectives. Third, 'regional governance', of most importance here, is a subset of global governance involving state, inter-state and non-state actors, which is applicable to a specific region (Armstrong and Gilson 2011a: 2–3). Hence, even though much governance happens through government, and applied to the regional level this means RIGOs (Scholte 2005: 140), global and regional modes of governance are not necessarily dependent on or controlled by states. This implies a different system of rule, with diffusion of some power away from states to, for example,

NGOs, which are increasingly present within various governance structures (Grugel 2004: 32–33).

Governance, then, provides an opportunity to get out of the conceptual prison of state-centrism and think in terms of more complex and multi-level modes of governance instead of national government. Governance implies that the nation state is being reorganized and that non-state actors assume many responsibilities and functions traditionally reserved for the state (Godsäter and Söderbaum 2011). Therefore, regional governance should be conceptualized as the result of an ongoing interaction among state actors, CSOs and private firms on a regional level in which regional development and related practices and policies are constantly negotiated (Shaw et al. 2003: 198–199).

Söderbaum (2004b) has conceptualized two variants of regional governance in Africa: sovereignty-boosting and neo-liberal. In sovereignty-boosting regional governance, political leaders use regional governance to strengthen their regimes and the sovereignty of the state, which may or may not promote the development interests of the broader public. This means engaging in a rather rhetorical game of signing various regional documents such as free trade agreements and water protocols in order to praise the values of regionalism, which in turn enables political leaders to increase legitimacy for their often authoritarian regimes (Söderbaum 2004b: 425–426). Neo-liberal regional governance emphasizes regional economic integration which is market driven and outward looking, in which obstacles to the free movement of goods, services, capital and investment within the region and to the rest of the world should be removed. The welfare and development ambitions of the state are side-lined and poverty reduction is limited to economic growth in which development projects must be profitable. The role of regional institutions is merely to facilitate trade through various liberalization schemes (Söderbaum 2004b: 423, 425). In essence this type of regional governance is policy driven and state centric and excludes civil society and the 'common man' (Shaw et al. 2003: 199). These two types of regional governance are highly applicable to Southern Africa, as will be discussed in Chapter 3.

Having been in an academic blind spot for most of the 20th century, the quite old concept of civil society was dusted off in the 1980s and since then has been used frequently in the social sciences and, in fact, has moved to the centre of the international stage in the last 15 years (Edwards 2009; Muukkonen 2009). A number of reasons can explain this development, such as the fall of communism leading to a democratization of society in the former East, the popular uprisings against dictatorial states in Latin America and the rapid rise of NGOs all around the world (Edwards 2009). There are a rich variety of definitions and meanings of 'civil society', and there is still no international or interdisciplinary consensus around the overall research questions in civil society studies (Scholte 2000, 2002; Muukkonen 2009). The different meanings of civil society reflect the fact that the state, society and the basic institutions of society are framed in vastly different terms by different research traditions (Muukkonen 2009: 685). According to one scholar, 'cited as a solution to social, economic and political dilemmas by politicians and thinkers from left, right and all perspectives in between, civil society is claimed by every part of the ideological spectrum as its own' (Edwards 2009: 2). However, some common denominators can be distilled. In the widest possible terms, civil society is a sector that exists between other established or basic social institutions (Muukkonen 2009: 684). In slightly more detail, civil society is often loosely defined as the public realm and the associational life existing between the state and the private sector. From this perspective civil society is seen as an arena where different associations can express their interests and engage with the state. Although not always conceptualized in this way, civil society is generally considered to be distinct from the state (e.g. Sjögren 1998; Scholte 2002; Söderbaum 2007).

Assuming the basic understanding of civil society highlighted earlier, my conceptualization of this ambiguous term stresses the in-built heterogeneity of this arena due to social conflicts between the involved actors, influenced by critical theoretical accounts of civil society (e.g. Cox 1999; Gill 2008). Actors within civil society can also be an obstacle for development, serving the needs of donors and political and economic elites rather than local communities (Godsäter and Söderbaum 2011). Based on this, the following definition of civil society is arrived at: an associational, heterogeneous and conflict-ridden sphere between the state and market sectors, where people act collectively within different types of associations for different ends, more or less in engagement with the state and sometimes for narrow material gains, which ultimately creates ideological and resource-based conflicts. This analytical conceptualization of civil society also has a descriptive element. Civil society includes a rich variety of actors such as NGOs, networks, community-based organizations, interest groups, trade unions, social movements, faith-based organizations, academic institutions, clan and kinship circles, lobby groups, youth associations, business organizations and more, which in this book are referred to as civil society organizations (CSOs).

A few words need to be said about the most relevant types of CSO actor on a regional level: 'NGOs', 'social movements' and 'networks'. Starting with 'NGO', as for the concept of civil society, there is no universal characterization of what it is and what it does or should do (Fowler 2011: 43). Nevertheless, a tentative definition is presented here, drawn from Vakil (1997): 'self-governing, private, not-for-profit organizations that is geared to improving the quality of life of disadvantaged people' (Vakil 1997: 2060). The latter has led some commentators to speak of 'non-governmental development organizations' (NGDOs) being formally labelled 'developmental' by the advent of foreign aid (Fowler 2011: 43). Hence, one important additional dimension of the NGO is the utilization of donor funds as a basis for its existence (Fowler 2011: 44–45). However, the 'positive' characterization of NGOs, ascribing them with developmental potential, does not go uncontested. The sometimes self-seeking agendas of NGOs and their use as instruments by governments to control civic actors have given rise to a range of related acronyms such as BRINGO (Briefcase NGO), MONGO (my own NGO) and GONGO (governmental NGO) (Fowler 2011: 43–44). Hence, sometimes driven by the same economic interests as market actors, the not-for-profit dimension of NGOs will be problematized in this book, as well as their self-governance, since NGOs and other parts of civil society are often intimately connected with state and donor actors, in many regards being controlled by the latter.

Furthermore, Vakil (1997) mentions one important descriptor of NGOs relevant for this book, namely orientation, referring to the type of activities NGOs engage in. NGOs engaged in development activities support the capacity of local communities to provide for their own basic needs. For membership organizations, the beneficiaries are the organization's members themselves. Service providers are NGOs that act as intermediaries in delivering various types of social services to other organizations or directly provide services to people on the local level, for example related to housing, education and health care. An advocacy orientation refers to a striving to influence policy or decision-making related to particular issues and to mobilize support for these claims among other organizations or the wider public. Last, a research orientation implies the intention to conduct research on topics related to development and provide this to various stakeholders. Needless to say, one and the same NGO can perform many of these functions at the same time.

The 'social movement' is an informal network made up of a multiplicity of individuals and organizations, oriented towards social change and engaged in political and social conflicts, often on the basis of shared collective identities. Social movements often adopt confrontational and disruptive tactics. In order to capture the attention of the public and to put pressure on policy-makers for certain ideological causes, they have to amplify their often marginalized voices through challenging law and order. This implies an unusual form of strategy, often linked to protest, which connotes non-conventional forms of action such as civil disobedience. Social movements tend to become more and more institutionalized; hence the popular term social movement organization (SMO). SMOs are increasingly organized on the transnational level, have acquired a good deal of material resources and a certain public recognition and tend to replace protest with lobbying and less contentious methods (Della Porta and Diani 2011: 69–74).

Furthermore, a 'network', in its broadest terms, is defined as a formal or informal structure that links individuals or organizations that share a common interest connected to a certain issue and/or who are united around specific values or ideologies (Perkin and Court 2005: 2). Of special interest in this book are civil society networks, especially advocacy and facilitating networks. The former contains CSOs that have come together to seek to influence a certain policy process. This network is often based on shared values. The other type of network, the facilitating network, helps members carry out their activities more efficiently, for example through offering certain resources and technical assistance (Perkin and Court 2005: 10–11). Networks are often formally organized as NGOs; hence the term 'networking-oriented NGO' is appropriate (Vakil 1997: 2063). However, as shown, social movements are also a type of network, but one where collective identity and collective contentious actions are more important.

Last, a few words on regional CSO (RCSO) are warranted, since this type of organization is the focus of this book. This applies to all the sorts of CSOs mentioned – NGOs, social movements and networks – whose activities are strongly oriented towards the region and who have created regional structures across national borders. In more detail, drawing on Scholte (2005), five criteria for CSOs to be called regional are proposed. First, CSOs with an organizational form that is regional in character, for example having offices or members in several countries in the region, are considered regional. Second, regional organizations deal with cross-border issues that are constructed as having a regional scope, for example HIV/AIDS and trade. Third, CSOs that somehow engage with state-led regional governance, for example via RIGOs, can be said to be regional. This implies performing regional governance and acquiring regional policy-making and service-providing functions but also contesting and resisting formal regional institutions. Fourth, regional CSOs are motivated by sentiments of transnational, regional solidarity and have developed supra-territorial or non-territorial identities that are somehow related to the region. Fifth, regional CSOs tap into and depend on the availability of donor funds deployed for regional activities. The CSOs involved in this study more or less fulfil these criteria. However, it should be noted that some CSOs are weaker on one or a few of these criteria. For example, many CSOs are particularly weak in terms of the identity aspect.

Methodology

Case selection

The justification for the choice of the Southern Africa region as the overarching case of civil society regionalization is both empirical and theoretical. In terms of the former, the focus on Southern Africa is justified due to the distinct history of civil society interaction in this part of the world during de-colonization, the recognized and quite distinct overall regionalization dynamic and the multitude of state forms with different links to their respective civil societies. The most comprehensive understanding of 'Southern Africa' covers the SADC group of countries, (currently) Angola, Botswana, Democratic Republic of Congo (DRC), Lesotho, Madagascar, Malawi, Mauritius, Mozambique, Namibia, Seychelles, South Africa, Swaziland, Tanzania, Zambia and Zimbabwe. This list has changed over the years, hand in hand with growing membership. In line with a mainstream state-centric understanding of regions, this is the most conventional delimitation of Southern Africa in current research, but there are also other informal and dynamic sub-regions within this definition. Civil society interactions do not always follow the membership of inter-governmental regional organizations. Therefore, in line with the social constructivist argument that the hegemonic conceptualization of regions is always in flux and constantly contested, our definition of Southern Africa should not be taken for granted.

The choice of Southern Africa is further motivated by the fact that, compared with other regions, there is a lack of studies on African regionalism in general and civil society regionalization in particular. Mainstream, rationalist regionalism theories have mostly been developed in a Western European context, and when exported and applied to other non-European regions the main focus has been on North America and the Asia-Pacific (Söderbaum 2004a; Baez, Söderbaum et al. 2014). As shown, the emerging research output in terms of civil society regionalization partly follows this trend. In comparison with, for example, South-East Asia and Latin America, which get increasing attention, there are still few studies on civil society regionalization in African sub-regions. The southern part of Africa is particularly under-researched in this sense. This greatly warrants a thorough study on civil society regionalization in Southern Africa.

Furthermore, choosing the most suitable kind of sub-cases for analyzing the overall case of civil society regionalization in Southern Africa is not easy. George and Bennett bring up two important criteria for case selection. First, the cases should be of relevance to the research objective of the study and, second, provide variation (2005: 83). Before further discussing these two points in relation to this book, it should be noted that the choice of cases is made on empirical grounds and assumes the generally accepted issue areas, also referred to as 'sectors', among CSOs, donors and policy-makers on the development scene. Among a vast number of such sectors, the trade and HIV/AIDS sectors were chosen.[4] In terms of the first criterion, these sub-cases are considered most suitable for studying the overall case of civil society regionalization in Southern Africa in which they are embedded. In these cases, organizational and issue-related boundaries are particularly solid, which makes it easy to tease out relevant CSOs. Regional co-operation in these sectors also appears to be rich, a prerequisite to understanding regional co-operation. As indicated, according to my database study, CSOs dealing with HIV/AIDS and economic development (of which trade is central) issues in particular 'go regional'. As will be shown later in the book, the involvement of donors in these sectors is also high. In fact, donor support to civil society regionalization generally tends to focus on CSOs dealing with HIV/AIDS and trade issues. Hence, in order to capture the CSO–donor dynamics, these sectors are a good choice. CSOs related to HIV/AIDS and trade also tend to be fairly involved in regional governance, which is important due to the fact that this book has great interest in RIGO–civil society relations. Furthermore, in terms of the second criterion, variation, these sectors seem to be rather heterogeneous, with representation from different types of CSO, such as advocacy and service-providing NGOs and social movements. The different configurations of regional civil society in the two issue areas, producing different forms of regionalization dynamics, facilitate comparison. This is also related to the fact that CSOs seem to play different roles in regional governance in the trade and HIV/AIDS areas respectively. All in all, these sub-cases share some fundamental common features, such as the type of actors involved and the strategies used for regional co-operation, but nevertheless display reasonably different regionalization dynamics, which makes them what Yin calls 'logical subunits' (2009: 50).

Furthermore, in terms of the theoretical rationale for the choice of these sub-cases, one serious gap in the study of civil society regionalization is neglect of the internal motivations of CSOs to engage regionally. The choice of the HIV/AIDS and trade sectors is warranted by the importance of ideas, such as issue-framing, within civil society regionalization in these sectors. In order to be able to contribute to theory-building and to strengthen theoretical understanding of the role of non-state actors in the study of regionalization, regional CSOs in the trade and HIV/AIDS sectors provide important empirical data about issue-framing and, to a less extent, identity-making.

Research techniques and material

For a valid and comprehensive analysis of the regionalization of civil society, a variety of perspectives need to be included: insider views, that is CSOs themselves, as well as external stakeholders such as donors and RIGOs and outsider views, such as other researchers (e.g. Heinrich 2004: 25–26). The material in this book is both of a primary and secondary nature. The main primary sources are interviews and various documents from CSOs, RIGOs and donors, such as annual reports, policy documents, information brochures and Internet resources. The main secondary sources consist of academic books and articles, research reports, newsletters (often electronic) and evaluations. As already mentioned, in general there is a lack of research and hence reliable data on civil society regionalization in Southern Africa. Therefore, most data had to be collected by myself.

The bulk of the field research for this book took place during two major trips to Southern Africa in 2008 and 2009. Supplementary interviews were also conducted in Sweden and Norway in 2012. Sixty-four semi-structured interviews were carried out with representatives from regional CSOs in the trade and HIV/AIDS issue areas, some of their national members and partners, other regionally active CSOs, various SADC institutions, research institutes and foreign donors involved in regional integration. Also, some complementary information was received through e-mail. Semi-structured interviewing suited this research project well. This type of interview technique is generally used in qualitative studies and in the field of social movement/NGO research in particular, where the goal is to explore and/or interpret complex social events and processes (Blee and Taylor 2002: 93) such as civil society regionalization. Furthermore, there is a rich flora of primary civil society, RIGO and donor written material. Reports and participant lists from regional civil society, donor and SADC workshops, conferences and campaigns, e-mail communication, regional CSO e-mail lists, CSOs' and donors' annual reports, strategic plans, evaluations and statements were collected and analyzed (see the reference list for further details).

Last, a small statistical analysis of CSO directories in South Africa, Tanzania and Zimbabwe was carried out in order to present figures about the percentage of CSOs regionally active in relation to the total number of CSOs listed. This gives an indication of the magnitude of the regionalization process. The databases were PRODDER in South Africa, the CSO Directory in Tanzania and Kubatana in Zimbabwe. In total, 3,941 CSOs from various sectors were counted and analyzed: 1,386 in South Africa, 2,305 in Tanzania and 250 in Zimbabwe. The targeted sectors were 'economic development', 'environment', 'education', 'HIV/AIDS', 'community development', 'health' and 'human rights'. Various regional characteristics of CSOs were analyzed in terms of the information given in the databases. More specifically, CSOs listed as having 'regional' geographical scope, activities, target groups and/or objectives were counted as regionally engaged.[5]

Outline of the book

Arguing that most theoretical understanding of civil society lacks an interest in the agency of CSOs, Chapter 2 brings in social constructivist thinking, which highlights ideational mechanisms such as issue-framing and identity-making. The chapter also argues that the centrality of statist-capitalist social structures related to world order is important to understand civil society regionalization, in line with critical theoretical theory-building. The chapter then presents the theoretical framework, which is built on five dimensions: relations between IGOs and CSOs, relations between donors and CSOs, relations between CSOs, CSOs issue-framing and CSOs and identity-making.

Chapter 3 situates the process of civil society regionalization within the statist-capitalist social order in Southern Africa. The chapter shows how deeper statist and capitalist social structures, emanating from the world order, are manifested in widespread state authoritarianism, neo-liberalism and state domination of civil society on a national level and SADC-led sovereignty-boosting and neo-liberal regional governance on regional level.

In Chapters 4 and 5, the two empirical chapters, the five dimensions of civil society regionalization are analyzed in terms of the trade and HIV/AIDS sectors respectively. The chapters are structured in a similar way. In essence, they discuss the influence on civil society regionalization first of the interaction between CSOs and SADC, CSOs and donors and between CSOs and, second, the internal motivations of CSOs to 'go regional' in terms of issue-framing and identity-making.

In the concluding Chapter 6, the two cases of civil society regionalization in the trade and HIV/AIDS sectors are compared in order to present a more overall picture of civil society regionalization in Southern Africa. The chapter, first, discusses the dynamics of civil society regionalization, analyzing similarities, and to a less extent differences, between the cases. Second, the chapter discusses the strength of CSO regional engagement. It will be argued that in terms of the sample of CSOs in this study and the specific five ways in which CSOs can be considered 'regional', civil society regionalization is quite a strong process. However, there are also many problems related to 'going regional', discussed next. Finally, remaining research areas are discussed.

Notes

1 FBOs are development-oriented organizations that are based on religious beliefs.
2 For an overview of the NRA, see Hettne et al. (1999), Söderbaum and Shaw (2003), Söderbaum (2004a), Farrell (2005) and Van Langenhove (2011).
3 Social structures can also operate on other scales. For example, many indigenous cultures have structures that do not operate beyond local spaces.
4 The words 'sector', 'case' and 'sub-case' are used interchangeably throughout the book. This implies that, when it is not otherwise stated, 'case' is referred to as the trade or HIV sector.
5 See www.prodder.org.za/, www.csodirectory.or.tz/ and www.kubatana.net/html/dir/dir_cont.asp for further details about these directories.

Chapter 2
Theoretical considerations

The importance of social structure and agency for the study of civil society

As indicated in the previous chapter, the role of agency in the understanding of civil society is often missing in contemporary analysis. This book attempts to somewhat fill this gap. Civil society actors must be studied in their own right and not only in terms of the functions they perform with regards to, for example, substituting for the reduced welfare state or contesting the capitalist order. This implies the importance of understanding how CSOs are formed and by what means; that is the process of group formation, in line with social constructivist scholars such as Keck and Sikkink (1998). If we do not deepen the understanding of the construction of civil society actors, in line with social constructivist thinking, it is then difficult to comprehend internal civil society dynamics and civil society's relation to external actors – key focus areas of this book. However, as indicated earlier, CSO agency never takes place in isolation but is always influenced by social structures. Conflicts and battles within the arena of civil society, as well as the complex relations between civil society and state and donor actors respectively, are ultimately influenced by the underlying capitalist and statist social structures.

Hence, the understanding of civil society dynamics, regardless of whether they are taking place on the local, national, regional or global level, needs to take into account the operation of these structures. This is something that is recognized by critical theoretical perspectives on civil society, touched upon in the previous and discussed further in this section. Agency and social structure will now be discussed in more length, starting with the latter.

Social structures establish a fundamental ordering framework for the actions of and interrelations between actors on various societal levels, in the sense that they influence how actors understand their interests and identities. Social structures affect international actors just as much as they affect local and national ones. Therefore, in a globalized world, social structures are seen as features of the world order (Scholte 1993). Actors are normally but not always affected by social structures in different ways. Being a state or non-state actor, the class or gender a certain actor represents and the values and ideologies adhered to determine its position within those social structures (Scholte 2011). Therefore, it is argued here that studying civil society, including the regional level, without relating it to overarching social structures is difficult.

24 *Theoretical considerations*

The important role of social structures in international relations is addressed by a range of different theoretical schools, of which neo-realism and critical theory are highlighted in this book.[1] Neo-realists conceptualize power structures within the auspices of a state-centric anarchic world order in which states are seen as the most powerful actors, pursuing their material interests *vis-à-vis* other states, with some states dominating others because of greater military and economic strength (e.g. Gilpin 1987; Waltz 1988). According to one commentator, states 'continue to run the world' (Hawthorn 2000: 196). On the other hand, critical theory emphasizes global capitalist structures, where some privileged classes, states and CSOs dominate other less privileged ones due to the mechanisms of the capitalist world order. Inter-state hegemony plays an important role in this process, in which international institutions and hegemonic states set the rules for the maintenance of the world order (e.g. Cox 1996; Gill 2008).

Neo-realism has two major shortcomings: the focus on states as the only actors that matter in world order and the narrow perception of hegemony and power structures. In terms of the former, it is only recently that neo-realists have started to acknowledge the existence of transnational civil society organizations and their ability to shift political issues partly away from the state (Lamy 2005: 219). However, this is greatly downplayed in their analysis of the world order and is far from representing a theory of global civil society. Second, neo-realists have a strict territorialist approach to power which reduces hierarchies in world affairs to relations between countries, for example in terms of north–south divides, bipolar camps and the hegemony of a leading state (Scholte 2012). Hence, neo-realists focus on the relational power of hegemonic states (Strange 1994: 24). Instead, it is argued in this book that international relations are governed by structural power which ultimately emanates from the capitalist system. In terms of interaction within global and regional governance frameworks, for example, structures of power need to be understood more broadly than in traditional realist paradigms (e.g. Godsäter and Söderbaum 2011; Scholte 2011, 2012). In line with Strange (1994), structural power is conceived of as the power to shape the structures of the global political economy within which not only states and their international institutions but also economic enterprises, civil society organizations and social groups such as classes operate. This implies a more multi-faceted understanding of social structures in world politics besides state power that takes seriously the multitude of different types of state and non-state actors in global politics which are operating on a range of different levels.

Critical theory, especially Coxian Critical Theory (CCT), influenced by the writings of Robert Cox (e.g. Leysens 2001, 2008), delivers such a broad understanding of structure. According to CCT, 'structure' is perceived in terms of 'historical structure', a kind of social meta-structure related to a particular historical epoch (the current one being modern capitalism). Historical structure is often referred to as a framework for action, implying that all social action has to be understood within this structure (Leysens 2008: 48). Any historical structure is made up of three interrelated components: material capabilities, ideas and institutions. Material capabilities depict the productive and also destructive potential of the historical structure in terms of the overall technological and organizational capabilities, natural resources, industries, armament and wealth that manage these (Cox 1981). This aspect of historical structure is not directly relevant for this book and will not be further discussed. On the other hand, ideas and institutions are highly relevant here. There are broadly two kinds of ideas: inter-subjective meanings and collective images of social order. The former implies commonly shared popular notions and social discourses of the nature of social relations, for example the notion that people are organized and commanded by states (Cox 1981)[2] or the ideology of 'free trade' inherent in the neo-liberal discourse (Leysens 2001: 225), that influence habits and expectations of behaviour. Collective images of social order are more specific notions held by different popular groups, which may differ and stand in opposition to each other (Cox 1981). However, this understanding of 'ideas' is not used in the theoretical framework to come. Hence, in this book, when discussing structural influence on civil society regionalization, ideas in terms of more general inter-subjective meanings are referred to. Last, in CCT institutions, often linked to the state, are seen as instruments for maintaining a specific hegemonic order, promoting and reproducing particular images of this order. Institutions always reflect the prevailing power relations inherent in the world order (Cox 1981). International institutions linked to IGOs are particularly important. The dominant ideas and institutions, derived from the current capitalist mode of production, determine the general forms of behaviour for states and those forces of civil society that act across national boundaries (Cox 1983). In essence, together with material capabilities (not discussed here), ideas and institutions make up the structure of the current hegemonic world order (Taylor 2001). From this it should be evident that CCT's understanding of social structure is more eclectic than the one delivered by neo-realists and more suitable for this book. CCT's understanding of structure implies acknowledging both state and non-state actors, even though the former is seen as most prominent. In highlighting institutions and ideas it also brings up both material and ideational structural aspects of world order. The power of social structures is indeed important to include in the understanding of international relations.

However, actors themselves and their actions greatly matter (Scholte 2012), something which is largely overlooked by critical theorists and other structurally oriented scholars such as Wallerstein (2004a, 2004b). Critical theorists such as Cox do not get to the internal motivations behind the formation of various transnational civil society alliances (Grovogui and Leonard 2008) and therefore devote little attention to how civil society actors actually operate. In the social constructivist camp it is widely argued that CSOs, such as TANs, do not emerge solely in connection with structural changes of some sort but are also actively created by people themselves (e.g. Keck and Sikkink 1998). The actor-perspective is therefore paramount. This implies that the study of how actors are formed, in this book regional CSOs, and the process around this formation is important. There are several theories which focus on civil society agency, of which two are highlighted here:

resource mobilization theory (RMT) within broader social movement research and social constructivist theories dealing with the ideational construction of so-called new social movements and transnational advocacy networks.[3]

The idea that civil society actors are driven by material incentives and are rational actors engaged in instrumental action to secure material resources is an essential point of departure for RMT (e.g. McCarthy and Zald 1977; Jenkins 1983). RMT examines the variety of resources that must be mobilized for social movements and other collective actors to be sustained, and the flow of resources toward and away from specific social movements is conceptualized in terms of the liberal idea of supply and demand (McCarthy and Zald 1977). It is argued that collective actors differ in terms of the resources they command, their ability to make resources available and how skilled they are in using their resources effectively (Klandermans and Staggenborg 2002: x). This explains why certain movements persist and others perish. All in all, agency is understood as a rational and adaptive response to the benefits and costs of different types of action (Jenkins 1983; Buechler 1995), for example what resources should be mobilized from whom and what tactics should be used to achieve what objectives. However, RMT has been widely criticized for an obsession with material resources and a one-dimensional view of CSOs as first and foremost rational actors acting in accordance with the utilitarian economic model, neglecting norm creation, identity-making and other cultural processes (e.g. Buechler 1993; Fantasia and Hirsch 1995; Taylor and Whittier 1995; Klandermans and Staggenborg 2002). According to Fantasia and Hirsch, 'resource mobilization has not been of much use in understanding the subjectivity and inter-subjectivity of movement participants or the cultural dynamics of movement processes' (1995: 144). As others have pointed out, in fact '[s]ymbols, rituals, patterns of affective orientation, values, discourse, and language – to mention only a few elements of culture – have always been part and parcel of social movements' (Johnston and Klandermans 1995: 20).

RMT is at odds with the meta-theoretical constructivist approach towards agency adopted in this book, which is informed by the inter-linkage between material incentives and ideational forces such as norms and identities. As underlined earlier, while not denying that material interests exist, these are also always interpreted and given meaning by social actors. Indeed, actors' interests, motives, ideas and identities are not necessarily exogenously given and structurally determined (for example by foreign donors), which more materialistically inclined theories such as RMT and critical theory claim, but are also socially constructed by reflective actors (e.g. Buechler 1995; Taylor and Whittier 1995; Söderbaum 2004a).

Even though material aspects such as the availability of donor funds and the behaviour of international institutions do indeed affect the transnational mobilization of civil society, constructivists argue that ideational forces are equally important to understanding how and why actors are formed, what kinds of action are taken and how efficient these actions are (e.g. Wendt 1994; Keck and Sikkink 1998; Risse 2002). This directs attention to the role of ideas, norms, identities and social understanding in shaping actor behaviour (Chandler 2004: 30; O'Brien and

Williams 2010: 36). This is in line with CCT, which, as was shown in the previous section, acknowledges the role of ideas in the reproduction of the world order. However, due to the general neglect of studying CSO agency in terms of CCT, it fails to account for the specific ways in which overall ideas related to, for example, neo-liberal norms are incorporated into CSO agency and inform the consolidation of transnational networks and coalitions.

Moving on, in studies about social movements and transnational advocacy networks the roles of issue-framing and identity-making have particularly enjoyed increasing theoretical recognition (Buechler 1995: 441; Keck and Sikkink 1998; Risse 2002), and here these are considered important dimensions of civil society regionalization. In the words of two scholars, 'transnational civil society ultimately emerges, consolidates and operates in a process governed by collective identity creation and construction of common values' (Risse and Sikkink 1999: 14).

In more detail, the act of 'framing' is an important social act in all sorts of communication and social relations. Individuals make sense of the world by applying frames to situations they encounter, most often unconsciously (Johnston and Klandermans 1995: 8). In the words of one commentator, frames are 'interpretive schemata that enable participants to locate, perceive, and label occurrences' (Johnston 2002: 64). In terms of collective actions, framing exercises are often conscious and highly strategic actions by CSOs (Johnston and Klandermans 1995: 8) to create and recreate meaning of what they know and how they should act (Finnemore and Sikkink 2001: 409). More specifically, 'issue-framing' implies portraying issues in a thoughtful way in order to successfully mobilize people around certain causes and persuade policy-makers to make policy reforms (Risse 2002: 268).

Identities, second, are consciously constructed and manipulated by collective actors in order to justify and boost their actions (Fine 1995: 132). Hence, the starting point for analyzing the role of identity-making for civil society regionalization is the social constructivist argument that social identities, be they individual or linked to social groups, are not pre-socially given or existing in some objective reality. Instead, identities emerge in social processes whereby people gradually make sense of who they are and what they want. This requires that studies about social identities take the self-understanding of social actors seriously (Risse 2010: 20). In fact, identity-making is partly an autonomous process that provides much of the basis for the choice of action on behalf of various actors. According to one scholar, 'people engage with one another in society not only to obtain resources [. . .] but also to discover who they are, where they belong and what they might become' (Scholte 2005: 146–147; see also Söderbaum 2004a). At the same time, self-discovery is intimately connected with material interests, in line with the meta-theoretical foundations of this book. Linked to regionalism, 'regional identity' is not, then, something people possess but rather an instrument used in certain regional discourses, often in order to gain certain material benefits (Van Langenhove 2011: 73). All this implies that a social constructivist approach to the study of identities does not deny that rational choice is relevant. Therefore, 'the significant question is [...] how identities and interests interact with each other' (Risse 2010: 21). Drawing from the foregoing, in terms of agency two specific motivations for CSOs to regionalize are highlighted in this book: issue-framing and identity-making.

Last, it should be underlined that, in line with the meta-theoretical understanding of the interconnection between structure and agency in this book, even if partly an autonomous process, issues are never framed and identities never constructed apart from social structure. Instead, as will be evident when studying civil society regionalization, issue-framing and identity-making are heavily influenced by the dominant ideas in the current world order related to neo-liberalism and statism, discussed further in what follows.

Studying the dynamics of civil society regionalization implies understanding the *interconnection* between structure and agency in this process. This will conceptually be done in the remains of this chapter, building on the previous discussion of social structure and agency. To begin with, in line with the thinking of CCT, agency is not perceived as being *determined* by social structures (Leysens 2008: 48), as structuralists such as Wallerstein claim (2004a, 2004b), but still as *under the influence* of structure. In the words of one commentator, 'while [structures] constrain human action, they can be transformed by human action (Leysens 2008: 48). This implies that CSO agency is to some degree an autonomous process and can partly be understood in terms of internal, intra-organizational mechanisms, in line with social constructivist thinking, but is nevertheless affected by structure. It is difficult to comprehend the relations between RIGOs and CSOs, between donors and CSOs and between CSOs, as well as relations within CSOs, without taking the deeper statist and capitalist social structures inherent in the world order into account. This is the task of the next section.[4]

The statist-capitalist world order

In broadest terms, 'world order' is here understood as a social order that is global, formed by structural and ideational conditions in terms of the material interests, political power relations, military capacity and discursive control that shape transnational interaction between various state and non-state actors (Hettne 2005). More specifically, it is understood in line with the CCT. According to this thinking, the world order is maintained not only through coercion by dominant states in terms of materialist power, that is military might and economic dominance, but also by consent. This implies that the dominant actors in the international system, to a large extent powerful states but also multinational corporations, manage to generate broad support for a world order that suits their interests (Hobden and Wyn-Jones 2005: 239). Consent is produced by the operation of cultural hegemony whereby dominant states disseminate ideas and ideologies in order to uphold the prevailing order (Woods 2005: 336–337). Multilateral institutions also play a vital role in consolidating hegemony and 'propagate and ensure the continuation of a particular hegemonic project by the mediating and legitimising function that they perform' (Taylor 2001: 18). In essence, the current hegemonic project is statist and capitalist, and these two features will now be discussed.

CCT's perception of the world order privileges the interstate system (Saad-Filho and Ayers 2008: 116). Even though '[a] hegemonic world order is not *only* an inter-state system' (Leysens 2001: 225, my emphasis), according to Cox, 'the crucial role [in world order], it turns out, is played by the state. [S]tates [. . .] create the conditions in which particular modes of social relations achieve dominance' (1987: 399). Hence, one important element of the world order is statism. In more detail, statism is a deep social structure that profoundly affects the action of various actors on all levels of society. Statism implies that the regulatory operations of territorial national government determine most forms of societal governance. To a great extent, then, the formulation, implementation, monitoring and enforcement of societal rules take place directly through the state and through inter-state relations (Scholte 2005: 186). Statism is intimately linked to the ideology of nationalism, deeply affecting identity-making across the globe in terms of constructing identity as national. The prevailing identity structure in the current world order is linked to the nation state (Scholte 2005: 186). Hence, nationalism, linked to the general notion that the state offers people the best organizing principle, is a powerful idea important for the reproduction of the state-centric element of the world order.

In terms of international institutions, the statist legacy is a powerful feature (e.g. Vale 2003; Scholte 2011). The state retains a significant degree of importance and is given a central role in creating and maintaining global governance (Higgott et al. 1999: 1; O'Brien and Williams 2010: 426). Therefore, according to one scholar, '[u]nder statist governance, macro-regional and global regulatory mechanisms are small in scale [. . .] and fall more or less completely under the thumb of country governments' (Scholte 2005: 186). Furthermore, in contemporary global and regional governance frameworks, CSOs are greatly affected by processes dominated by states and IGOs, for example in terms of being facilitated to or obstructed from participating in international policy-making forums (Boli and Thomas 1999: 29; Grugel 2004; Bowden 2006). In Grugel's words, 'one cannot escape the centrality of the state [. . . State] institutions are mainly vigorous [and] [t]he space for civil society activism is not neutral terrain but is shaped by [. . .] states' (2004: 38). On the whole, then, IGOs find it difficult to include civil society in various ways (Scholte 2011: 336). Hence, in line with CCT, the hegemonic international institutions are important instruments for maintaining a state-centric world order and reproduce the prevailing power relations between states and CSOs.

Capitalism is another fundamental social structure deeply embedded in the contemporary world order. Capitalism is here understood as 'a circumstance where social relations are pervasively and thoroughly oriented to the accumulation of surplus' (Scholte 2011: 338), which, in short, implies that wealth is owned privately and that market principles determine the organization of economic life (Heywood

2011: 84). In the contemporary world order, practices, ideologies and policies based on capitalist thinking pervade a wide range of social, economic and political life and have become more or less institutionalized and 'mainstream' (Gill 2008). Since the 1980s the latest stage and contemporary form of capitalism has been neo-liberalism (Ayers 2008; Gill 2008), a world-wide ideology which promotes the free market as the principal form of governance. In more detail, neo-liberalism is closely related to the 'project' of economic globalization and entails market efficiency, discipline and confidence; economic policy credibility and consistency; and limitation on democratic decision-making processes (Gill 2008: 138). These dominant neo-liberal ideas are cemented across the globe, including in Southern Africa, are more or less referred to as 'common sense' and play an important role in reproducing the capitalist world order.

Neo-liberal ideology is institutionalized at the macro level by various regional and global governance frameworks (Gill 2008: 138) and fundamentally affects civil society dynamics and state–civil society complexes (Gill 2008: 139). In line with CCT, this is related to the fact that capitalism deeply shapes the rules that govern relations between most actors in the world order (Scholte 2011: 338). Various multilateral institutions and IGOs form an important part of global and regional governance frameworks. In the neo-liberal era of globalization, some categories of non-state actors are closely integrated into the process of governance, which, as was indicated, revolves around states. This implies that some state authority is passed on to firms, business associations, NGOs and INGOs in order to reproduce the system of capitalist accumulation in a new, globalized condition. In this process, some non-state actors are actively supported and even created by states, donors and business to act as instruments to secure Western states' dominance of the world order and to further the neo-liberal project (Higgott et al. 1999: 6). In many regards, socialized into the dominant neo-liberal market model and being used for 'stabilizing the social and political *status quo*' (Cox 1999: 11, original emphasis), civil society can be seen to reflect the dominance of state and corporate economic power (Cox 1999: 10). On the whole, international institutions within global and regional governance frameworks are important instruments for serving the current capitalist hegemonic world order. One commentator concludes that the current world order 'is the consequence of a "fit" between ideas/ideology (support for "free" trade) [and] institutions (International Monetary Fund)' (Leysens 2001: 225).

Hence, hegemony is not only state based but also involves transnational social forces which control the capitalist mode of global production (Leysens 2008). In fact, since state policy-making within global governance often reflects the preferences of powerful corporate elites, 'states and markets have to be understood as two different expressions of the same configuration of [capitalist] social forces' (Higgott et al. 1999: 6). In more detail, in line with CCT, these social forces can be conceptualized in terms of a transnational managerial class, which reflects global corporations, national industries, global finance, government agencies and an established highly skilled workforce (Leysens 2008: 57). At the same time, many social groups are underprivileged in the world order and disadvantaged by neo-liberal globalization, such as semi-skilled and contract workers in the core states and industrial workers, state employees, peasants and urban dwellers in peripheral states (Leysens 2008: 57). Hence, the current world order is fundamentally maintained by structural social inequalities not only based on class, as shown, but also race, ethnicity, gender, sexual orientation and other social groups. This creates power relations where some actors dominate others, which is determined by the structural position of these actors in the world order (Scholte 2011).

In terms of civil society participation in global governance, CSOs represent different social groups, residing in different parts of the world, and which, because of social inequalities, are not equally successful in governance processes. It is mostly CSOs representing privileged classes, often somehow linked to the transnational managerial class, that are included in the global governance framework, even if they are still being instruments for the reproduction of the capitalist world order as discussed. Hence, 'civil society engagement of global governance agencies has widely manifested and reinforced class hierarchies. Thus professional and wealthy social circles have generally obtained greater accountability from global governance through CSOs than underclasses' (Scholte 2011: 337). However, being dissatisfied with the current social order, subordinate classes are potential challengers to the neo-liberal ideology and might constitute a basis for a 'counter-hegemony' (Leysens 2008: 58). Organized across borders, these social forces are sometimes referred to as global social movements (GSMs). GSMs attempt to alter the prevailing taken-for-granted neo-liberal assumptions of the current world order and to change policy outcomes. For example, they demand democratic accountability at the international level (Higgott et al. 1999: 4). Even though social stratification *per se* is not included in the analysis, the *hegemonic struggle* between CSOs derived from different social groups, which emanates from global social inequalities, is nevertheless part of my analytical framework. Hence, the ways in which different types of CSO relate differently to the neo-liberal ideological project and hegemonic international institutions are important to include in the study of civil society regionalization.

The influence of the statist and capitalist social structure on civil society regionalization, in terms of how hegemonic ideas related to statism and neo-liberalism and hegemonic international institutions affect the relations between IGOs and CSOs, between donors and CSOs and between CSOs, as well as within CSOs, will be further conceptually discussed in the next five sections.

Relations between RIGOs and CSOs

In this section, the ways in which the statist and capitalist social structure affects relations between RIGOs and CSOs will be discussed. This is manifested by RIGO issue preferences, RIGO focal-point creation for CSOs and CSO inclusion and exclusion in RIGOs which will be addressed in order.

RIGO issue preferences

In order to protect their economic, financial, security and other primary interests, in line with the reproduction of the statist and capitalist world order, states and IGOs often control the access of civil society to international policy-making processes and dominate global governance frameworks. This partly implies that state actors decide which policy-making issue areas CSOs can be involved in (Grugel 2004; Bowden 2006). In some policy areas IGOs offer extensive opportunities for engagement, whereas in other areas CSOs are closed out (Jönsson et al. 2012). The nature of these dynamics is ultimately determined by the capitalist social structure. Hence, most CSOs are barred from more sensitive policy areas such as security and trade (Grugel 2004; Bowden 2006) as well as finance (Jönsson et al. 2012) in order to retain power in the hands of states and business for the furthering of the statist and capitalist world order, while more are included in social policy areas such as health and labour (Jönsson et al. 2012). In terms of the latter, in line with the dominant neo-liberal ideas, outsourcing of service provision to civil society and mitigation of the negative effects of economic globalization for poor people are important for the world order to function smoothly. The neo-liberal discourse also affects what more specific policy issues within trade, health and other areas are prioritized by IGOs. For example, IGOs are generally reluctant to adopt issues connected with the so-called rights-based approach (RBA) because many of their member states resist the proliferation of the human rights framework (Schmitz 2012), which can threaten their power.[5] In addition, more resources are generally invested into trade and finance-related institutions than into those dealing with social issues. All in all, the nature of the agendas driven by IGOs, in terms of the focus on certain broad issue areas as well as on more specific policy issues at the expense of others, paves the way for which CSOs are included and excluded in various governance institutions, discussed in what follows.

Furthermore, in order to guard themselves from those parts of global civil society which challenge the statist and capitalist world order, for example in terms of the operations of global governance institutions, demands such as institutional democratic reform and incorporation of social issues into governance agendas are absorbed and written into the official documents, policies and procedures of IGOs. However, this is only a strategic game in which the rhetoric of IGOs changes, but in reality capitalist and neo-liberal principles still determine the substance of their actions (Paterson 2009: 47). An example is in terms of implementation, where emphasis is put on problem-solving projects and programmes that deal with business, wealth creation, market facilitation, trade integration, economic development and service delivery. In effect, this implies that various civil society demands for social and economic justice and democracy are hi-jacked and tuned in with the capitalist discourse (Paterson 2009: 53). In turn, this greatly affects who is included and excluded in international governance-related policy-making and project implementation.[6]

In terms of civil society regionalization in Southern Africa, the later task at hand is to study the extent and ways in which the regional governance agenda focuses on certain issue areas and neglects others and how this might influence CSO participation in regional governance and, ultimately, regional CSO consolidation.

RIGO focal point creation for CSOs

As we have seen, state domination can effectively bar CSOs from inter-governmental meetings and forums. However, this marginalization can also be an incentive for international civil society action. Hence, inter-governmental forums, even if rather closed, can act as focal points around which parallel international civil society platforms can emerge (Florini 2000). The very act of gathering alongside global and regional governance institutions means that state agencies can have a strong influence on civil society networking in terms of the ability to perform and operate (Gilson 2011a: 134). One commentator concludes in relation to international organizations that 'the fact remains that as the constitutive elements and ultimate enforcers of those regimes, states remain the central actors – and the focal point for transnational action' (Santa Cruz 2004: 28). Furthermore, IGOs can have a more direct role in facilitating transnational civil society networking when arranging and in other ways supporting international civil society conferences and meetings, as well as multi-stakeholder forums involving both state and non-state actors.

The creation of regional focal points linked to RIGOs, facilitating civil society regional co-operation, is an important dimension of civil society regionalization. This will be analyzed later in the empirical sections.

CSO inclusion and exclusion in RIGOs

States not only determine in what policy areas CSOs can have an influence but also decide in which specific institutions CSOs can have a say in order to protect the statist and capitalist hegemony. Hence, IGOs decide which actors to include and exclude in policy-making processes in various institutions (Gilson 2011a: 13). When they open up to non-state actors in various deliberations, IGOs are generally very selective in terms of who to involve and rarely operate without limitations on the participation of those actors. Civil society participation is often strictly formalized through an accreditation system. Actors are involved in terms of their usefulness to the international organization in question, for example in delivering various types of expertise and as providers of information and policy alternatives (Boli and Thomas 1999; Jönsson et al. 2012), serving the interests of states. In the words of Dupuy and colleagues, '[s]tates are gatekeepers for NGOs; they regulate the barriers to entry, affect the cost of operations and organization [. . . and] establish the specific issues that NGOs can work on' (2012: 9).

In terms of which institutions of a particular IGO CSOs are allowed to participate in, according to Jönsson and colleagues non-state actors' access is much higher in monitoring and enforcement, implementation and policy formulation institutions such as committees, secretariats and courts than in decision-making forums such as councils of ministers and summits, which are dominated by the traditional state model of representation (2012), in line with the statist social structure. This is related to the fact that state officials often invoke a traditional discourse of sovereign statehood in order to exclude civil society initiatives from influencing international organizations (Scholte 2011: 336). The consequence of this is that shallow forms of civil society involvement are more common than deep and influential forms of participation (Jönsson et al. 2012).

Furthermore, the centrality of capitalism in global relations has far-reaching implications for which CSOs are involved in regional and global governance (Scholte 2011). Those actors that work within the parameters of the rules of capitalism and hence legitimate the current world order, for example by accepting private property rights, monetized social relations, the market-based economy and offering instrumentalist ways of 'solving problems', are most successful (Scholte 2011). They are used as instruments by international institutions to reproduce the current hegemony. Drawing on Cox (1993), problem-solving means, for example, offering solutions to correct dysfunctions in the current world order such as market failures, malfunctioning political institutions and lack of social services for poor people in the South. On the other hand, civil society actors that seek structural transformation of the current capitalist system remain at the margins of global politics (Scholte 2011). Hence, business associations, orthodox trade unions, mainstream think tank organizations and reformist NGOs are more involved in regional and global governance than counter-hegemonic anti-capitalist social movements, peasant groups and radical environmental movements (Jönsson et al. 2012).

Applied to the regional level, the extent to which the inclusion and exclusion of CSOs in regional institutions affects civil society regionalization will be analyzed later. Being included in regional governance can strengthen the operation of CSOs, whereas excluded ones might be weakened, which affects overall regionalization.

Relations between donors and CSOs

As indicated earlier, civil society regionalization is greatly affected by donor–CSO relations in terms of CSO dependency on regional donor funds and donor influence on CSO regional agenda, which will be discussed next.

CSO dependency on regional donor funds

Being influenced by the hegemonic neo-liberal discourse, CSOs are moulded into an economistic way of thinking, based on a neo-liberal understanding of development, issues based on economic growth and outsourcing of service-provision to 'private' civil society actors (Mittelman and Chin 2000). Donors play an important role here. CSOs in the South are greatly dependent on donor funds for their operation, a fact well known in the academic world (e.g. Michael 2004; Bob 2005; Fowler 2011) and which results in donor agencies dictating the procedures and forms of fund-giving in line with the hegemonic capitalist discourse (Michael 2004). Hence, market principles are increasingly the basic organizing principles of civil society (Dagnino 2011), and CSOs are forced to adopt an economistic rationale in their development work that is based on supply and demand and the accumulation of capital, even though on paper development is a non-profit domain (Bob 2005).

Donor dependency and the socialization of neo-liberal, market-oriented and profit-oriented thinking can create organizations that merely serve as instruments for narrow private economic gains. Even if so-called 'briefcase NGOs' may fulfil certain functions, their main purpose is to extract resources from those (donors) willing to pay. The quest to make money also leads to NGOs being professionalized and increasingly headed by members of the middle class (Godsäter and Söderbaum 2011).

Applied to the regional level, the availability of donor funds for regional activities, as well as the neo-liberal socialization of CSOs by donors, greatly affects civil society regionalization, which will be shown later.

Donor influence on the CSO agenda

CSO–donor relations are fundamentally shaped by the statist and capitalist world order. CSOs in the South are greatly dependent on donor funds for their operation and, in line with critical theoretical thinking, such donor dependency is used to uphold and reproduce the current dominant capitalist social structures. The relationship between donors and their CSO recipients is therefore best characterized by a power asymmetry in which the former have the upper hand (Bob 2005). This implies that the neo-liberal agendas and goals of the dominant partner in the relationship, the donor, are forced upon the receiving partner, the CSO, and accountability procedures are geared toward the needs of donors rather than local needs. In that way, and linked to the previous section, donors are crucial for socializing CSOs into the neo-liberal/capitalist discourse (Katz 2006) in terms of determining what type of development agenda is furthered and what type of development issues addressed. In other words, the aid channel is the 'transmission belt of a dominant discourse tied to Western notions of development' (Tvedt 2004: 140 quoted in Katz 2006: 335).

Furthermore, due to the workings of the capitalist global order, the distribution of donor funds does not benefit all types of CSOs equally. Those CSOs that buy into the neo-liberal agenda and adopt problem-solving strategies are more successful in fundraising than CSOs that challenge the current neo-liberal order using contentious methods. However, there are also donors who are challenging power relations between donors and recipients and the mainstream problem-solving rationale behind development work, even if they are in a minority. These alternative donors adopt what some scholars call an 'accompaniment approach', based on a deep commitment to the processes of social change. Accompaniment donors want structural change of the world order and seek to identify shared, counter-hegemonic interests between people from the South and North (Macdonald 1994).

In the empirical chapter it will be discussed how donor funding influences the nature of CSOs' regional work and in extension also the composition of regional civil society.

Relations between CSOs

The capitalist world order creates deeply diverging interests between different CSOs, which results in very complex internal dynamics within an inherently heterogeneous global civil society. As already indicated, CSOs have different functions in global politics, either reproducing or challenging the capitalist system, and correspondingly different relations to state and market actors (Cox 1999). This is a profound aspect of the global governance process where the global statist capitalist order indirectly ascribes different roles for CSOs to play in global governance institutions (Buckley 2012). According to Armstrong and colleagues (2004), three such roles can be discerned: civil society as a partner in global governance, taking part in service provision, project implementation and policy development; civil society as legitimating global governance, making IGOs legitimate and accountable to the public; and civil society as contesting global governance, questioning the current global order and seeking structural change. In the end, the heterogeneous nature of global civil society creates tension between CSOs with different ideological inclinations and different functions (Cox 1999; Buckley 2012). Applied to the regional level, the heterogeneity of civil society regionalization will be discussed in the empirical chapter including what role intra-civil society ideological rivalry plays in civil society regionalization.

CSOs and issue-framing

Leaving the external forces behind civil society regionalization, this and the next section will focus on the motivations of CSOs to 'go regional' in terms of issue-framing and identity-making. In terms of the former, regional issue-framing and the construction of regional target groups will be discussed first.

Regional issue-framing

As indicated, being weak in material terms in relation to state actors, the greatest tool for CSOs to attempt to influence various policy-making processes on a local, national, regional or global level is information and knowledge. Civil society networks and campaigns that manage to provide information that would not otherwise be available, from sources that are normally not heard and make it comprehensible and useful to activists, publics and those in power tend to be powerful (Keck and Sikkink 1998). The power of knowledge is linked to the amount of and type of knowledge an organization possesses, of which two crucial aspects are expertise and experiential evidence. Expertise is often related to rarity, that is unique knowledge about a specific issue that is sought after by policy-makers and the general public and therefore is often referred to as technical expertise, which in turn often draws on the legitimacy of the academic and political worlds (van Rooy 2004: 81). Experiential evidence, on the other hand, draws from the legitimacy of the grassroots. Organizations with close links to the field derive their knowledge from direct experience of people's own understandings of poverty, gender inequality, environmental problems and other issues (van Rooy 2004: 92). Possession of knowledge helps strengthen CSOs active internationally and adds to their consolidation.

However, the possession of knowledge in itself does not necessarily explain the degree of success for transnational civil society action, for example in terms of regional advocacy campaigns. In order to influence policy-makers and the general public and to successfully consolidate as NGOs and networks, knowledge claims have to be framed in strategic ways (Keck and Sikkink 1998). Here, issue-framing comes into the picture. Issue-framing implies the ways in which CSOs render events or occurrences meaningful to their target groups (such as policy-makers), members and partners by organizing experiences and guiding action in a certain pedagogical and sometimes provocative way. This means bringing complex issues to the public agenda by framing them in innovative ways (Keck and Sikkink 1998).

For issue-framing to lead to collective action and possibly policy change (McAdam et al. 1996) two things are required. First, issue-framing must communicate the conviction that it is possible to change some undesirable conditions through collective action. Issue-framing, then, 'suggest[s] not merely that something can be done but that "we" can do something' (Gamson 1995: 90). Second, if this 'we' is a transnational network or NGO that targets a transnational audience, issue-framing has to build on 'transnational' notions of development, trade, HIV/AIDS, the environment and so forth. In fact, most importantly, it is argued in the social constructivist camp that the ability to frame issues as transnational can partly explain the formation of transnational networks. Linked to this, if the issues dealt with are framed in ways that resonate well with already existing transnational agendas, issue-framing is an even stronger incitement for transnational action. CSOs are likely to be influential in issue areas where the values in question coincide with national and regional state and public interests (Keck and Sikkink 1998).

In terms of the regional level, issue-framing as a force behind civil society regionalization will be further analyzed in the empirical chapter. It will be shown that CSOs active on a regional level frame their issues in a regional setting and adhere to regional agendas and how this is informed by hegemonic ideas and international institutions.

Construction of regional target groups

Issue-framing can be linked to some sort of injustice in the sense that moral indignation is felt over something. When the source of feelings of injustice is linked to clearly identifiable persons or social actors, such as states or corporations, who are accused of bringing harm and suffering to some parts of the population or the environment, this can spur collective action. The more concrete the target is, the more likely this will spur collective action. The ability to link these concrete targets to broader socio-economic forces, bridging the concrete and the abstract, is also important for mobilizing success (Gamson 1995: 90–92).

Hence, issue frames are often adversarial: some 'we' stands in opposition to some 'they' who are responsible for certain injustices and/or have the power to make a change (Gamson 1995: 101). If issue-framing is codified in resolutions and other policy frameworks, advocacy success can increase further (van Rooy 2004: 95–97). This is often manifested in so-called 'shaming', whereby CSOs remind state actors of their obligations and demand that they live up to certain norms and realize implementation of policies and programs (Risse 2002: 268). Most importantly here, if the perceived target is an international actor this can spur transnational civil society activities. Furthermore, if international targets are framed and shamed in adversarial ways, this can lead to the construction of an exclusive, resistance type of identity, discussed in what follows.

In terms of the regional level, if the target group of advocacy campaigns and lobbying is understood in terms of regional policy-makers and is framed as responsible for regional injustices this can facilitate regional civil society consolidation and action. This will be further discussed in the empirical chapters.

Last, since it is not possible to 'stand apart from the prevailing order', social activities such as issue-framing must be located within the context of the whole (statist and capitalist) system (Leysens 2008: 40). Hence, issue-framing and target-group construction are not autonomous processes, taking place in isolation, but are deeply informed by hegemonic statist and neo-liberal ideas, as well as the power relations within international institutions, related to the world order. Since CSOs relate differently to neo-liberal ideology and hegemonic international institutions, based on their different positions in the global social hierarchy, they play different roles in the world order. Some CSOs serve to legitimize the prevailing world order, and others contest it 'because of a dissatisfaction with the prevailing order' (Cox 1987: 403). These processes can fundamentally affect civil society regionalization, which will be shown later.

CSOs and identity-making

In terms of identity, the focus of this book is on group identities, which are often referred to as collective identities. Here people recognize themselves and are recognized by others as part of broader groupings (Della Porta and Diani

2006: 91). Sometimes collective identity is defined in reference to some social trait, such as class, religion, gender, ethnicity or sexual orientation. This type of identity can be quite strong. However, identity can also be more loosely based on shared orientations, values, attitudes, world-views and lifestyles without members of the group sharing a particular social trait (Della Porta and Diani 2006: 92). More specifically, collective identity is 'an interactive and shared definition produced by several individuals (or groups at a more complex level) and concerned with the orientations of action and the field of opportunities and constraints in which the action takes place' (Melucci 1995: 44). This implies that collective identity is always constructed through interaction between members of the group (Taylor and Whittier 1995: 172). At the same time as the evolution of collective action produces and reproduces collective identity, collective identities also guide collective action. The two are intimately connected (Della Porta and Diani 2006: 93). It should also be emphasized once more that identity-making is often instrumental, in the sense that identities are forged in order to safeguard certain material interests, for example seeking donor funds.

Furthermore, it is argued here that collective identity is often linked to territorialism as the prevailing structure of social space, which is linked to the statist social structure (Scholte 2005). This means that collective identity is spatially dependent in the sense that it is based on a distinct territory, be it the 'local', 'national', 'international', 'regional' or 'global'. However, collective identity can also be formed on a supra-territorial basis that transcends territorial boundaries, as in the case of transnational class, religious, gender and ethnic solidarity. In this vein, Scholte (2005) highlights three types of collective identity relevant for this book: national, supra-national and non-territorial. In the case of national identity, the basis of identity is nationalism. This implies a situation where people construct their being and belonging first and foremost in terms of national affiliation and a national territorial pattern of social space. Claims are made to the difference and uniqueness of one national group *vis-à-vis* the rest of humanity (Scholte 2005: 147–148). Important manifestations of the structure of nationalism are the construction of states, firms and also CSOs as 'national' organizations. Hence, the idea of nationalism goes hand in hand with statism (Scholte 2005: 225), fundamentally affecting CSO identity-making.

In the second case, supra-national identity implies an idea of nationhood 'above' the nation-state, often constructed on a basis of a supra-state macro region. Shared experiences of, for example, the slave trade, colonialism, common cultural heritage and/or religion are claimed to provide deep historical roots for the supra-national, regional identity. However, this type of identity still rests on the notion of territoriality as well as statism, albeit stretched above any one nation-state (Scholte 2005: 236–237).[7] On the whole, the first two examples of identity are influenced by the hegemonic idea of the nation-state as the primary instrument for ordering social relations inherent in the current world order.

Last, whereas territorial identities based on nationalism or supra-nationalism are linked to a particular geographical area, other aspects of being, such as class, religion and gender, are not bound to territorial location. Constructing the self and group affiliations in terms of class interests, religious beliefs or being a woman, non-territorial identities transcend territorial place, distance and borders to encompass people all around the world (Slocum and Van Langenhove 2005: 149).[8]

Inherent in the construction of collective identity is the maintenance of boundaries between 'we' and the 'other'. Collective identity cannot occur in the absence of a 'we' characterized by a particular social trait or adherence to some specific values and principles. This is referred to as a positive identity (Della Porta and Diani 2006: 94). In terms of networks, common in regionalization processes, their strength can come from relationships among the networked organizations producing one coherent 'voice' based on some social traits, representation of a particular constituency and/or some common principles and goals. The voice of the network, then, is not the sum of all the individual voices in the network but the product of an interaction of voices and is also different from any single voice of a network member (Keck and Sikkink 1998).

Most importantly, the social sphere in which identity is formed ultimately affects on what level CSO action is taking place. In other words, adherence to national, supra-national or non-territorial collective identity determines the spatial nature of agency. Hence, when having a national identity, NGOs, networks and social movements tend to focus their activities on a national level, while a supra-national identity warrants macro-regional action, and a non-territorial identity spurs transnational action, which can be global but also regional.

One important aspect of transnational collective identity is the concept of 'solidarity'. When civil society activists share an understanding of their collective actions as being an act of solidarity with the suffering of some oppressed, distant or not-so-distant group or section of the same social constituency, this can effectively add to the consolidation of collective identity (Thörn 2009: 207–208). If these oppressed groups reside in neighbouring countries in a particular region this can spur regional mobilization in support of those groups.

Collective identities built on common social traits, shared values, world-views, lifestyles and/or other types of common experiences of actions, somehow linked to the 'region', is a rather weak dimension of civil society regionalization, which will be discussed in the empirical chapters.

International events such as conferences, protest campaigns and workshops where CSOs meet intensively and their members are frequently activated are important venues for both issue-framing and identity-making. International events serve as arenas for what Fine calls the 'staging of culture' (1995: 133), that is the framing of core issues, the interpretation of material interests and the construction of a group identity. At these events, the reconstruction of social actors and the constitution of group identities and ideas are strengthened through various types of collective action (Klandermans et al. 2002: 337–338). Contentious events are particularly strong venues for issue-framing and identity-making, that is a series of protest events, civil disobedience campaigns and boycotts where specific rituals are continually performed, for example in terms of demonstrations or speeches. Here the uniqueness and difference of the collective actor is demonstrated in terms of communicating a certain world vision or demonstrating a basic historical experience (Della Porta and Diani 2006: 109). The extent to and ways in which regional events affect the regionalization of civil society in terms of framing issues in a regional setting and constructing regional identities will be addressed in the empirical chapters.

Notes

1 There are other theoretical schools addressing other dimensions of power structures in the world order. For example, critical feminists highlight gender as a specific form of structural inequality reproduced by patriarchal institutions and ideologies (e.g. Whitworth 1994; Tickner 2001), and post-colonial theories address power relations based on race and ethnicity (e.g. Inayatullah and Blaney 2004; Krishna 2009).
2 Referring to the 'state' as an idea and not a fact, contingent with a particular historical era, one commentator argues that 'the historical structures of the feudal manor and the fief that confronted serfs and lords in mediaeval times appeared as real and as enduring as do our modern historical structures of the nation-state and interstate system' (Gale 1998: 271, quoted in Taylor 2001: 17).
3 The Political Opportunity approach is another theory which emphasizes civil society agency, particularly with regards to social movements. This approach studies how social movements and other CSOs strategically use the limitations and opportunities of existing political structures, for example the composition of the formal political architecture in a particular country, to reach their goals, and how this affects their internal consolidation (e.g. Tarrow 1998; Meyer 2004).
4 However, the focus in this project is not on world order *per se*. In other words, this is not, by any means, a study about world order. World order is only included in the analysis of civil society regionalization because of its (indirect) fundamental influence on this process in terms of the deeper statist and capitalist social structures. Linked to this, this book is indeed theoretically influenced by CCT and its world order framework but should not be seen as formally belonging to this research tradition. Hence, this study does not qualify as being a 'critical theory of civil society regionalization', so to speak, fully applying the CCT framework and method to this topic.
5 The RBA to development seek to frame poverty and other social issues in the language of international human rights standards. From this perspective, poverty is not primarily due to lack of resources but is a result of discrimination and the political decisions of policy-makers. The role of external actors such as donors and their CSO recipients is no longer to substitute for absent government services but instead to focus on mobilizing individuals and the legal system to hold the state accountable for delivering social services (Schmitz 2012: 1).
6 In terms of the trade arena, relevant for this book, Paterson (2009) argues that the World Trade Organization (WTO) deliberately involves certain CSOs at the expense of others. Certain partner-CSOs are used to legitimize the capitalist ideology and procedures of the WTO, especially market-oriented NGOs (Ma-NGOs), for example in terms of drafting official documents, giving policy advice and carrying out programmes. Ma-NGOs are created by corporations to campaign for their interests in important global policy-making institutions in the trade arena, such as the WTO. In most respects, the WTO has focused its NGO engagement on partner and Ma-NGOs. On the other hand, so-called alter-globalization NGOs, demanding greater transparency and social participation in global

governance, are formally excluded from policy-making, implementation and monitoring processes within the WTO and are unable to put their issues on the negotiating table due to only being granted accreditation status in forums far from decision-making bodies (Paterson 2009: 43, 52–53).
7 'Regional identity' has become a catchphrase in academia since the 1980s, not the least in regionalism studies, and has been recognized as an important element in the making of regions (e.g. Hettne 1999; Katzenstein 2005; Slocum and Van Langenhove 2005). It has been argued that belonging to a specific region may raise a sense of identity that challenges hegemonic national identity narratives (Paasi 2009). It is argued that regional identity is becoming a new identity structure that affects how people and organized actors view their belonging. In the EU in particular, a regional identity is emerging hand in hand with increased regional integration, which has become the object of intense scholarly debate and benchmarking by policy-makers (Katzenstein 2005: 77; Slocum and Van Langenhove 2005; Paasi 2009; Risse 2010). Furthermore, even though the literature on regional identity focuses on Europe (Slocum and Van Langenhove 2005: 148), other world regions are beginning to register on researchers' radar. In Asia, for example, and within ASEAN in particular, it is claimed that the presence of a common cultural heritage has facilitated the emergence of regional identity (Bøås and Hveem 2001: 123) and that discourses of 'the Asian way' and 'Asian values' are used for political purposes (Katzenstein 2005: 79), for example in terms of building a foundation for states-led regionalism.
8 One important example of non-territorial identity-making is the voting patterns among worker representatives at International Labour Organization (ILO) conferences. In a recent study it was shown that worker representatives often vote together with worker representatives from other countries and against the national position of their home state. In fact, workers are guided by interests, values and beliefs that are in line with their transnational class identity and not their national identity (Koenig-Archibugi 2012). The extent to which non-territorial identity-making, in line with community-building between workers in the ILO, as well as construction of regional identities also affect regional consolidation of CSOs in Southern Africa will be discussed in the latter half of Chapters 4 and 5.

Chapter 3
The statist-capitalist regional order in Southern Africa

Björn Hettne, among others, argues that the statist and capitalist social structures inherent in the world order are manifested on many different levels, of which the regional is one. Hence, according to him, it is possible to talk about specific regional social orders (2002, 2005) at the same time also being part of the world order, which was briefly discussed earlier. Southern Africa qualifies as a regional hegemonic order with a distinct state-society regional complex, in line with the conceptualization of CCT (Leysens 2001), taking into consideration the neo-liberal hegemony, the evolving regional political economy and state domination (particularly South Africa) which mark the region. Hence, the regional order in Southern Africa 'replicates the ideas/ideology of the current global hegemonic order' (Leysens 2001: 231). In other words, being embedded in the statist and capitalist world order, the regional order in Southern Africa shares many of its features, which is discussed in this chapter.

Implications of the statist social structure

In this section, the implications of statism in Southern Africa will be discussed. First, the authoritarian African state and, second, its dominating tendencies *vis-à-vis* civil society and how this affects the latter. Third, an account of regional governance in Southern Africa will be made in terms of its sovereignty-boosting element.

The authoritarian state

The literature on the post-colonial African state is rich. With few exceptions, states in Africa are considered highly problematic in a democratic sense (Freund 2010). The African state has been characterized by high levels of authoritarianism (Nwabueze 2003), despite the democratization that has been taking place in many countries during the last two decades: 'Africa is still far from being a bastion of democracy [... Political elites] support pluralism because it is a method of retaining or gaining power' (Thomson 2010: 247). African states are highly centralized in the sense that power has accumulated in the executive branch, often within the office of the president, king or prime minister, at the expense of parliaments and judicial branches. Individuals belonging to the executive, on local and national levels, tend to dominate and monopolize formal politics within society. To a large extent, then, African governments have developed a monopoly over political decision-making within their countries. Often, the centralization of the state is related to 'neo-patrimonialism', whereby power is concentrated in the personal authority of an individual leader. On a national level this is the head of state. For neo-patrimonial leaders, the various concerns of the state are seen as their own personal affairs (Thomson 2010: 247). This is often manifested by the extraction of resources from the state for personal enrichment. State resources are also deployed as an instrument to maintain support and legitimacy for the regime through nurturing key political, administrative and economic allies (Söderbaum and Taylor 2008: 22).

Moreover, in order to maintain the concentration of power in the hands of the political elite, opportunities for organized opposition, for example through opposition parties, are limited. This also includes restrictions for and manipulation and co-option by the government of actors within civil society such as labour unions, professional groups and other voluntary associations. In the process of centralization the state therefore enjoys a superior position *vis-à-vis* civil society, whose members are increasingly constrained. For example, CSOs are often denied the possibility of providing advice and feedback on policy or of suggesting alternative approaches in various sectors (Thomson 2010: 122–123). The political elite within the authoritarian state sometimes use less civil ways to maintain power: '[t]he state takes on the peculiar character of an instrument for the domination, oppression and repression of the people [. . .] by a regular, systematic application of organized force' (Nwabueze 2003: 353–354). In fact, state elites even consciously create disorder in society in order to maintain power (Freund 2010: 52).

As in other parts of Africa, Southern African states have fostered a regional political culture of authoritarian rule, and the dominance of personal rulers is strong, which is a great obstacle towards deepening regional integration in the SADC (Peters 2011: 165). Authoritarianism and the centralization of the state have cemented a regional order based on states. In such a statist regional order, the prime objective for states and corresponding political elites is to exercise control over their sovereign affairs and maximize the 'national interest' (Vale 2001, 2003), which often equals the political and economic interests of the ruling elites.

Similar to the world order at large, an important element of the state-centric regional order is the widespread nationalist and statist notion of community in the region, promoted and cemented by political leaders, which has created a national identity structure. Southern African states invest little time in developing strategies for creating regional consciousness among the region's citizens or promoting a sense of regional identity (Williams 2006), and the question of free movements of people and people-centred regional citizenship is not a priority for the political elite in the region (Radebe 2008). States see migration mainly through security lenses, and regional policy-making linked to facilitating the movement of people is overshadowed by protectionist immigration laws on a national level and the widespread criminalization of foreign migrants in most states in the region (Matlosa 2006). Due to the lack of commitment by political elites to supporting regional citizenship and identity-making for people in the region, 'the forging of a regional consciousness is likely to take place at a glacial pace if at all' (Kornegay 2006: 45).

On the whole, then, the understanding of identity in Southern Africa is limited to, and dominated by, the states of the region. According to one scholar, 'the interpretation of regional community in SADC remains a prerogative of the narrow interests of regional elites [. . .] which implies that states provide the only path to regional community' (Blaauw 2007: 230). Additionally, the lack of common political and democratic values in the region among political elites plays against the promotion of regional community and citizenship from above (Peters 2011: 165). One commentator concludes that the 'means of promoting a sense of regional identity, loyalty, homogeneity, and participation is not available to Southern Africa' (Schoeman 2001: 153). Furthermore, the predominant perception of regional community-building in Southern Africa as based on the community of states is spread throughout society (Radebe 2008: 28). Nationalist notions among citizens and CSOs in the region are common, and the concepts of the nation-state and national identity have become an integral part of their identities (Radebe 2008: 49). According to one scholar, this implies a separation of 'the people from their shared history and their shared concerns' (Vale 2003: 114). According to a major survey about popular attitudes towards migration in the region, the Southern African Migration Project, the majority of people interviewed saw the migration of people more or less as a problem. Therefore, the study concludes that any sense among people of regional solidarity with other countries in the SADC is absent (Williams 2006: 12). Another national survey undertaken in Lesotho, Zimbabwe and Mozambique indicated that 62% of people agreed with the importance of a national border to separate their country from others (Leysens 2001: 228). One tragic implication of these nationalist and statist notions is widespread hostility towards foreigners in most countries in the region, not the least in South Africa and Zimbabwe, where suspicion towards foreigners and xenophobic stereotypes are ripe in society (Matlosa 2006). Two scholars conclude that identification with the SADC as a regional community is underdeveloped among the populations of the region (le Pere and Tjönneland 2005: 45). The extent to which national and statist notions of identity affect the regionalization of civil society will be discussed in the concluding chapter.

State domination of civil society

The statist deeper social structure in Southern Africa has greatly influenced state–civil society relations, to the detriment of CSOs. Many governments in the region have an innate distrust of civil society and often undermine its ability to play a meaningful role in democracy and development. According to one scholar, 'the relationship between national NGOs and national governments is acrimonious at best' (Blaauw 2007: 246). In Mozambique, for example, the space for influencing policy is limited by the state. The state is dominating in its interaction with civil society, and there is widespread manipulation of civil society, for example in terms of taking sides in party political disputes and *ad hoc* informal consultation with (some) CSOs in policy-making without any real commitment to the provision of policy influence to civil society more broadly (FDC 2007). In Tanzania as well, the culture of authoritarianism is entrenched in wider society, and the government controls all society's activities. This fundamentally affects state–civil society relations (Ndumbaro and Kiondo 2007). When NGOs challenge the Tanzanian government for political space, in terms of advocating for policy change and human rights, government suspicion of NGOs is expressed in overt and less overt ways (Michael 2004). In Zimbabwe, this tendency is even more pronounced. Contrary to the Mozambican situation, where advocacy activities are at least allowed by law, Zimbabweans do not have the freedom to form and participate in civic groups and associations as they wish. Furthermore, many CSOs have been severely restricted in their activities due to repressive legislation that governs civil society, for example in terms of criminalizing activities such as popular meetings that would allow citizens to participate in governance processes. The implication of this is that there is very little civil society participation in the development of public policies (Sachikonye 2007: 54–55). As will be discussed in the last section of this chapter, the negative attitude of states towards civil society spills over to the regional level and the SADC.

The SADC and sovereignty-boosting regional governance

The statist social structure also deeply affects the regional integration process in Southern Africa. Historically, regionalism in Southern Africa has been the preserve of states and governing elites, and popular participation in regional integration frameworks has been very weak (Tsie 2001: 132). The SADC, as the current main manifestation of regionalism and the most important RIGO in Southern Africa, is deeply state centric and elite driven (Matlosa and Lotshwao 2010: 52) and a good example of sovereignty-boosting regional governance.[1] Before this is discussed further, a few general words about the SADC as a regional organization are warranted.

The Southern African Development Community (SADC) was formed in 1992 and is the prime RIGO in Southern Africa. As of 2016 it has 15 members, namely Angola, Botswana, the DRC, Lesotho, Madagascar, Malawi, Mauritius, Mozambique, Namibia, Seychelles, South Africa, Swaziland, Tanzania, Zambia and Zimbabwe. The headquarters are based in Gaborone, Botswana. The SADC institutions are the Summit of Heads of State or Government; the Summit Troika of the Organ the Council of Ministers; the Sectoral & Cluster Ministerial Committees; the Standing Committee of Senior Officials; the Secretariat; the SADC National Committees; and the SADC Tribunal (SADC 2016a). The institutions relevant for this book are briefly discussed in what follows.

The summit is the SADC's supreme policy-making institution. It consists of the heads of state or government of all members states, meeting at least once a year. The summit is responsible for the overall policy direction and control of the organization and takes decisions by consensus. The Council of Ministers (COM) consists of one minister from each member state, normally the one responsible for foreign affairs, and meets at least four times a year. The COM reports and is responsible to the summit, advising the latter on policy issues and further development of the organization, for example recommending to the summit the approval of protocols and treaties. The Secretariat is the SADC's principal administrative and executive institution. Among its chief tasks are strategic planning and policy analysis; monitoring, coordinating and supporting the implementation of SADC programmes; implementation of the decisions of supreme decision-making bodies; and general promotion of the SADC (SADC 2016a). The Secretariat is headed by the executive secretary, and under him/her are two deputy executive Secretaries responsible for regional integration and finance and administration. The work on regional integration is divided into a number of directorates. The TIFI Directorate encompasses the sectors of trade, industry, finance, mining and investment; the IS Directorate the infrastructure and services sectors; the FANR Directorate the food, agriculture and natural resources sectors; the SHDSP Directorate the social and human development sectors and special programmes; and the Directorate of the Organ the peace, security and defence sectors. Since the trade sector is one of the focuses in this book, a few more words about TIFI are warranted. TIFI's main functions are to facilitate the implementation of the trade protocol, to analyze and promote macroeconomic policy convergence in the region, to initiate industrial-development promotion policies, to promote the development of mining, and to promote efficient and development-oriented financial sectors (SADC 2016b).

Last, and based in Windhoek, Namibia, the Tribunal is the SADC's supreme judicial body. The prime tasks of the Tribunal are to make sure that the treaty and corresponding protocols are adhered to and to deal with disputes related to their interpretation. However, the Tribunal also has a broader mandate to protect the interests and rights of SADC member states as well as their citizens and to adjudicate disputes between states and natural and legal persons. The implementation of decisions is subordinated to the member states through the summit (Oosthuizen 2006: 209–210).

The SADC Treaty was signed in 1992 and amended in 2001, formally establishing the SADC as a regional legal entity. It is not an overstatement to say that the SADC agenda was originally very ambitious. According to the SADC Treaty, the (quite diverse) objectives of the SADC are to:

a) achieve development and economic growth, alleviate poverty, enhance the standard and quality of life of the people of Southern Africa and support the socially disadvantaged through regional integration;
b) evolve common political values, systems and institutions;
c) promote and defend peace and security;
d) promote self-sustaining development on the basis of collective self-reliance and the interdependence of member states;
e) achieve complementarity between national and regional strategies and programmes;
f) promote and maximize productive employment and utilization of resources of the region;

g) achieve sustainable utilization of natural resources and effective protection of the environment;
h) strengthen and consolidate the long-standing historical, social and cultural affinities and links among the people of the Region (SADC 1992).

Also referred to as the SADC common agenda, these objectives have given the SADC a strong focus on regional economic integration, as well as on opening up new political areas such as peace, security and the promotion of democracy (le Pere and Tjönneland 2005).

Furthermore, the Regional Indicative Strategic Development Plan (RISDP) was adopted in 2003 and is often referred to as SADC's main plan for implementing goals related to socio-economic development. It provides strategic direction with respect to SADC programmes, projects and activities over a period of 15 years (2005–2020) (SADC 2003a). The RISDP 're-affirms the commitment of SADC member states to good political, economic and corporate governance entrenched in a culture of democracy, full participation by civil society, transparency and respect for the rule of law' (SADC 2003a), signalling the importance put on implementing the plan in a democratic way and involving non-state actors. In 2007, in order to make the SADC more efficient, four priority areas were approved: peace and security co-operation as a pre-requisite for economic integration; trade and economic liberalization through progressive market integration; infrastructure in support of regional integration; and special programmes, for example food security, gender equality and HIV/AIDS (Giuffrida and Muller-Glodde 2008). In terms of the latter, realizing that HIV/AIDS had become a real threat to widespread development, in 2003 the SADC took on the challenge of combating the pandemic, which was to be addressed in all SADC activities. Therefore, an HIV/AIDS Unit within the SHDSP Directorate was formed the same year, responsible for implementing the special programme on HIV/AIDS, for mainstreaming HIV/AIDS in the SHDSP directorate and for supporting other directorates in their HIV/AIDS work, as well as for overall HIV/AIDS policy development and harmonization within the SADC (Oosthuizen 2006).

Leaving the organizational nature of the SADC, since the overriding motivation for regional governance in Southern Africa is for leaders to maintain the existing statist order, to a large extent the pursuit of regional integration in the SADC in practice centres on member states exerting their specific national interests and goals. The national rationale for regional integration is clear. In the words of two scholars, 'planning and budgeting of key regional integration programs are an imminent political, interest-led process of negotiating and agreeing in order to add value and visible benefits to the ongoing national plans and programs' (Giuffrida and Muller-Glodde 2008: 21). Hence, 'national sovereignty becomes paramount [. . . and is] a powerful tool in international relations and the way states relate to each other at regional levels' (Matlosa and Lotshwao 2010: 46). SADC leaders tend to use regional governance to strengthen their regimes and the sovereignty of the state. It is not a coincidence, therefore, that the weakest states in Southern Africa are members of many more African inter-governmental regional organizations than relatively stronger states such as South Africa and Namibia (Söderbaum 2004a). In many respects, therefore, the SADC is a good example of sovereignty-boosting regional governance.

Furthermore, despite a restructuring of the SADC from 2001 onwards which attempted to give more supra-national powers to the Secretariat (at least on paper), member states still seem reluctant to give up national sovereignty and to transfer policy-making to the regional level (le Pere and Tjönneland 2005; Mulaudzi 2006). To a large extent, decision-making power is centralized in the heads of state and government (Matlosa and Lotshwao 2010: 46). Even though members, at least formally, have ceded some policy-making powers to a few SADC institutions, such as the Secretariat and the Tribunal, it is more correct to speak of 'change in the locus and context of exercising sovereignty, rather than a loss of sovereignty' (Oosthuizen 2006: 162). In reality, most SADC institutions, including the Secretariat, are controlled by direct representatives of member states, and those not controlled in this way, such as the Tribunal, have no real authority. In fact, the SADC Summit 2010 decided to suspend the activities of the Tribunal and review its mandate (SADC 2016a), preceded by the refusal of the Zimbabwean regime to recognize the Tribunal's earlier ruling against the country (Afadameh-Adeyemi and Kalula 2011) On the whole, the interests of individual member states are supreme in the SADC, and 'member states to a large extent still control the [SADC-led] process of regional integration' (Afadameh-Adeyemi and Kalula 2011: 20).

The negative consequences of this for deeper regional integration are many. For example, since member states make sure that they refer to the principle of national sovereignty in all SADC policy documents (Matlosa 2006), the various regional policy documents signed by the member states are in practice not binding, which results in a lack of political commitment to implement agreed conventions, norms and standards. Additionally, SADC member states hardly put any effort into translating regional protocols, declarations and codes of conducts into practice, which requires legal reforms (Malaudzi 2006: 12; Matlosa and Lotshwao 2010: 47–48). Last, the consensus model of deliberations practiced in SADC decision-making organs such as the summit ensures that the SADC is a traditional inter-*governmental* body as opposed to a supra-national entity (Blaauw 2007: 194). On the whole, the unwillingness of SADC member states to share sovereignty and promote regional citizenship from above, as also discussed earlier, are great impediments for building a common regional community in Southern Africa. This fundamentally affects the relationship with civil society.

The SADC frequently and strongly proclaims the need to involve civil society in regional integration. The need to forge partnerships with CSOs is addressed in the SADC Treaty:

> SADC shall seek to involve fully, the people of the Region and non-governmental organisations in the process of regional integration [. . .] SADC shall co-operate with, and support the initiatives of the peoples of the Region and non-governmental organisations, contributing to the objectives of this Treaty in the areas of co-operation in order to foster closer relations among the communities, associations and people of the Region.
>
> (SADC 1992: §23)

Subsequent amendments to the Treaty in 2001 also make reference to the role that civil society such as NGOs and workers' organizations should play in regional integration efforts (Blaauw 2007: 207). However, this and other proclamations are mainly rhetorical statements which are not materialized in reality. Since the SADC is built on political state systems where democracy has not matured, as in other parts of Africa, it is not part of the member states' and the SADC's political culture to interact with non-state actors.[2] The SADC is largely driven by power politics and logically does not voluntarily give up that power to the benefit of CSOs.[3]

In more detail, the role of civil society within the SADC is not yet clear. The Treaty fails to define exactly what status civil society has in the envisaged partnership (Balule 2009). The SADC has not defined any clear criteria for interaction with civil society, and it is uncertain which CSOs can actually qualify for co-operation.[4] The SADC has failed to develop concrete overall modalities and mechanisms for collaboration with civil society (Balule 2009). For example, there is not yet a formalized SADC participatory framework which takes into consideration all the possible avenues for public participation in the SADC (Nzewi and Zakwe 2009: 43). To conclude, 'civil society involvement and participation is limited in a structural way'.[5]

It is widely recognized by civil society and academic commentators that civil society is in practice deliberately marginalized in SADC-led regionalism and that consultation with CSOs in various sectors is more or less minimal, if not non-existent.[6] In fact, the SADC itself is very honest about the reluctance to engage with CSOs. According to one SADC representative, the SADC has no interest in interacting with researchers and CSOs. Interaction and consultation only takes place when it is meaningful and advantageous for the SADC: 'If it is convenient for you, we are really too busy and just don't have time for you. SADC is a closed institution that has not prioritized to work with civil society'.[7] All in all, according to Matlosa and Lotshwao, '[t]he integration agenda still remains state-centric, elite-dominated and exclusionary. Ordinary people still remain objects, and not subjects, in a regional project ostensibly aimed at improving their lives' (2010: 49). Hence, the statist social structure has deeply influenced SADC-led regional governance. In other words, the SADC is an important regional institution for reproducing a statist regional order in Southern Africa.

Implications of the capitalist social structure

In this section, the capitalist social structure in Southern Africa will be discussed, first in terms of the general neo-liberalization of the region, which has resulted in, second, a largely problem-solving civil society. Third, the implications of the capitalist social structure for regional governance will be addressed.

The neo-liberal project

Besides statism, capitalism, manifested by the neo-liberal discourse, has made substantial imprints on social order in Africa. In order to further strengthen the hegemonic world order, peripheral regions are gradually integrated into the world economy, and Africa is not an exception to this. In fact, quite the contrary is true. Africa is at the forefront of the globalized project of neo-liberal reform and has undergone extensive and protracted neo-liberal social engineering during the past 30 years (Harrison 2010). Despite many experiments with alternative political systems in Africa after independence, of which Nyerere's African Socialism in Tanzania is perhaps the most famous example, most African countries eventually resorted to market capitalism (Thomson 2010: 44), in line with the global hegemonic idea of the 'free market'. Even if many governments initially wanted to control market forces and therefore developed state capitalism in which the regime encouraged private enterprise but in many ways retained control over the market (Thomson 2010: 44), widespread neo-liberal privatization and liberalization gradually gained a stronghold in many countries. In fact, the rigour and persistence of these reforms on the continent is a good example of what one scholar calls 'scientific capitalism' (Ferguson 1995). Driven by international financial institutions (IFIs) such as the World Bank and International Monetary Fund (IMF), as well as foreign donors, the neo-liberal economic and political packages of trade liberalization, the privatization of national assets and resources, the commodification of social services and the marketization of goods and services have become intrinsic in policy-making in African states. At the same time, a large part of the African political, economic and intellectual elite has voluntarily accommodated this neo-liberal discourse (Shivji 2007), gradually joining the transnational managerial class. To a large extent, the implementation of neo-liberal reform has been mandatory for African states subject to the World Bank's Structural Adjustment Programmes (SAPs) and has left them with little choice to embark on alternative economic frameworks. According to one scholar, 'the extent of interventions to promote the putative free market has been remarkable over the past 30 years [. . .] and place the highest priority on freedom of manoeuvre for private capital' (Fine 2010: 73). Furthermore, neo-liberal reforms have been infused with social programmes to ease difficult neo-liberal transitions. In essence, this means providing safety nets for weak parts of the population that lose out during the shift to a neo-liberal political economy (Harrison 2010: 102), in line with the dominant problem-solving rationale. Civil society plays an important role here, as will be discussed in the next section.

The global neo-liberal pressure is particularly strong in Southern Africa. Neo-liberal reforms have taken place in almost all countries in Southern Africa, often through external coercion. Many states in the region have been forced to implement SAPs and the successor programme, Poverty Reduction Strategy Papers (PRSPs), which have imposed upon them neo-liberal economic reform packages under the supervision of IMF and the World Bank. At the same time, there is a big element of free will in the neo-liberal adoption. Many states have voluntarily adjusted their domestic economic policies in line with changing global economic conditions in order to better benefit from economic globalization. One good example is the South African pro-market Growth, Employment and Redistribution Programme (GEAR). The neo-liberal reforms, as in the rest of Africa, mean trade liberalization, the privatization of public enterprises, currency devaluation, price decontrol, the reduction of state expenditure, achieving real interest rates and maintaining macroeconomic stability in order to create the foundations for market-led development and integrate the regional economies into the world capitalist system (Tsie 2001; Kanyenze et al. 2006). Neo-liberal reforms have great implications for the evolution of civil society in the region, including the regionalization of civil society, which will be discussed later.

Besides the neo-liberal stronghold, another striking feature about the Southern African region is the economic dominance of South Africa (Odén 2001; Tsie 2001). The widespread and deep neo-liberal economic reforms in the region since the beginning of the 1980s can be seen as the latest stage in the historical evolution of a regional capitalist political economy in Southern Africa that revolves around that country. During the colonial era, a form of regional capitalism emerged that was based on structural integration among South Africa, the centre, and the neighbouring states, which became peripheral service economies. The regional political economy has gradually been constituted and integrated through production, capital transport and labour patterns. South African investments in regional infrastructure, mineral production and cash crops throughout the region, in combination with labour migration, tied the entire region together into a system that reinforced the interests of South African mining and plantation capital (Söderbaum 2004a: 64–65). Since then, economic development has been marked by uneven penetration of capitalism in the region, and South Africa remains the key locus of capital accumulation in the region (Matlosa 2006: 5).

The historical polarized patterns of accumulation ensure that the rest of the SADC economies remain dependent on South Africa for trade routes, food imports, labour migration, foreign investment and a number of manufactured goods. In the current regional political economy, the economies of individual countries such as Mozambique and Zimbabwe are connected to and deeply affected by regional processes revolving around South African capital.[8] The GNP of South Africa is four times that of the other SADC members combined, and South African business completely dominates trade in the region (Blaauw 2007: 43). On the whole, regional economic integration in Southern Africa is highly asymmetric, where there is a heavy dependence on the export of primary commodities for weaker economies against the import of basic goods and services from South Africa. In this unequal exchange of goods, weaker countries suffer because they cannot compete in the current market-driven regional order (Pressend 2010). The extremely asymmetrical trade flows 'clearly reveal that South Africa is a semi-industrialized country juxtaposed to a backward, underdeveloped periphery which is nevertheless of paramount importance to its future growth and prosperity' (Tsie 2001: 134). The tendency, then, is that South Africa plays a dominating role, hindering regional development instead of acting as the regional motor from which all parts of the region can benefit (Odén 2001). In the words of one scholar, 'in the affairs of the region, South Africa continues to dominate' (Vale 2003: 137). In fact, this has created hostility among other member states, fearing that South Africa will re-colonize the region (Mulaudzi 2006: 15). The implications of South African dominance for civil society regionalization will briefly be discussed in Chapter 6.

One important implication of the capitalist social order in Southern Africa for ordinary people is the evolving informal sector. The privatization or dismantling of industries as a consequence of SAPs have caused widespread unemployment in the region and left urban dwellers with no other source of income. Forgotten by the state and untouched by development policy, in order to secure livelihoods many poor people often resort to informal economic activities, of which informal cross-border trade (ICBT) is one good example (Matlosa 2006: 9; Mijere 2009). Here, informal traders buy their goods in informal markets and travel with their goods between states (IOM 2010a). According to some new studies, the informal sector in fact employs the largest proportion of the total labour force, and ICBT forms a substantial percentage of economic activity in the Southern African economy, albeit highly undocumented (e.g. Matlosa 2006; SARDC 2008; Mijere 2009; IOM 2010a). In fact, ICBT could possibly make up almost 40% of total trade in the region (SARDC 2008).

Problem-solving civil society

Since the late 1980s, civil society has indeed become one of the leading concepts in African development, expected to help in both improving the quality of the African state and contributing to development and democratization (Opoku-Mensah 2008: 75).[9] According to one scholar, '[w]hen NGOs emerged in the 1980s and 1990s to play a central role in development they were greeted as a "magic bullet", the panacea to failed top-down development' (Hearn 2007: 1096). In line with the prevailing neo-liberal discourse, this reflects that the state is blamed for lack of development in Africa. The failure of African governments, their institutions and structures in addressing the problems of welfare, poverty and human development has paved the way for NGOs to take the place of the state (Dibie 2008: 2). This goes hand in hand with a period of widespread political liberalization in Africa, which has also legitimized civil society as a relevant arena for democratization (Dibie 2008: 2).

Providing social services to poor and marginalized areas but also improving policies related to the facilitation of market forces, non-state actors such as NGOs and business associations have become important partners to states, hand in hand with the shrinking of public sectors and the dismantling of welfare systems. To a large extent, social welfare and the provision of basic needs and services to the community are assigned to NGOs and are no longer the responsibility of the state or the private sector (Shivji 2007: 40). According to one commentator, NGOs 'were born in the womb of neo-liberalism [. . . and] are inextricably imbricated in the neo-liberal offensive [. . .] playing the role of ideological and organizational foot soldiers of imperialism, however this is described' (Shivji 2007: 40, 29). Hence, the function of civil society in Africa is greatly influenced by the neo-liberal project.

In most regards, African NGOs generally buy into the mainstream problem-solving agenda inherent in the prevailing global neo-liberal ideology, in which development problems inherent in the dysfunction of the social order, such as lack of services and the malfunction of certain political structures and markets, are to be 'solved' by state–NGO partnership. Hence, civil society in Africa is focusing more on meeting immediate societal needs than on having political functions in terms of influencing the overall policy environment on a deeper level through lobbying and advocacy and addressing the root causes of development problems. Therefore, civil society plays a weak role in public policy-making (Opoku-Mensah 2008). Furthermore, due to their incorporation into the overall neo-liberal ideology, the model for the successful NGO is the corporation. The success of an NGO is to a large extent measured by its efficiency, a criterion borrowed from the corporate sector. According to one commentator, 'NGOs are ever more marked and judged against corporate ideals' (Shivji 2007: 33). Therefore, the strategic planning of an organization is often tied to log frames in which development interventions are tabulated and quantified (Shivji 2007: 33).

As is the case of Africa at large, civil society in Southern Africa largely plays a problem-solving role and is generally active in poverty alleviation through providing various social services to the poor, filling the service-provision gap of the state. In Tanzania, for example, the charitable and voluntary dimensions dominate the character of CSOs, which are often referred to as welfare organizations (Michael 2004; Ndumbaro and Kiondo 2007). CSOs here play a heavy role in service delivery, foremost related to gender, the environment, education and health, but lack engagement with the wider issues of the root causes of underdevelopment and are rather absent in advocacy work (Michael 2004). Similarly, in Mozambique CSOs are by far more committed to providing services, sometimes as an extension of public administration services, than to participating in political life. Service provision is mostly related to the sectors of development and housing, health, the environment, social services and culture, education and recreation. In general, CSOs have a weak lobby and advocacy capacity, and resorting to more radical contentious forms of struggle such as strikes, demonstrations and petitions is virtually unknown in Mozambique (FDC 2007). Most South African CSOs are also engaged in service activities, which is partly due to the fact that the South African government since 1994 has bolstered its relationship with civil society in policy development and implementation and has welcomed dialogue and cooperation (Swilling et al. 2004: 117), in line with the political but also economic liberalization in the country. At least parts of civil society are considered to be a partner in development, and civil society is perceived as an extension of the service-delivery and policy-making capacity of the state. In addition, civil society is somehow encouraged by the government to perform a watchdog role, pushing the state to deliver what it has promised. However, this liberal attitude towards civil society only applies to those sections of civil society that buy into the current overall macro-economic government policy in the country in terms of privatization, trade liberalization, limited state intervention in the economy and the rationalization of public services. The dynamics of the capitalist social structure have also created critical NGOs and social movements that challenge and contradict government policy, for example in terms of the privatization of water and market-based land reform, and which demand increased and improved public service delivery to the poor. These actors are often seen as enemies by the state and *vice versa*. Often, contentious strategies such as demonstrations, civil disobedience and mass mobilization are used outside of the formal and accepted ways of interacting with the state (Ranchod 2007).

Funding NGOs, donors play an important role in the 'neo-liberal offensive' in the region. Being highly dependent on the prevailing (neo-liberal) donor agenda when designing their development programmes, NGOs are becoming increasingly donor driven (Shivji 2007). In other words, 'NGOs are set up to respond to whatever is perceived to be in vogue among the donor-community at any particular time' (Shivji 2007: 32). Therefore, many African NGOs are seen merely as an extension of the dominant donor aid agenda and as agents of Western interests. One commentator concludes that many NGOs have become 'local managers of foreign aid money, not managers of local African development processes' (Hearn 2007: 1107). In Mozambique, most CSOs have emerged as a result of donor funding and generate 70% of their income from foreign donors (FDC 2007). CSOs are drawn into sectors where there is a lot of money at the time. As a result they adopt the agenda of their donors and the working strategies donors put forward to the CSOs, meaning they are tied into the guidelines and discourse of the donor.[10] Similarly, in Tanzania, almost half of CSO revenues come from donors (Ndumbro and Kiondo 2007), and in Zimbabwe most CSOs rely mainly on donor funding (Sachikonye 2007).

As indicated earlier, deeply influenced by the capitalist social structure, civil society in Africa has become 'the place to make money' (Hearn 2007: 1102), generating briefcase NGOs driven primarily by economic self-interest, material gain and careerism rather than by altruism (e.g. Dicklitch 1998: 8; Michael 2004; Shivji 2007). These NGOs are led by representatives from the economic and political elites, not infrequently former government bureaucrats who joined or started NGOs when donor funding was being directed there (Shivji 2007: 321). This deeply affects questions of accountability and legitimacy for CSOs. In Mozambique, for example, CSOs are considered less democratic due to weak transparency, the lack of a culture of accountability and weak public confidence in CSOs that have a limited role in promoting social capital at the grassroots level (FDC 2007). In Zimbabwe, likewise, accountability to the grassroots has been a problem for CSOs. Some of them have failed to account for funds they have obtained, many CSO leaders are accused of corruption, and several CSOs lack legitimacy due to limited grassroots participation in their activities (Sachikonye 2007: 66). In Tanzania it is claimed that 'some people treat NGOs as their private property and, in this sense, are limited in membership' (Ndumbro and Kiondo 2007: 29). In one study it was found that at least 5% of registered NGOs are 'pocket organizations', mainly established to cater for private interests. Many NGOs also show low levels of transparency, and many organizations are reluctant to disclose their revenues and expenditures (Ndumbro and Kiondo 2007: 37). The (lack of) legitimacy of civil society on the regional level will be briefly discussed in the concluding chapter.

The SADC and neo-liberal regional governance

Regionalism in Southern Africa has to be seen within the context of regional economic neo-liberalism and economic globalization (Söderbaum 2004a), besides being deeply affected by the statist social structure discussed in the first half of this chapter. As indicated in the opening paragraph of this chapter, regionalism in Southern Africa and other African sub-regions should be seen as a regional manifestation of the current neo-liberal global architecture and is often referred to as 'open regionalism' (Harrison 2010). This signifies the ambition to synchronize regional market integration with economic globalization (Söderbaum 2004a: 78).

Consequently, the SADC is largely driven by the neo-liberal logic, in which trade is highly prioritized (Söderbaum 2004a), and a true version of neo-liberal regional governance. In more detail, this implies emphasizing regional economic integration which is market driven and outward looking, in which obstacles to the free movement of goods, services, capital and investment within the region and to the rest of the world should be removed (Söderbaum 2004a: 75). Hence, free trade areas, such as the one the SADC launched in 2008, constitute stepping-stones towards regional and inter-regional free trade (Söderbaum and Taylor 2008: 25). In most aspects, then, the neo-liberal type of regionalism the SADC supports today is greatly influenced by the global free trade paradigm (Pressend 2010). In fact, this is so entrenched among SADC leaders that 'rarely are the nature of free trade and its assumptions challenged' (Pressend 2010).

Neo-liberal regional governance is more concretely manifested in a number of ways. For example, the emphasis on so-called 'development corridors' is claimed by the SADC to bring globalization to Southern Africa and at the same time enhance regional economic integration (Söderbaum and Taylor 2008: 25). The best example is the Maputo Development Corridor (MDC), initiated by the SADC as an important regional development project to reconstruct, revitalize and formalize economic cross-border relationships between Mozambique and South Africa, even though it also aims to gradually benefit Swaziland, Botswana and Zimbabwe. The basic idea behind the initiative is the implementation of a large number of investment projects related to infrastructure and economic development in order to foster cross-border trade. Most important is the rehabilitation of the road and rail links between Maputo and the Gauteng area in South Africa (Mulaudzi 2006; Söderbaum and Taylor 2008). In terms of organization and implementation, the MDC lies formally outside the SADC framework, even though it co-operates with the IS Directorate on infrastructure-related projects. The MDC is frequently referred to in various SADC policy documents. For example, among the chief principles guiding the RISDP is that implementation should take place within the context of existing development corridors in the region (SADC 2003a). The most important institution for the coordination of MDC-related projects is the Maputo Corridor

Logistics Initiative (MCLI), an independent membership organization comprised of private investors, service providers and public actors (Söderbaum and Taylor 2008: 47).

Furthermore, the 'openness' of neo-liberal regional governance in Southern Africa is manifested by the Economic Partnership Agreements (EPAs) between the EU and the SADC. EPAs refer to contractual and reciprocal trade, development and cooperation agreements negotiated between the EU as one party and six regional groups of African, Caribbean and Pacific countries as the other party (Shilimela 2008). On a more general level, EPAs are said to foster the integration of SADC countries into the world economy in terms of trade and private investment. Hence, the EU–SADC co-operation aims at 'enhancing the productivity, supply and trading capacity of the [SADC] countries as well as their capacity to attract investment [. . .] strengthening trade and investment policies' (Lorenz 2011: 5).

Therefore, one important role of regional institutions related to the SADC is to facilitate trade through various liberalization schemes, since the private sector is seen as the driving force behind regional development (Söderbaum 2004a, 2004b: 423, 425). As a result, one main task of the SADC is to facilitate the movement of goods and capital by the removal of tariff and non-tariff barriers (Matlosa 2006: 7–8). However, it is mainly elites and corporations that benefit from trade liberalization, to a large extent those residing in South Africa, at the expense of, for example, informal traders. This will be further discussed in Chapter 4. Regional free trade pushed by neo-liberal regional governance frameworks is mainly but not only in the interests of South African capital, especially those sections that are globally integrated and therefore benefit the most from open regionalism (Leysens 2001).

In line with the emphasis put on the reduction of the state in order to boost the private sector, the welfare and development ambitions of the state are increasingly rolled back, and poverty reduction is reduced to economic growth in which development projects must be profitable. Therefore, in order to build consent among state and non-state actors in the region around a regional order that mostly benefits South African capital, according to one scholar, South Africa, as the political-economic hegemon, has pushed the SADC to adopt a 'universalist [development] language used in SADC documents [. . .] to compensate, reward or simply placate the subordinate/marginalized social forces' (Leysens 2001: 232) which lose out from the current hegemonic regional order. In line with the overall neo-liberal agenda of easing the pain of economic restructuring, pushed by South Africa the SADC has therefore designed some corrective measures to mitigate the negative consequences of regional integration for poor people (Mittelman 1999; Kanyenze et al. 2006) such as the spread of HIV/AIDS, environmental degradation and the informalization of the economy, discussed further in the empirical chapters. However, the developmental rhetoric of the SADC hides a hegemonic capitalist order dominated by South Africa (Leysens 2001). With the focus on market integration, the SADC in practice puts little emphasis on social issues, despite the inclusion of various social charters in integration agreements (Mittelman 1999). In other words, 'in rhetoric [. . .] there appears to be some degree of commitment to the idea of taming the market and embracing developmentalism. In practice, the evidence seems to point in a different direction' (Ajulu 2007: 37).

The neo-liberal inclinations imply that the SADC views business as particularly important in the process of regional integration (Matlosa 2006: 7–8). Through public–private partnerships (PPPs), business in the region is playing a critical role, for example in building infrastructure, in the promotion of the SADC region as an investment centre and in job creation (Blaauw 2007: 205). Hence, of the regional non-state organizations associated with the SADC, either informally or through a formal agreement, the majority are business related (Blaauw 2007: 205).[11] Furthermore, even though policy-making and social programmes related to HIV/AIDS, gender, the protection of workers' rights and environmental education are quite weak and suffer from poor implementation, they do involve collaboration with certain service-providing and research NGOs active in these areas. Such CSOs engage with regional interstate frameworks on a consultative basis, mainly in order to solve joint problems related to, for example, policy development and the lack of social services, as will be further discussed in Chapters 4 and 5.

On the whole, the SADC as a regional institution serves the purpose of legitimizing and reproducing a capitalist regional order dominated by South Africa.

Notes

1 The Common Market for Eastern and Southern Africa (COMESA) is another important RIGO in the region with Burundi, Comoros, DRC, Djibouti, Egypt, Eritrea, Ethiopia, Kenya, Libya, Seychelles, Madagascar, Malawi, Mauritius, Rwanda, Sudan, Swaziland, Uganda, Zambia and Zimbabwe as member states. The regional Secretariat is situated in Lusaka, Zambia. The overall aim is to achieve sustainable economic and social progress in all member states through increased co-operation and integration in various fields of development. According to the home page, COMESA's current strategy can be summed up with the words 'economic prosperity through regional integration' (COMESA 2013). However, due to the little engagement with COMESA by the targeted CSOs in this book, it will only sporadically be included in the discussion in Chapters 4 and 5. For the same reason, another RIGO, Southern African Customs Union (SACU), is left out in the empirical analysis. SACU is a customs union among Boswana, Lesotho, Namibia, South Africa and Swaziland with a regional secretariat situated in Windhoek, Namibia. It aims to facilitate trade in terms of maintaining the free interchange of goods among member countries. It provides for a common external tariff and a common excise tariff to this customs area. SACU also wants to be a vehicle for deeper development integration within the broader Southern African region (SACU 2013).
2 le Pere, interview, 27 November 2008.
3 Ncube, interview, 8 December 2008.
4 le Pere, interview, 27 November 2008.
5 Barnard, interview, 26 November 2008.
6 E.g. Osei-Hwedie, interview, 5 December 2008; le Pere, interview, 27 November 2008; Ashley, interview, 17 December 2009; Landsberg 2012; SADC-CNGO 2009a.
7 Ncube, interview, 8 December 2008.
8 Castel-Branco, interview, 24 November 2008.

9 Civil societies in Africa are gradually expanding in number and scope and in terms of influence over development processes on the continent. During the last 25 to 30 years, the number of NGOs has increased dramatically in Africa (e.g. Michael 2004; Hearn 2007). One scholar goes as far as calling the growth of NGOs 'explosive' (Dibie 2008). In fact, it is claimed that of all regions in the South, Africa is the one which has experienced the most pronounced proliferation of NGOs (Michael 2004: 7). In Tanzania, according to one study from 2007 there were about 58,000 registered CSOs (Ndumbaro and Mvungi 2007), in South Africa 101,000 (Swilling et al. 2004), and in Kenya in 2005 there were amazingly 350,000 registered CSOs (Kanyinga and Mitullah 2007). These numbers have most certainly increased since then.
10 Castel-Branco, interview, 24 November 2008.
11 Gilson (2011b) and Ameli (2011) have observed the same trend in civil society engagement with regional governance processes related to the Asia-Europe Meeting (ASEM) and the Organisation of the Islamic Conference (OIC) respectively. Here, business-related groups have better access compared with development-oriented NGOs and social movements.

Chapter 4
Civil society regionalization in the trade sector in Southern Africa

As was shown in the previous chapter, structure matters. This was very clear when analyzing the state of states and CSOs in Southern Africa, including the (sovereignty-boosting and neo-liberal) nature of regional governance. It was shown how states dominate civil societies in the region and the problem-solving character of the latter, due to the statist and capitalist social structure. This has made a deep imprint on civil society regionalization in the trade and HIV/AIDS sectors. However, at the same time, even if CSOs are influenced by the regional social order they are not passive actors subsumed under the statist and capitalist structures but actively participate in regional governance, advocate for policy reform, tap into regional funds, frame regional issues and construct regional identities. Hence, CSOs are active participants in building the Southern African region. This will now be discussed, starting with the trade sector in this chapter, moving on to the HIV/AIDS sector in the following one.

Key RCSOs

In this section, 11 important regional NGOs and networks related to trade will be briefly presented. To start with, the Association of SADC Chambers of Commerce and Industry (ASCCI) is a non-profit private-sector regional network, based in Gaborone, Botswana, which brings together 18 national chambers of commerce organizations, trade associations, employer organizations and confederations of industries from all SADC states. ASCCI aims to facilitate the effective participation of organized business in the SADC and to enhance the role of the private sector in regional integration. Its driving principles are private-sector growth, an improved business and investment climate, and development of a free market economy system in the SADC (ASCCI 2016). In terms of the analytical distinction between different types of network, discussed in the conceptual section in the introductory chapter, ASCCI is a good example of a facilitating network with an advocacy element.

The SADC Private Sector Forum (SPSF) (formerly SADC Employers Group, SPSF) is a network of 11 national employers' organizations in Southern Africa. The secretariat is hosted by one of the members, the Botswana Confederation of Commerce, Industry & Manpower (BOCCIM), in Gaborone, Botswana. SPSF seeks to be a leading regional private-sector organization that contributes to the SADC regional integration programs. It aims to improve the trading and investment environment in the region, to strengthen relationships between members and to participate in regional policy-making (SPSF 2016). SPSF is an example of a combination of a facilitating and advocacy network.

The SADC Council of Non-Governmental Organizations (SADC-CNGO) is a regional civil society network made up of 15 national networks of NGOs, from all SADC countries, with a secretariat in Gaborone, Botswana. SADC-CNGO seeks to influence development policies in the SADC, to accelerate their implementation and to advance NGO interests and perspectives and more specifically to create conditions that favour people-centred regional economic integration. SADC-CNGO wants to coordinate and provide leadership to civil society in the region and to improve capacity to engage with regional integration and development issues within the SADC (SADC-CNGO 2009a). SADC-CNGO is a combination of a facilitating and advocacy network.

The Southern African Research and Development Centre (SARDC) is a regional resource centre based in Harare, which produces and disseminates information about development processes and regional integration in the SADC region to various state and non-state actors.

SARDC's research concerns regional trade and development issues (SARDC 2016). SARDC is a combination of a service-providing and research NGO.

The Southern and Eastern African Trade Information and Negotiations Institute (SEATINI) is another regional research/training/lobby group, with a similar outlook to SARDC. SEATINI works in 21 countries in the Southern and Eastern African region, with regional headquarters in Harare, Zimbabwe, and a national office in Kampala, Uganda. SEATINI tries to strengthen the capacity of policymakers, CSOs and the media to play a more effective part in global, regional and national trade and financial processes. SEATINI monitors developments in the trade area, undertakes research related to trade and development and disseminates information to the public (SEATINI 2016). SEATINI is a broad NGO in terms of its activities and has elements of service provision, research and advocacy.

Another regional research and training centre is the Trade and Development Studies Centre (Trades Centre), based in Harare, Zimbabwe. Trades's aim is to analyze trade and development issues from the perspectives of Southern Africa's poor communities and to explore the implications of the various international, regional and bilateral trade agreements. More specifically, Trades carries out policy-relevant training, research and analysis for government, private and civil-society actors, particularly focusing on the nexus between trade and development, aid and development and poverty alleviation and welfare (Trades Centre 2012). Trades Centre is mix of a service-providing and research NGO.

The Southern Africa Trade Union Coordination Council (SATUCC) is a regional network of 18 trade union federations in the SADC and is based in Gaborone, Botswana. SATUCC's aim is to strengthen solidarity amongst trade unions in the sub-region and to give voice to labour issues at the regional level. SATUCC is a platform for trade unions and workers to engage with and influence policies nationally and regionally through the active and effective participation of affiliate national federations (SATUCC 2016). SATUCC is a good example of an advocacy network.

The Southern African People's Solidarity Network (SAPSN) is also heavily involved in trade, labour and social rights issues and fights for an alternative development and regional integration agenda. The secretariat is currently hosted by the Malawi Economic Justice Network (MEJN) in Lilongwe, Malawi. The SAPSN network involves 26 CSOs from nine countries in the region, such as trade unions, social movements, CBOs and NGOs. SAPSN's mission is to mobilize regional solidarity, to build members' capacities and to support people-based regional cooperation in the fight against the debt crisis, global trade injustices and neo-liberal policies. SAPSN regularly holds regional workshops and produces evidence-based research (SAPSN n.d.a). SAPSN is another example of an advocacy network.

The Economic Justice Network of FOCCISA, the Fellowship of Christian Councils in Southern Africa (EJN), is the most important ecumenical regional network, involving 11 national councils of churches in Southern Africa. The head office is in Cape Town, South Africa. EJN wants to strengthen the commitment of the church in advocacy work on economic justice, lobbies national and regional policy-makers such as the SADC on trade-oriented issues such as EPA and ICBT and acts as a catalyst for engaging people in the promotion of just economic and social structures in the region (EJN 2016a). EJN is also an advocacy network.

The Zambia Cross-Border Traders Association (CBTA) is a membership organization of informal traders based in Lusaka, Zambia. The main focus lies in Zambia, but CBTA is also active in Eastern and Southern Africa, with 40 branches throughout the region. The aim of CBTA is to represent informal traders in negotiations with government and regional institutions and to provide social assistance to informal traders (Nchito and Tranberg Hansen 2010: 171, 173). CBTA is a combination of a facilitating and advocacy network.

Until recently, CBTA was the main organization for advancing the interests of informal traders in the region. However, in 2012 the Southern African Cross-Border Traders Association (SACBTA), a more pure *regional* organization, was formed in order to strengthen the regional representation of informal traders. The SACBTA is a membership organization with five national cross-border traders' associations as members. The regional secretariat is hosted by the SADC-CNGO in Gaborone, Botswana. The overall objective is to protect the rights of informal traders through, for example, engaging with and influencing national and regional policy-makers, building the capacity of national members and promoting networking (SACBTA 2012). As for CBTA, SACBTA is also a combination of a facilitating and advocacy network.

Relations between the SADC and CSOs

This section will discuss how the statist-capitalist informed social relations between SADC institutions and various RCSOs influence civil society regionalization in the trade sector in three different ways. First, the trade-related issues prioritized in the SADC agenda and how this affects the regional work of CSOs are targeted. Second, focus is put on the direct and indirect creation of regional platforms for CSO collaboration. Third, intimately related to the SADC's issue preferences, the inclusion of certain CSOs and the exclusion of others in various SADC institutions will be analyzed in terms of how this affects civil society regionalization.

SADC issue preferences

As indicated in the last chapter, the SADC type of regional governance is inherently neo-liberal and market oriented, with a great focus on fostering regional economic co-operation in general and trade integration in particular. Hence, despite grand declarations about fostering regional social and economic equity and human rights in various regional documents, such as the SADC Treaty and RISDP, in reality the main focus is on trade (Peters-Berries 2010; TRALAC 2012). One important component of RISDP is the 15-year framework for intensified regional economic integration, which sets time-bound targets for the trade-driven regional integration approach of the SADC (Peters 2011: 146). According to the framework, the plan is to have a Free-Trade Area (FTA) by 2008, an SADC customs union by 2010, an SADC common market by 2015, an SADC monetary union and central bank by 2016 and a regional currency by 2018 (SADC 2008a).

So far, only the first target has been achieved. The FTA was launched in August 2008 (TRALAC 2012), coupled with a lot of prestige on behalf of SADC leaders, and is considered the most important event in the history of the SADC (Salomao 2008). Significant challenges have emerged in the trade integration process, for example related to the reduction of trade barriers, which contributed to the failure to launch the SADC Customs Union in 2010 (TRALAC 2012). Despite the challenges, trade integration is at the heart of SADC-led neo-liberal regional governance, and challenging this agenda therefore means contesting the foundation of the SADC.

Due to the dominance of neo-liberal regional governance in Southern Africa, manifesting the capitalist regional order discussed in the previous chapter, in the trade integration agenda important social issues connected to trade, such as ICBT and labour rights, are downplayed. In terms of ICBT, this is not taken seriously by the SADC. Most trade-related policy-makers at national and regional levels continue to ignore the informal dimension of trade, partly due to its perceived illegal character and the consequent perspective that it should not be facilitated (e.g. SARDC 2008; Makombe 2010; Mwaniki n.d.; Masango and Haraldsson 2010). This is despite the fact that ICBT is an important instrument for efficient poverty-alleviation in the region, since it creates livelihood opportunities for a great number of poor people (e.g. Masango and Haraldsson 2010). However, the linkage between informal trade and development falls outside the remit of traditional trade-related policy-making. According to the

TIFI representative, the SADC considers trade integration ultimately to be about goods.[1]

The SADC's overall policy document, the SADC Treaty, does not mention informal trade or the informal economy more broadly in any way. In terms of RISDP, it is briefly stated that the informal sector should be acknowledged and taken on board in regional integration in terms of both trade liberalization and actual production (Southern African Trust 2008: 9). However, in terms of more specific regional policy documents related to trade, 'the ICBT sector continues to be marginalized' (Southern African Trust 2008: 9). For example, the important SADC Protocol on Trade does not address the social dimension of trade and ignores ICBT issues (Makombe 2010). Even if the provisions of the protocol are relevant and important for informal traders, addressing issues of high relevance to them such as transportation, exemption from customs, customs legislation, import and export restrictions and the like, it does not recognize the sector or respond to its needs (Makombe 2010). This has to do with the fact that the measures for facilitating regional trade are designed only for established companies and by consequence are of little relevance to informal traders. One important study concludes that 'the SADC trade protocol does not benefit ICBT in any significant ways, if at all' (SARDC 2008). Similarly, according to SACBTA, at an overall SADC level 'regional economic policies are not conducive to informal cross border trade' (2012: 5). Since the Trade Protocol is essentially premised on the free trade paradigm (Pressend 2010), this and other policy documents related to trade are not deliberate policies on ICBT but on established business. It is argued that there is a need to come up with a separate policy framework which specifically targets ICBT (SARDC 2008).

Last, in terms of labour issues, according to the former general secretary of SATUCC, to a certain extent the SADC has put instruments in place in order to promote regional labour standards. One major achievement is the Charter of Fundamental Social Rights in the SADC often referred to as the Social Charter, adopted in 2003, which among other things aims to promote the establishment and harmonization of labour policies and measures that facilitate labour mobility, social security schemes and regulations relating to health and safety standards at workplaces across the region (SADC 2003b). However, as is the case for movement of people and ICBT, implementation lags behind.[2] It is very uncertain how seriously SADC members take the rhetorical emphasis put on social issues such as labour rights in practice. For example, social issues tend to be downplayed in key SADC policy-making institutions such as the previously existing Integrated Committee of Ministers (ICM).[3] Since no guidelines exist in terms of which ministers should attend ICM meetings, ministers of finance and trade dominate the structure at the expense of social sector ministers, who are marginalized (SATUCC n.d.). In order to develop and institutionalize the employment and labour agenda as articulated in the RISDP and Social Charter, SADC designed an Employment and Labour Protocol (SADC 2011b), which was signed at the Summit in 2014 after a consultative process. The Protocol is intended to facilitate the harmonization of labour and employment policies/legislation in the region; facilitate the promotion of productive employment creation; and to ensure minimum labour standards, social protection and social dialogue (SATUCC 2015). However, as of February 2016, the Protocol has not been ratified by the member states and is not yet operational.

It is argued here that the general ignorance of the SADC towards the more social aspects of trade ultimately boils down to the state-centric and capitalist regional order. Despite grand declarations on the importance of involving CSOs in regional integration, including the trade area, the ignorance of ICBT and other social dimensions of trade in practice partly relates to the fact that SADC policy-makers invoke a traditional discourse of sovereign statehood in order to dodge social issues and avoid serious interaction with CSOs that might compromise the market-oriented neo-liberal agenda. In the words of the director of SADC-CNGO, 'SADC, through the Secretariat, continues to hide behind sovereignty of member states' (SADC-CNGO 2010e: 5). Ignoring ICBT and other social aspects of trade profoundly affects SADC–civil society interaction, discussed later.

However, it should be noted that during the past few years increased attention has been given to social issues. For example, the SADC has shown a growing interest in the ICBT sector and opened up for interaction with relevant CSOs. In a recent civil society awards ceremony in 2014, organized by the Southern Africa Trust and Mail & Guardian, the SADC Executive Secretary claimed that '[t]he important contribution of informal cross border trade to alleviating poverty in the region cannot be over-emphasized' and highlighted the SADC Advocacy Strategy on Informal Cross-Border Trade from 2011 (SADC 2014: 7), which provides a clear policy area for creating an enabling environment for informal cross-border traders. It seeks to create a mechanism for informal traders to engage with governments at national level and support women to have full access to productive resources for a better quality of life (SADC 2011a). An action framework has since been developed (SACBTA 2012: 4). Also in 2011 the SADC Labour Ministers drafted a Protocol on Workers in the Informal Economy, which one prominent commentator considers a major breakthrough in terms of officially recognizing workers in the informal economy, including informal traders.[4] However, as for February 2016 the action framework linked to the strategy is still not implemented, and the protocol has not yet been signed by the SADC Summit, and therefore has no legal status. It should also be said that the strategy, as a separate SADC policy framework which specifically targets ICBT, has a very low policy status in relation to SADC charters, declarations and protocols. Only time will tell if these developments represent a paradigm shift in the SADC's view on regional trade integration to the benefit of informal traders and workers.

The link between poverty eradication and trade is also gaining increased attention, albeit in a problem-solving fashion. One example is the SADC's arrangement of an International Conference on Poverty and Development in Mauritius, which SADC leaders, donors and a few international leaders participated in. The conference aimed to forge regional consensus on the key elements of poverty eradication. It also sought to develop an Action Plan on Poverty and Development, outlining a series of specific tasks and actions and monitoring and evaluation mechanisms (SADC 2012a). The most important outcomes of the conference were the SADC Declaration on Poverty Eradication and Sustainable Development, the Regional

Poverty Reduction Framework (RPRF) and the establishment of a new institution, the SADC Regional Poverty Observatory (RPO).

In the Declaration, SADC leaders acknowledge that, despite great efforts to achieve economic development, more than 40% of the SADC population still lives in extreme poverty. In line with overall neo-liberal regional governance, the linkage between poverty eradication and the standard strategies of economic growth, regional trade liberalization and promotion of business are emphasized throughout in the Declaration. Nevertheless, trade is not the only prescription for combating poverty; providing various social services, promoting education and achieving food security are also highlighted (SADC 2008b). What is most interesting is the focus on implementation and practical work on poverty eradication and the new regional framework for this. The RPRF articulates key intervention areas, strategies and activities and functions as the key implementation mechanism of the RISDP in terms of operationalizing poverty eradication. The RPRF also constitutes the basis for indicators to measure poverty and poverty reduction within the RPO (SADC 2008c). Most importantly, the RPRF and RPO are signs of growing determination to match the rhetorical commitments to poverty eradication and development in the region with practical work on the ground. However, the RPRF has not been properly implemented so far due to weak political will of the SADC leadership and lack of funding (Southern Africa Trust 2014a). According to a representative from SATUCC, the RPRF '... is not a priority. It is being sidelined and not sufficiently operationalised' (Tendai Makanza, quoted in Southern Africa Trust 2014a). The RPO institutional framework will be discussed further in the next section.

SADC focal point creation

The SADC is an important focal point around which CSOs consolidate regionally. The SADC has also played a more direct role in terms of facilitating regional civil society co-operation. These two points will now be discussed. In terms of the former, a number of civil society meetings running parallel to the annual SADC Summit have been held since 2000. In fact, there are two different such meetings: the SADC Civil Society Forum and the People's Summit. The forum is organized by the SADC-CNGO and principally involves NGOs, church groups and trade unions. In recent years it has been run in collaboration with EJN and SATUCC. The overall aim is to improve regional collective civil society engagement with the SADC and to influence SADC leaders in order to enhance regional development (Osei-Hwedie 2009). The first forum was held in conjunction with the SADC Summit in Gaborone, Botswana, in 2005; the second one in Maseru, Lesotho, in 2006; the third one in Lusaka, Zambia, in 2007; the fourth one in Johannesburg, South Africa, in 2008; the fifth one in Kinshasa, DRC, in 2009; and the sixth one in Windhoek, Namibia, in 2010. In 2011, the seventh forum was supposed to be held in Luanda, Angola, but due to reasons explained in what follows was moved to Johannesburg, South Africa. In 2012, the forum was held in Maputo, Mozambique, in 2013 again in South Africa, in 2014 in Harare, Zimbabwe and in 2015 in Gaborone, Botswana.

The People's Summit, organized by SAPSN, has also been held in relation to the SADC Summits. The first meeting occurred in 2000, but the process immediately waned and was only restarted in 2006. Since then, the People's Summit has taken place every year. The People's Summit has a more radical agenda when compared with the forum and attracts a different clientele: principally social movements and advocacy-based CBOs and NGOs. The summit aims to transform and reclaim the SADC for the people and to achieve people-centred regional integration, which is manifested in the so-called 'People's Declaration', issued at the end of every meeting and delivered to the SADC Summit.[5] Even though the forum and summit have different objectives and relate differently to the SADC, they are nevertheless both centred on the latter. In other words, as the prime target group for both the forum and the summit, to a large extent the SADC has informed their creation. This will be further discussed in the next section. In conjunction with each forum and summit, preparatory as well as evaluation meetings have also been organized by the arranging organizations: for example, there was a post-forum feedback meeting in Namibia in 2010 where outcomes of the forum and the way forward were discussed (SADC-CNGO 2010c).

Regarding more direct facilitation of civil society regionalization, through the RPO the SADC has created a platform which facilitates regional state–donor–civil society co-operation around poverty and development issues, including the social aspects of trade. The RPO was formally established after a decision at the SADC Summit in August 2010. It acts as a forum where all stakeholders working in poverty eradication at the national and regional levels, that is civil society, business, government and foreign donors, periodically meet to evaluate and monitor the implementation of the objectives, targets and actions that have been specifically assigned to public and private sectors within the RPRF (SADC 2008c). The RPO is located at the Secretariat, as an individual center, and is often referred to as the RPO Unit. The RPO Steering Committee provides direction to the RPO and plays an advisory role. It consists of one senior official from each member state, five representatives from the regional apex civil society organizations, three experts on poverty and development and two representatives from the donor community. The Regional Stakeholder Forum, made up of all relevant stakeholders, is also convened every two years to deliberate on trends on poverty and development (SADC 2008c). The RPO process has generated a number of possibilities for regional civil society consolidation.

Emphasizing the participatory nature of the RPO, according to the SADC it 'is designed as a multi-stakeholder forum because it has been observed that the involvement of all key stakeholders is key to the success of programs aimed at eradicating poverty in the region' (SADC 2012b: 5). Therefore, the planning process leading up to the creation of the RPRF and the RPO was marked by consultation with civil society,[6] creating a number of regional planning meetings for CSOs to join hands. For example, a major regional conference for member states, SADC officials and CSOs was held in Kinshasa, DRC, at the end of 2009 (SADC 2012b). RCSOs have also been critically involved in the development of the SADC Common Poverty Matrix, with common poverty indicators, which has resulted in several regional civil society meetings (SADC-CNGO 2011a). Furthermore, a Southern Africa Civil Society Reference Group on the RPO was formed to coordinate civil society participation in the planning process and to make concerted input to the new framework. Members of the reference group, that is representatives of women's organizations, social movements, church organizations, trade unions and NGOs, have met regularly to deliberate on the content and operation of the RPO (SADC-CNGO 2011a). EJN, SATUCC and SADC-CNGO, as well as their partners and members, are key players in these processes.

CSO inclusion in the SADC

Regardless of the statist character of the SADC discussed in the last chapter, generally excluding civil society in regional integration, some CSOs in the trade sector have nevertheless been able to participate in various SADC institutions. These CSOs more or less buy in to the SADC's neo-liberal trade agenda and provide policy advice and other services in issue areas where such assistance is wanted by the SADC. Highlighting their proximity to the SADC, both geographically and ideologically, ASCCI and SPSF, together with SADC-CNGO and to some extent SATUCC, are often referred to as SADC subsidiary organizations (Ncube 2009). This implies that (most of) these organizations are located in Gaborone, that they share, more or less, the SADC's regional agenda and that they have formal relations with the Secretariat.

Regional business organizations generally enjoy a fair amount of attention from the SADC and are regularly involved in policy discussions in various SADC institutions. SPSF, for example, is involved in various SADC Technical Committees and working groups, such as the SADC Employment and Labour Task Force, which is comprised of government, labour and employer representatives and discusses regional labour and employment issues. SPSF has regular contact with the SADC Secretariat, for example through TIFI, and is regularly invited to various regional meetings arranged by the SADC, such as the SADC Customs Private Sector Partnership Forum. SPSF has also managed to directly address both the SADC Summit (2008) and SADC COM meetings (2010) with their issues (SPSF 2010).

Furthermore, ASCCI has entered into a memorandum of understanding (MoU)[7] with the SADC on partnership in terms of promotion of business in the region, a core aspect of the SADC's neo-liberal trade agenda. ASCCI regularly arranges regional conferences for SADC officials and government and business representatives to discuss the trade agenda and speed up regional integration (ASCCI 2016). ASCCI, through various sub-committees, also prepares position papers and reports on trade-related issues which are presented at COM meetings of trade ministers and SADC Summits, with the aim of influencing policy and legislation in the region. Last, ASCCI conducts the Regional Business Climate Survey to assess how conducive the environment for trade is in various SADC countries. The survey results are used to lobby the SADC Secretariat and governments to further facilitate regional trade integration (B2B Renewable Energies 2012). According to ASCCI themselves, there is a general willingness from the SADC Secretariat to engage with them, and their interaction with the TIFI and IS Directorates is successful (ASCCI 2012: 10, 14). This is partly due to the fact that the deputy executive secretary for regional integration 'is a strong champion for private-sector involvement within the SADC

Secretariat' (ASCCI 2012: 19), unsurprising considering the SADC's neo-liberal, market-oriented agenda. In fact, in most regards, the SADC and the private sector agree on the present neo-liberal type of regional governance and share the conviction that trade liberalization will create the foundation for economic development and prosperity in the region. In a statement by the SADC private sector at the SADC Summit in 2008, SADC promotion of intra-regional trade and investment through deepening regional economic integration was strongly endorsed (Nkosi 2008).

Furthermore, regional resource and research centres such as SARDC, Trades Centre and SEATINI also participate regularly in SADC-led regional governance and view themselves as partners in a common quest for regional trade integration and development. SARDC works closely with the SADC Secretariat and has signed a MoU which formalizes the relationship. SARDC plays the role of pushing the SADC and governments to assist in pinpointing potential bottlenecks in the implementation of various policy documents, such as RISDP, through providing policy-relevant information.[8] SARDC also researches and disseminates information on the impact of key economic development processes on regional integration in Southern Africa, in close collaboration with the SADC Secretariat and other partners, for example through the *SADC Today* newsletter and a series of policy review briefs covering a wide range of issues such as trade, transport and agriculture. Currently, SARDC is also implementing a regional project called 'Communicating Energy in Southern Africa' together with the Southern African Power Pool (SAPP), an SADC project aiming at connecting the power grids of all member states, and with the SADC Secretariat. The aim is to promote the development of national and regional policies that allow for private-sector investment in the power sector (SARDC 2012). In general, according to the representative of SARDC, the SADC and governments take SARDC seriously, and in many final declarations it is clear that SARDC's advice is incorporated.[9]

Trades Centre specializes in demand-driven research and training on trade and development issues, and their target groups are national and regional policy-makers, as well as business and civil society in the Eastern-Southern Africa (ESA) region. According to the director of Trades, 'SADC takes us as a think-tank. When they have issues that they need special analysis and assessment [. . .] they engage us'.[10] Central for Trades are providing the SADC and other partners with technical support and strengthening their position in regional and multilateral trade negotiations (Trades Centre 2011), assisting the SADC in improving and harmonizing regional trade policies and participating in the design and implementation of multilateral trading regimes such as EPAs (Trades Centre 2010). For example, their research output has been used by government and the business community to enhance benefit from trade liberalization, has helped members of the COMESA take firm positions in the EPA negotiations and has made recommendations on how the FTA can contribute to poverty eradication and development (Trades Centre 2010). All in all, '[t]he research papers from the Centre are highly sought by government, business sector, civil society, parliamentarians, to name a few' (Trades Centre 2010: 5), and 'because of the high quality [. . .] a lot of interest [is] generated by [. . .] regional trade organizations such as SADC, COMESA and EAC' (Trades Centre 2011: 5).

SEATINI has organized and participated in a number of national and regional workshops and lobby meetings in Eastern and Southern Africa with members of parliament, CSOs, government officials and representatives of the SADC and EAC Secretariats in order to influence bilateral and regional trade negotiations, for example EPAs, and to promote sustainable development. SEATINI has also produced a number of research publications and information material about trade and development issues, including EPA, which have been distributed to various policy-makers on national and regional levels, for example the SADC (SEATINI 2011). Most importantly, SEATINI regularly participates in various government trade delegations at regional and global levels (SEATINI 2010), for example the ESA group in the EPA negotiations.[11] In fact, 'SEATINI has [. . .] been recognized by governments as one of the leading NGOs involved in trade issues' (SEATINI 2010: 6).

Since 2004 SADC-CNGO has tried to interact with SADC institutions. In the previous year, 2003, SADC-CNGO and the SADC Secretariat entered into a formal partnership through a MoU. The MoU aims to provide a framework for cooperation between the two parties and promote collaboration in the implementation of SADC-CNGO programs on poverty eradication and sustainable development (SADC-CNGO 2003). There are ongoing discussions with the Secretariat, including the executive secretary, to operationalize the MoU, and a more concrete framework of collaboration has been proposed (SADC-CNGO 2010d: 3) but not yet implemented as of February 2016. SADC-CNGO sits at some open spaces for engagement with the Secretariat and sometimes receives formal invites to certain meetings and consultations (Southern Africa Trust 2014b). In relation to trade and development, SADC-CNGO has participated in the formation of the SADC RPO and has made input to the RPRF. According to the SADC-CNGO representative, 'we do feel we have been able to contribute not only to the process but even to the substantive issues [. . .] So if you read [the RPRF] many issues reflect our opinions and views'.[12]

SADC-CNGO and its partners have scored some success in terms of engaging SADC Summits and other high level meetings. It is often present at the opening and closing ceremonies of the summits and on the side-lines (Southern Africa Trust 2014b). At the 4th Civil Society Forum in South Africa in 2008, civil society through SADC-CNGO was allowed to address the summit (EJN 2010), albeit not directly. An SADC representative participated in the forum to clarify the SADC's position and debate with civil society on various issues.[13] The greatest success came later the same year at the Mauritius conference on poverty and development. The director of SADC-CNGO was allowed to attend the meeting and directly address the heads of governments and states (Osei-Hwedie 2009: 10). All in all, according to Forum Nacional das Organizações Não Governamentais em Moçambique (TEIA), a national NGO forum in Mozambique and one of the founding members of SADC-CNGO, the doors to the official SADC meetings are now opening up[14]; in the same vein, SADC-CNGO claims that 'we do see ourselves making several inroads'.[15]

The choice of SADC-CNGO as a regional civil society partner to the SADC, representing development-oriented NGOs in the region, stems from the fact that SADC-CNGO shares much of the SADC's neo-liberal view on regional integration. For example, this is manifested by the Forum Statement at the 5th SADC Civil Society Forum held in Kinshasa, DRC, in 2009 and issued by SADC-CNGO and its partners. In this statement, it is claimed that civil society in the region reaffirms commitment to the aims and ideals of regional cooperation and development as spelt out in the SADC Treaty. The forum also noted the progress that the SADC is making in a number of areas, for example in terms of trade, but was concerned about a number of impediments for regional economic integration and called upon member states to accelerate regional infrastructure development projects (SADC-CNGO 2009b). This problem-solving approach was further consolidated at the SADC Civil Society Forums in South Africa 2011. The forum urged member states to:

> address key challenges to intra-regional trade and regional economic integration, particularly simplification of rules of origin; macro-economic convergence; harmonization of trade, industry and finance policies; tariff and non-tariff barriers; customs administration and mitigating the effects of regional economic integration such as loss of customs of revenue.
>
> (SADC-CNGO 2011b)

More specifically, the forum pushed governments to implement the Trade Protocol (Pressend 2010). In other words, the forum called on the SADC to accelerate implementation of already established protocols, plans and programs.

SATUCC also seeks close collaboration with SADC institutions and wants to have influence on regional policy-making. SATUCC is the only trade union confederation with a formal status in the SADC (SATUCC 2016), and their relationship is more formalized when compared with SADC-CNGO. First of all, SATUCC is a member of the SADC Tripartite Meeting in the Employment and Labour Sector, held once a year and often referred to as the ELS Meeting. The ELS Meeting brings together the SADC ministers responsible for employment and labour and social partners in the employment and labour areas, that is SPSF representing employers and SATUCC representing workers, to discuss related policy issues (Osei-Hwedie 2009). Within the ELS Meeting, SATUCC has been part of designing various policy documents, such as various codes, labour standards and declarations and charters, including the Code of Conduct on HIV/AIDS and Employment; the SADC Declaration on Productivity and Social Security; the Protocol on the Free Movement of Persons; the SADC Protocol on Gender and Development. Most importantly, SATUCC was instrumental in developing the SADC Charter of Fundamental Social Rights, as indicated above, which is seen by SATUCC as a major achievement.[16] Furthermore, SATUCC sits on a number of technical committees at the Secretariat. All in all, according to the former secretary general of SATUCC, over the years it has built up a cordial relationship with the SADC.[17]

CSO exclusion in the SADC

In the context of the overall statist and capitalist regional order, SADC–civil society interaction must be problematized. The SADC controls which CSOs to include in regional governance related to trade, at the expense of others. There are regulatory obstacles that make it difficult for anyone who wants to engage with the SADC on a more formal level to do so. Formal engagements with the SADC are regulated by MoUs, which are limited to a few CSOs that are considered key representatives of civil society and business in the region and/or as possessing valuable policy-related knowledge, such as ASCCI, SARDC, SATUCC and to a certain extent SADC-CNGO. With the Secretariat's limited capacity, coupled with a reluctance to talk to those CSOs that challenge the SADC's neo-liberal agenda, it is efficient and convenient for the SADC to single out a limited number of civil society partners. The SADC representative confesses that this system bars many important CSOs from accessing the SADC. For example,

> since it is SADC-CNGO and no-one else that SADC has a MoU with, it is impossible for other actors to come in, regardless of how important they are. This is one negative effect of a bureaucratic institution such as SADC: the only interaction is with those on the list.[18]

According to one prominent researcher with great insight into SADC affairs: '[i]f this is the [SADC] attitude and they told us this themselves [. . .] to get an institutionalized relationship is extremely difficult'.[19]

Due to the capitalist regional order that supports those actors who somehow enhance capital accumulation, some CSOs are more involved in regional trade governance at the expense of others. Those CSOs, mostly business and research NGOs, that offer technical expertise in various trade-related areas where the SADC lacks competence and which share the same market-oriented development agenda, for example related to business development and capacity building of trade negotiators, are generally much more included in various SADC institutions than advocacy-oriented RCSOs which demand people-centred regional economic integration and policy reform of SADC policy documents to include ICBT or the like. Therefore, even some RCSOs with an institutionalized relationship with the SADC have struggled to have real influence on trade-related policy-making when occasionally raising a more critical voice. Critical proposals by SATUCC, for example, pushing for critical policy reform of the neo-liberal agenda within the ANSA framework, are taken lightly by the SADC, not to mention SAPSNs resistance agenda (see what follows). CSOs with a different take on regional integration, for example relating trade to labour rights, ICBT and poverty, which are not priority areas for the SADC, are to a varying degree marginalized in SADC–led regional trade governance.

For SADC-CNGO, the space for real policy influence is narrow. According to one scholar, the partnership between SADC-CNGO and the SADC as envisaged in the MoU 'exists in the world of theory. It has not yet been translated into practical reality' (Matlosa and Lotshwao 2010: 41). There is no formal consultative process between SADC and SADC-CNGO around various components of regional integration. Therefore, SADC-CNGO struggles to efficiently engage the SADC, especially on trade-related matters. According to the representative, the relationship is strong with some directorates and very weak with others such as TIFI: 'By and large civil society engagement with SADC has been uneven. In some pockets very well, such as in the HIV/AIDS-groups, in some cases [such as trade and security] very bad'.[20] In general, engagement between SADC-CNGO and the Secretariat is varied, with spaces open in some mainly informal and technical consultation areas and closed off in more formal policy processes (Southern Africa Trust 2014b). Furthermore, there is no formal mechanism for declarations and outcomes of the Civil Society Forum to be formerly discussed in Council of Ministers and summit meetings, which are the main decision-making forums in the SADC. SADC-CNGO inputs at the SADC Summits are rarely taken up by member states (Southern Africa Trust 2014b); hence '[d]eclarations and communiqués [. . .] have [. . .] had very minimal impact on SADC Policy decisions' (SADC-CNGO 2010c: 11). The director of SADC-CNGO has noted that, despite a breakthrough for SADC-CNGO in 2008, during past forums it has been difficult to get officials from the SADC Secretariat into the meeting (EJN 2010). This culminated in 2011, when the leaders of EJN, SADC-CNGO and SATUCC were denied entrance to Angola, where the SADC Summit was held, despite having valid visas. This was considered 'a blatant attempt to deny leaders of civil society to interact with and add voice to SADC structures' (EJN 2011).

The marginalization of SADC-CNGO partly has to be viewed in relation to the network's increasingly critical approach. In recent years, SADC-CNGO has broadened its concept of trade integration. For example, in the Forum Declaration in South Africa in 2013, taking a more critical stance, the forum notes that SADC needs to move away from the current neo-liberal paradigm, focusing on free trade, market orientation and business investment, which is directly harmful to the people living in the region (SADC-CNGO 2013). This critical standpoint was further accentuated in the 2015 Declaration where SADC member states were urged to 'formulate macro-economic policy frameworks that are conducive to . . . structural transformation and the realization of sustainable livelihoods' (SADC-CNGO 2015: 5). Also, SADC needs to take the necessary measures to protect the rights of informal workers (SADC-CNGO 2015). Besides the fact that the SADC is allergic to more critical voices, SADC-CNGO itself is also to be blamed for its increased marginalization due to a weak knowledge foundation for its policy claims, discussed later.

All in all, SADC interest in collaborating with CSOs such as SADC-CNGO is shallow and exists provided that they do not mount too much critique and, as one commentator puts it, 'rock the boat', but instead align themselves with the interests of the SADC.[21] Hence, even though the SADC allows SADC-CNGO to come to some of its meetings, it is expected to be compliant with the SADC agenda. In fact, 'SADC-CNGO is almost like a bureaucratic appendix of [. . .] the Secretariat and there is now a growing critique of that'.[22] One CSO representative goes even further and claims that SADC-CNGO is 'a classic case of institutionalized cooption, [SADC] trying to legitimize certain processes regionally through consultations with civil society'.[23] These critical comments raise serious concerns about the autonomy of SADC-CNGO and the risk of being co-opted and neutralized by regional policy-makers such as the SADC. This is a complex process. On the one hand, as shown, by getting too close to those in the SADC it wants to influence, SADC-CNGO risks being drawn into the neo-liberal SADC agenda and playing a legitimizing role. One sign of this is the quite diverse and even paradoxical approach to SADC-led regional integration. For example, the forum has criticized trade liberalization for not bringing widespread development but at the same time recognizes the importance of the neo-liberal Trade Protocol. These two standpoints might not be mutually exclusive, but they are certainly not natural companions. The other side of the neutralization coin is sheer exclusion. As we saw, the more critical SADC-CNGO gets, the more marginalized it is in the SADC structure.

Furthermore, even though SATUCC supports the SADC-led regional integration agenda and wants to improve the interaction with various SADC institutions, it also makes some critiques. In some respects, SATUCC is quite critical of the SADC agenda and sometimes openly contests SADC policies, which, as will be shown, has made it difficult for some of its policy proposals to be taken seriously. In more detail, SATUCC is critical of the *laissez-faire* aspect of the current trade liberalization framework, and it argues that the SADC must include market regulation schemes to protect the most vulnerable people.[24] SATUCC, together with national trade union partners, has also developed concrete policy alternatives to the present SADC-led regionalism within the ANSA-project (Alternatives to Neo-liberalism in Southern Africa). Seeking fundamental policy reform of the current regional scheme, ANSA puts forward alternative policy proposals for a range of areas. In terms of trade, an alternative trade policy 'aims to involve the region's citizens in the ownership, production and trade structures of the economy in a much more meaningful and sustainable way' (Kanyenze et al. 2006: 271). Because of its critical standpoint, SATUCC struggles to find new entry-points to SADC besides the ELS-meeting (SATUCC n.d.). In fact, according to the former director, the formal space granted to SATUCC in policy-making processes has never been an automatic route to policy influence. SATUCC constantly has to claim its space,[25] which has proven more difficult in recent years in line with an increasingly critical stance. Besides having influence on the SADC-led employment and labour agenda in terms of participation in the design of various SADC policy instruments, there is no evidence that points to SATUCC's alternative policy proposals being taken into consideration by the SADC (Osei-Hwedie 2009: 14), for example in terms of the critical ANSA policy framework. All in all, 'the space for trade union participation [in SADC] has narrowed down' (SATUCC n.d.), to the benefit of SADC business, which is gaining momentum, as shown by the examples listed.

In terms of specific trade issue areas, due to the weak emphasis put on social aspects of trade such as ICBT issues as discussed earlier, in line with neo-liberal regional governance the SADC considers interaction with CSOs dealing with these issues less important, which results in exclusion. For example, CSOs doing advocacy around informal trade, social rights and trade justice are generally largely excluded and ignored by the SADC. One example is EJN, which has a specific regional programme on SADC Advocacy, of which one aspect is ICBT. The most important output so far is research on ICBT in Southern Africa, which generated evidence of the (weak) status of informal traders in the region. The results have been used to strengthen ICBT associations to advocate for fair trade policies at the SADC and elsewhere (EJN 2009). EJN has shared its results with SADC officials in order to influence national and regional policy-making (EJN 2016b) and demands that SADC member states recognize ICBT in regional trade-related policy-making and create the necessary conditions for it to flourish (Damon and Jeuring 2010). According to the director of EJN,

> If one talk of regional integration you will have to talk about informal cross-border traders because informal trade is a big part of trade integration [...] We have done research on the issues and we are pushing SADC for informal trade as part of regional integration.[26]

Nevertheless, despite being knowledgeable on the matter, EJN is still denied access to the SADC Secretariat and summit in terms of policy influence in the trade arena.

Another important regional player in the ICBT field is CBTA. CBTA is accredited to COMESA and the SADC (SARDC 2008: 64) and lobbies various SADC institutions to support and facilitate cross-border informal trade and to enable free movement of informal traders between SADC countries through press statements and written submissions. Yet CBTA has not managed to form a strong relationship with the SADC or COMESA (Nchito and Tranberg Hansen 2010: 181). The hope for greater policy influence on the SADC in the future is brought by the newly established SACBTA. SACBTA seeks to lobby the SADC for recognition of the needs of informal cross-border traders in important regional policy instruments such as the Trade Protocol and the Protocol on the Movements of Persons and strive to organize regular meetings with SADC officials, for example at TIFI (SACBTA 2012: 12). However, it seems as if not much cooperation between SACBTA and the SADC Secretariat has taken place so far (Southern Africa Trust 2014b). However, SACBTA has recently partnered with COMESA in the implementation of the Simplified Trade Regime initiative, designed to be used by small-scale cross-border traders to facilitate easy import and export of their goods in East and Southern Africa, in areas such as awareness raising (Southern Africa Trust 2014b).

The TIFI Directorate would be a natural partner for civil society engagement with the SADC on ICBT issues, as it is responsible for trade issues at the SADC Secretariat. However, according to the TIFI representative, engagement with informal trader interest groups is not prioritized as TIFI, focusing on the facilitation of formal trade, only works with business organizations such as ASCCI and SPSF that are dealing with the movement of goods, productivity and investment. In his own words,

Yes, I could say that in a nutshell we have a particular constituency of civil society we deal with, mainly the people that do the import and export of goods are our focus. We don't deal much from a trade perspective with the pressure groups.[27]

Other regional civil society actors are even more critical towards SADC-led regional integration and consequently more excluded. Their radical agenda makes them 'mortal enemies to SADC'.[28] SAPSN is the best example here. SAPSN is deeply committed to structural change of the present regional and global order and criticizes SADC-led trade integration in Southern Africa for being intimately connected with the current global neo-liberal trade regime. SAPSN demands trade justice that puts the needs of the Southern African people before profits for big corporations (SAPSN n.d.b). Trade, in SAPSN's view, is interpreted quite differently when compared with business CSOs such as SPSF and ASCCI, as well as regional research centres, and is related to a wide range of issues such as social and economic rights, poverty eradication, debt and privatization. During the 2009 People's Summit in Kinshasa, where it was noted that the privatization of basic public services, promoted by the SADC's market-oriented trade integration agenda, violates the right to life as it goes against the common rights to education, health care, water and so forth and thereby worsens poverty in the SADC (SAPSN 2009).

Furthermore, in the People's Declaration from 2014 SADC member states are criticized for failing to guarantee access to nutritious food and essential social services and urged to protect the people of the region instead of corporate and elite interests (SAPSN 2014a).

Contesting the very neo-liberal foundation upon which the present SADC–led regional integration project is built puts it on the side-lines of the SADC. The radical standpoint of SAPSN makes the SADC unwilling to even listen to its critique. Because of the SADC suspicion towards SAPSN, it is claimed, SAPSN is barred from openly presenting communiqués to the SADC Summit and obstructed from organizing peaceful marches (SAPSN 2014b). SADC leaders are often invited to attend the People's Summit but never show up (EJN 2010). Furthermore, due to their critical agenda, as a representative of social movements in the region SAPSN has not been invited to be a member of the RPO Steering Committee.[29] This is also related to its contentious methods, discussed later. However, it should be noted that the tense relations between SADC and SAPSN recently seemed to ease up. In May 2014 the SADC Secretariat met with a SAPSN delegation for the first time, and in order to establish more formal ties and a MoU between the two is in the making. By this, SAPSN hopes to become more involved in regional policy processes (SAPSN 2014c). In the Declaration at the People's Summit in 2014, SAPSN expressed appreciation of the improvements in the SADC Secretariat's engagement with CSOs (Southern Africa Trust 2014b). It remains to be seen to what extent SADC is willing to incorporate SAPSN's demands.

Relations between donors and CSOs

This section will discuss how the statist-capitalist informed social relations between various donors and RCSOs influence civil society regionalization in the trade sector in two different ways. First, the role of donor funds in facilitating civil society regionalization and the problematic dependency this creates on behalf of CSOs will be analyzed and, second, the ways in which donor agendas shape the nature of regionalization. However, the section starts by discussing how, in more general ways, the capitalist social structure has affected donors' relations with CSOs, as well as listing the most important donors involved in the trade sector.

The funding rationale for donors

To a large extent donors are part of reproducing a capitalist regional order. Generally, donors mainly support CSOs that are engaged in service provision, solving problems related to the process of neo-liberalization in the region. Claiming that government service delivery is insufficient, donors think that CSOs should be supported to fill these gaps, acting as a voice for the poor and ensuring basic service delivery for the marginalized (Southern Africa Trust 2010b). In line with the economistic rationale of neo-liberal thinking, another incentive to support service provision is the fact that funders want concrete and tangible results. The results of such funding are easier to measure. In terms of advocacy-based organizations that try to change the foundations for service provision and make states take more responsibility, it is harder to see tangible results. The difficulty of measuring certain types of activities also applies to the general reluctance to fund networking, co-ordination and coalition-building, which do not lend themselves to the same kind of quantification as the provision of certain tangible services. This trend has been further enhanced by implementation of the Paris Declaration on Aid Effectiveness from 2005,[30] which has changed the aid architecture within the last 10 years towards more efficient funding, pooling of resources and joint donor programmes. Due to the Paris Agenda, more conditionality is tied to aid, and requirements for accountability and attention to measurable outcomes and results are further strengthened (Trust Africa 2008; Southern Africa Trust 2010b).

However, despite the overall trend of funding measurable service-providing activities, some donors support the advocacy activities of critical CSOs. These donors believe that civil society organizations should ultimately not be responsible for service delivery, as it is primarily government's role, and government must be held accountable if it does not fulfil this function. These donors dislike when CSOs take over the role of governments, filling gaps in service delivery, claiming that responsibility for service provision resides with the government. Therefore, they mostly fund those CSOs that advocate for improved service delivery by the state, for economic justice and for pro-poor development (Southern Africa Trust 2010b).

Key donors

Southern Africa Trust is a regional non-profit organization based in Johannesburg, South Africa. Its prime objective is to 'contribute towards supporting deeper and wider civil society engagement in regional policy dialogue to overcome poverty in Southern Africa' (Southern Africa Trust 2011). The trust therefore supports diverse CSOs from Southern Africa that are dealing with, for example, finance, trade, investment and pro-poor growth and that want to influence national and regional policy-making to become more pro-poor and developmental. The main strategies are capacity-building; strengthening policy dialogue among CSOs, state actors and the private sector; evidence-based advocacy; and grant making (Southern Africa Trust 2010a).

The Open Society Initiative for Southern Africa (OSISA) is a Johannesburg-based private foundation working in 10 Southern Africa countries. OSISA supports local, national and regional civil society activities, mainly on a project level. One thematic area is economic justice, and here OSISA supports NGO initiatives that, for example, support government trade negotiations, CSO advocacy, civil society initiatives that promote regional labour rights and research and advocacy on regional integration, trade and development. OSISA also promotes regional civil society networking (OSISA 2008).

Diakonia is an INGO from Sweden with a regional office in Kenya that is involved in supporting regional CSOs in Eastern and Southern Africa. Diakonia has a regional programme on Social and Economic Justice (SEJ) that focuses on overcoming the structural causes of poverty in Africa. Therefore, Diakonia supports regional CSOs that work with debt cancellation, trade, aid effectiveness, gender equality in economic issues and sustainable private-sector investments. More specifically, Diakonia wants to strengthen these organizations' abilities to do research, networking, mobilization and advocacy work in order to influence the policies and practices of national governments and regional institutions such as the SADC (Diakonia 2011).

Action Aid International (AA) is another INGO, based in South Africa and with an African regional office in Nairobi, Kenya. AA supports a range of regional civil society initiatives in not only Southern Africa but the whole African continent. Even though AA's primary focus in Africa is at the local level, it also engages with CSOs working at African regional levels, supporting the development of popular alliances to influence regional policy and empower citizens to demand protection of socio-economic rights. For example, AA strengthens the regional leadership, engagement and coalition-building of organizations and movements of poor people demanding the right to food and just trade and facilitates regional civil society meetings (Action Aid International 2005).

Norwegian Church Aid (NCA), an INGO based in Norway and with a regional office in Pretoria, South Africa, is deeply committed to supporting regional civil society engagement. NCA has developed a specific regional programme for Southern Africa on economic justice, for example dealing with resources and finance and livelihood and trade. In particular, NCA aims to strengthen CSOs to take part in regional policy formulation and advocacy, foremost within the SADC and AU frameworks. NCA facilitates efficient linkages between the two. In essence, NCA enhances the capacity of CSOs in the regional work they do, facilitates information sharing between partners and creates regional platforms (NCA 2010).

The German Agency for International Cooperation (GIZ), which includes the former German Technical Cooperation (GTZ), is an international enterprise owned by the German government. GIZ assists the government to provide international cooperation services for sustainable development on a global scale (GIZ 2012). In Southern Africa, GIZ has a regional programme in support of the SADC. The programme focuses on strengthening regional economic integration, consolidating cooperation on trans-boundary water resource management and promoting the conservation and sustainable use of natural resources. Besides enhancing the capacity of the Secretariat, the programme also promotes civil society and private-sector participation in the integration process, supporting some SADC-affiliated RCSOs (GIZ 2011).

Last, the European Commission (EC) aims to support the acceleration of economic growth and development in the SADC region through deeper levels of regional economic integration and political cooperation. This is mainly, but not only, done by providing broad-based support to deepen SADC economic integration and trade policies, including investment promotion, regional infrastructure and food security. One (small) component of EC support to regional integration in the SADC is direct support to private and civil society organizations for involvement in SADC policy-making and service provision. The SADC Secretariat is responsible for channelling funds to CSOs as part of the overall budget support (EC 2008).

CSO dependency on donor funds

In general, the regional level is becoming more and more important for various types of donors. According to the director of EJN, for CSOs 'there is definitely more money for regional work today'.[31] This perception is backed up by a major study carried out by the Southern Africa Trust about donor and civil society relations in Southern Africa. According to the study, there seems to be an increase in donor funding to civil society organizations that work towards advancing the regional agenda. These include CSOs and networks that act regionally or that have programmes focusing on regional issues (Southern Africa Trust 2010b: 12). This is particularly the case in the trade field, where donors increasingly emphasize support to regional civil society activities. However, according to this research project it seems like the granting of funds for regional activities is greatly skewed towards private funders such as foundations, trusts and INGOs, at the expense of bilateral and multilateral funders, who tend to focus more on other sectors, foremost HIV/AIDS. Few bilateral/multilateral donors are engaged in supporting the regionalization of civil society in the trade sector. As discussed in the last chapter, bilateral donors' motives for developing regional programs are often administrational in terms of promoting aid effectiveness and harmonization of country programs and do not reflect a deep commitment to regionalization. This plays against a genuine interest in supporting the involvement of CSOs in regional integration.

RCSOs in the trade sector are highly dependent on the availability of donor funds, which stems from the general tendency of RCSOs to be 'dependent on donor decisions, financial resources available and the overall change in aid architecture' (Southern Africa Trust 2010b: 39) for their operation. One well-known scholar emphasizes this dependency even more, claiming that many national and regional networks and NGOs are generally kept alive by donor money,[32] including trade-related ones. In the same vein, the director of the Southern Africa Trust, with major insight in the regional civil society arena, argues that some RCSOs that they support in the trade sector tend to 'go regional' mainly for the money and not because of a fundamental interest in dealing with regional issues. RCSOs, including those in this study, are partly driven by economic interests, which are intimately related to the current availability of donor money.[33] Therefore, according to another donor representative, CSOs

> sometimes [. . .] work in the region not necessarily because they believe in it but because this is where the funding is [. . .] So for organizations, such as any other business [. . .] you have to be realistic and go where the money is.[34]

Therefore, '[y]ou end up having people following resources rather than resources following ideas'.[35]

RCSOs are generally greatly dependent on the decision of donors to fund them or not. At the moment, the financial situation for the RCSOs in this study is quite good, due to the great interest by trusts, foundations and INGOs in supporting regional civil society work around trade and development issues. However, for some RCSOs this has not always been the case, proving the vulnerable situation they are in. SADC-CNGO, for example, has long struggled to sustain its activities and build up organizational capacity, and the network has 'emerged and then died out three times'[36] due to shifting donor commitments. In fact, it has not been until recently that SADC-CNGO established a fully fledged secretariat, thanks to donor support.[37] SATUCC also struggled for funds for many years (Southern Africa Trust 2010b: 39). During periods with weak donor funding, the regional presence of these networks has been considerably lower due to fewer regional activities. SAPSN has faced similar challenges and is widely criticized for being inactive between regional events such as the People's Summit. This is partly related to the occasional lack of donor interest. Up until recently, donors mostly funded particular SAPSN-led events and temporal campaigns, such as the People's Summit, and not wider programs and the capacity-building of the secretariat. According to the SAPSN representative, 'most donors only give support for specific projects and activities, which is very unfortunate'.[38] The SAPSN case is related to the wider donor propensity to fund specific projects, foremost those (service-delivery) ones whose results can be easily measured.

Donor influence on the CSO agenda

In general, donors tend to influence CSOs' agendas according to what they believe the regional development priorities should be. In connection with the foregoing argument, regional civil society organizations often find themselves in a situation where they need to navigate between shifting loyalties between financial support and defending their constituencies (Southern Africa Trust 2010b: 38).

Bilateral and multilateral donors have a great influence on their CSO partners, who are often steered in a particular ideological direction. One arena for donors to influence their partners' agendas is participation in the development of CSO policy documents. One example is the process of designing the 2010–2014 Strategic Framework of SADC-CNGO, in which the donors were greatly involved (SADC-CNGO 2009a: 24). Bilateral and multilateral funders primarily support problem-solving agendas in support of the present neo-liberal order. In essence, they want to strengthen the current type of SADC-led, market-oriented regional integration and, for example, facilitate trade and economic growth in the region. GIZ and the EC, for example, enhance the capacity of the SADC Secretariat to improve implementation of trade liberalization schemes. For GIZ and the EC, CSOs are also somewhat important to support in this endeavour, since they provide various services and policy advice that strengthens regional trade integration. Some examples are private-sector development (in terms of ASCCI); monitoring implementation of the SADC agenda (SADC-CNGO); capacity-building of trade negotiators and provision of policy-related research (Trades Centre); and dissemination of SADC-related information and news (SARDC). However, it should be noted that bilateral and multilateral support to regional civil society is much more common in the HIV/AIDS sector, where various types of service-providing activities dominate. This will be discussed further in the next chapter.

Those donors that are willing to fund more critical regional civil society agendas are themselves often critical of the current market-oriented regional governance in Southern Africa. The critical agendas of these donors greatly influence the work of their regional recipients. These donors are mostly private foundations such as OSISA and INGOs such as NCA, AA and Diakonia, which share the worldview and critical approach of their Southern African partners. For example, NCA has a clear preference for supporting critical advocacy in relation to service provision, in line with the RBA. It is claimed that, 'as the political space for civil society is shrinking in the region [. . .] NCA [needs to] strengthen our partners to take active part in the on-going political processes' (NCA 2010: 19) and to foster values-based co-operation between NCA and partners based on a common struggle for social and economic justice.[39] Similarly according to the representative of AA, 'we believe it is possible to transform the current structures to be able to accommodate the interests of the poor',[40] and here partners in Africa are important instruments. Last, OSISA strives to change the neo-liberal paradigm and start discussing alternative models, such as ANSA. One central role for OSISA, therefore, is to harness alternatives to the prevailing paradigm that reside in civil society, which informs its support to the People's Summit, EJN and other critical voices.[41] Hence, EJN, OSISA and other donors 'are more like partners in a common struggle'.[42]

INGOs, and to a certain extent private foundations and trusts, relate differently to the capitalist, neo-liberal global order than their bilateral and multilateral counterparts discussed earlier. Foundations, trusts and INGOs are private and not public, which gives them a degree of independence and autonomy. As funders they are then more willing and able to support more critical civil society strategies and agendas. From the foregoing it is also clear that, in a way, civil society is viewed as an instrument for donors to achieve the overall goals of trade justice, pro-poor development and critical reform of the current regional governance architecture. In this process, CSOs are stimulated to foster a critical agenda and develop a contentious attitude towards various policy-makers.

On the other hand, aid flows from bilateral and multilateral donors are dependent on foreign policy in their home countries (Southern Africa Trust 2010b). Therefore, according to one commentator, 'they are more reluctant to fund things that might embarrass their counterparts and can harm trade relations and political ties [. . . and] tend to be more conservative and cautious'.[43] One civil society representative goes as far as saying that bilateral donors are in fact mere extensions of their foreign affairs departments, carrying out state policies through aid.[44] It is no wonder, therefore, that bilateral donors find it difficult to fund rights-based organizations such as EJN, SAPSN and, to a certain extent, SEATINI that challenge government agendas, want to reform current regional trade schemes and argue for trade justice. In contrast to SARDC and Trades Centre, who cooperate with bilateral funders, because of their more critical agenda, SEATINI are foremost funded by private foundations such as Rosa Luxemburg Foundation and INGOs such as AA and Oxfam.

Relations between CSOs

It is widely acknowledged by donors, researchers and also CSOs themselves that the main watershed within regional civil society is related to ideology and strategy. Different types of CSOs often have fundamentally different views on Southern African regionalism *per se*, using different strategies to reproduce, reform or even transform it. This implies that CSOs ideologically relate differently to the current regional capitalist order and its various manifestations, such as SADC-led neo-liberal regional governance. On a broad level, it is possible to distinguish between 'insider' and 'outsider' CSOs (e.g. van Rooy 2004). On the one hand, 'insider CSOs' are those formal NGOs and research centres that acknowledge the present regional governance framework and want to engage governments and regional institutions to modify policies and accelerate implementation. On the other hand, social movements and certain more critically inclined NGOs, that is 'outsider CSOs', contest the current neo-liberal agenda and emphasize popular mobilization, protest and also disengagement from state actors. In this regard, one CSO succinctly states that '[w]e the social movements do the mass mobilization around the issues, they do the research and the formal proposals'.[45] The outsider CSOs are best exemplified by SAPSN and member organizations such as Alternative Information and Development Centre (AIDC) in South Africa and Zimbabwe Coalition on Debt and Development (ZIMCODD) in Zimbabwe. These and other critical actors, loosely connected to SAPSN, such as International Labour Resource and Information Group (ILRIG) in South Africa and the former Anti-Privatization Forum (APF), believe that the best way people can influence regional processes is not from inside these structures but from the outside. To a varying degree, they opt for disengaging from formal, institutionalized processes and refuse to join the 'NGO crowd'[46] for example related to the SADC, since they believe this would justify an unjust regional order: 'The insider lobbying, trying to change the policies of regional integration, leads nowhere'.[47] On the other hand, insider NGOs such as Trades Centre, SARDC and SEATINI believe the best option for having influence on regional governance is to act from within. According to one commentator, 'sometimes it is better to be on the inside and not always on the outside [. . .] There are some benefits you can get from being on the inside'.[48] In the same vein, the SARDC representative claims that

> [w]e don't see [. . . the SADC] as our enemy [. . .] we want to complement the government's work [. . .] If we are going to criticize, we are trying to do that as constructively as possible. We have realized that if you are too negative you are not likely to be heard.[49]

Many CSOs involved in the study testify about problems in interacting with each other, especially across the 'insider/outsider' divide. For example, according to the Trades representative, 'engaging with other CSOs is not without conflicts; conflicts are inevitable especially if you use different strategies'.[50] The negative effect this has on the ability of CSOs to reach overall regional development objectives worries many organizations involved in this study. For example, according to SADC-CNGO, '[c]ivil society has suffered from unnecessary and sometimes counterproductive divisions on ideological, methodological and sometimes personality grounds to the detriment of the common good' (2010c: 11). Furthermore, ZIMCODD emphasizes the challenge of collaboration even further. Addressing both insider and outsider CSOs, the director highlights the need to 'stop wasting time dividing ourselves between the NGOs and the social movement [. . .] It is much easier to get consensus amongst the leaders of the region than amongst civil society'.[51]

The most profound manifestation of intra-civil society rivalry is the very existence of two different civil society meetings parallel to the SADC Summit. The forum is more institutionalized, involving formal NGOs, and is more restrictive in terms of participation. It pursues more formal engagement with governments at the SADC Summit. On the other hand, the People's Summit is less formal, is organized more as a social forum, and is more open to various sorts of non-institutionalized local groups that believe in contentious engagement and even disengagement with the SADC and emphasize mass protest.[52] In essence, the two meetings play different roles, wherein the forum is intimately linked to the SADC agenda and the

People's Summit engages with issues related to social and economic justice more broadly.[53] Both meetings claim to represent civil society in the region, albeit in different ways. On the one hand, the forum claims to speak for NGOs in the region, and on the other hand the summit claims to be the voice of popular, grassroots-led organizations.[54] The two forums also issue separate declarations with, as shown, very different approaches to the SADC. One commentator concludes that '[i]n terms of political and ideological inclinations they are very different'.[55]

It is widely acknowledged among both CSO representatives and donors that due to their different ideological inclinations, choice of strategy and types of participants, relations between the SADC Civil Society Forum and the People's Summit are contentious.[56] According to one donor representative, 'there is a lot of animosity between the social movements in the Peoples Summit and the NGOs in the Civil Society Forum. There is no room for coming together'.[57] The refusal of social movements to interact with the SADC makes them very hesitant to co-operate with the SADC-friendly forum.[58] SADC-CNGO, the main organizer, is accused of not putting forward an autonomous agenda and merely being a civil society face of the SADC.[59] NGOs are also invited to join the marches of the People's Summit, but few have shown up so far[60] because NGO leaders generally don't want to be associated with contentious strategies such as demonstrations, which might play against them in engagement with SADC leaders. This in turn relates to the fact that SADC-CNGO and other NGO groups question what change popular mobilization activities really make.[61] NGOs in the forum also question the sometimes aggressive approach towards the SADC and other target groups. One prominent commentator with great insight into both processes concludes that 'civil society groups are largely split [. . . C]onflicting declarations [. . .] and a divided understanding of the implications of "free trade" [. . .] undermine collective goals towards social justice and building regional solidarity' (Pressend 2010). All in all, until recently there have been no meaningful structural relations between the two.[62]

Furthermore, the exclusion of social movements such as SAPSN from the forum is more or less institutionalized. SADC-CNGO, EJN and SATUCC have formed a MoU on general co-operation, which is referred to as the 'Pact of Regional Apex Organizations'. In the document, the particular view on civil society and who belongs to it is clearly stated: '[c]ivil society in this context refers to churches, Non-Governmental Organizations (NGOs) and trade unions' (SADC-CNGO 2010b: 1). Hence, social movements, CBOs or other types of popular, non-formal organizations are left out. At the same time, SAPSN has been invited to a number of planning meetings in connection with the summit, but it has not been until recently that it has shown an interest in participating. According to one commentator, social movements are hesitant to participate because they don't want to be co-opted: 'If you co-opt them, how do they march outside the SADC Summit? It will give SADC the power to say why do you march now when you are also sitting inside?'[63]

However, the icy relations between the forum and summit are beginning to melt. SAPSN has accepted joining a few planning meetings, for example a 2010 Apex meeting. At that, SAPSN agreed it was important to better link up with NGOs in the forum to ensure collaboration across the ideological divide (EJN 2010). The same year, SAPSN also invited SADC-CNGO to a workshop to build their capacity around effective engagement with the SADC (SADC-CNGO 2010d). At an SAPSN coordination committee meeting in 2009 it was also agreed that the two meetings should remain separate but that competition should be minimized.[64] Also, the increasingly friendly attitude towards the SADC Secretariat, discussed above, can be a sign of reducing the ideological gap between SAPSN and SADC-CNGO. It remains to be seen what this will lead to in terms of broader co-operation between forums.

CSOs and issue-framing

In this and the next section, focus will be put on the agency of RCSOs, albeit within the context of the statist and capitalist regional order, in terms of the ways they frame issues and construct identities for regional consolidation. Hence, as will be clear in the coming two sections, while being partly an autonomous process, the internal motivations of RCSOs to 'go regional' are influenced by external actors such as the SADC and donors. Relations between the SADC and CSOs particularly affect how regional NGOs and networks frame issues and construct identities.

Regional issue-framing

Regional issue-framing plays an important role in understanding the regionalization of civil society. According to one commentator, 'the issues are a major unifying factor, for example debt and trade'.[65] Networks such as SADC-CNGO, SATUCC, EJN and SAPSN are regionally consolidated partly because of a shared regional perception of the issues they work with.

For SADC-CNGO, in its Southern Africa Civil Society Poverty and Development Charter for example, the SADC region is seen as having many development challenges in common. These include weak and non-dynamic economies, high income inequalities, high unemployment, high economic informalization, recurrent food insecurity, inadequate social protection, inadequate infrastructure and weak regional integration (SADC-CNGO 2010b). These problems are inherently cross border and regional in character. In the latest strategic plan of SADC-CNGO, the regional commonality of development issues is further emphasized. Here, issues such as hunger, malnutrition, landlessness and food insecurity are viewed as regional issues, which characterize the SADC region as a whole, affecting citizens regardless of where they live. Therefore, these problems need to be tackled collectively (SADC-CNGO 2009a: 34–36).

SATUCC reaches similar conclusions. According to the representative, 'when it comes to regional issues we are not divided. We see things from a common perspective'.[66] SATUCC has worked hard to educate member organizations on regional socio-economic issues such as EPAs, and these issues are then debated in order to reach a consensus within the coalition on how to argue their case at regional and national levels. Hence, when the former SATUCC director went to various SADC meetings on behalf of SATUCC, he claimed to present one common SATUCC standpoint.[67] One important regional policy issue for SATUCC is employment, and it is claimed that unemployment and a growing informal economy are not local or national problems but affect people equally all around the region (Makanza n.d., SATUCC 2016). This common understanding within the network seems to be essential for regional consolidation.

Furthermore, for EJN one rationale for bringing together church organizations regionally to advocate for economic justice is the perception of regional development commonalities. According to one EJN representative, 'the poverty issues are common in the region and unite civil society'.[68] EJN claims that the regionalization of poverty and development issues ultimately stems from the overall regional neo-liberal, market-oriented trend in Southern Africa.

Regional civil society meetings are important platforms for the regional construction of trade and development issues and the further consolidation of regional networks. The SADC Civil Society Forum is important in this regard. The Civil Society statements, released at the end of every forum, embody the debates taking place. For example, the statements in connection to the SADC Summits in 2011 and 2013 set the agenda for a regionally active civil society. In the preambles it is stated that participants commit themselves to 'collectively engage SADC and member states on issues of common interest such as poverty eradication, promotion of democracy and good governance and justice' (SADC-CNGO 2011b: 1, 2013: 1). This indicates a perception that trade and development issues concern the whole region and therefore presupposes collective regional action.

Regional research NGOs such as SARDC and Trades Centre strongly emphasize the connection among 'local', 'national' and 'regional' development processes. For them, the regional and global perception of the issues they deal with is a strong incitement for regional engagement. SARDC argues that informal trade is inherently cross border in nature and intimately linked to regional development and integration. It is claimed that in order to understand and also support informal traders, its activities must be linked to the overall regional trade and poverty structures (SARDC 2008). SARDC is therefore dedicated to informing and influencing citizens and policy-makers in the region about ICBT issues and how they affect national and regional processes. In the same vein, Trades Centre argues that, since the poverty dynamics in Southern Africa are regional, there is a great need to develop existing regional strategies, such as the SADC RISDP, 'to guide the region out of poverty' (Trades Centre 2010: 2). This motivates the centre's strong emphasis on assisting regional policy-makers, such as the SADC Secretariat, to develop and implement regional policy instruments. Last, business CSOs also make, more or less, a regional analysis of private sector–related trade issues. For example, the mission of ASCCI is to 'promote an enabling environment for business development in the SADC region' (2012b: 8), which means pushing SADC institutions and members to harmonize standards to facilitate market penetration of innovative goods and reducing production costs (ASCCI 2012: 21).

Construction of regional target groups

It is clear from the foregoing that RCSOs often frame their issues around regional policy-making actors such as the SADC. As will be shown, the SADC is framed as an important target for regional lobbying, advocacy and social mobilization, as responsible for lack of implementation of various projects, for lack of development orientation and even for causing poverty and injustices in the region. In different ways, the SADC is in itself an important incentive for regionalization of civil society. According to one interviewee, 'what makes [. . .] a regional formation powerful is that they have clear targets and enemies in what they are doing, for example the SADC Secretariat'.[69] In the trade arena it is particularly easy to see where important political decisions are taken, and it is clearer who the 'bad guys' are.[70]

In the case of SADC-CNGO, to a large extent the member councils are bound together by issues related to the SADC.[71] In the words of the SADC-CNGO representative, 'we are telling SADC indeed we are a diverse group but we are bound by a common vision, which is to see a prosperous and democratic SADC'.[72] In fact, studying the strategic plan for 2010–2014 it is clear that the rationale for SADC-CNGOs work is spelt s, a, d and c. The coalition's perception of regional integration, development and trade revolves around the SADC, and most activities have some link to the SADC agenda (SADC-CNGO 2009a).

However, regardless of effort to align its goals with the SADC agenda, as discussed, in practice SADC-CNGO is somehow excluded in various policy-making forums in the SADC, particularly in the trade sector. This is partly related to the fact that SADC-CNGO is considered by some people to have weak knowledge about trade and development issues. In other words, SADC-CNGO is not that knowledgeable about the issues it frames as regional. As discussed in the theoretical chapter, the framing of issues in particular ways needs to be backed up by serious claims to knowledge in order to be taken seriously by target groups such as the SADC and to gain influence. This is not the case for some CSOs in this study. Hence, according to one prominent commentator, when SADC-CNGO is invited to SADC meetings it does not really use that opportunity to influence:

> They merely sit there, and are happy with that, but don't contribute with substance. And, SADC knows that these RCSOs will not make a difference in policy-making, nor participate significantly in implementation of programs. In essence, in the eyes of government they lack credibility.[73]

SADC-CNGO also struggles to document evidence from local realities in its advocacy work.[74] The people participating at the SADC civil society forums are normally not the ones working directly with the various issues discussed and have grassroots experience but are uninformed representatives of national networks. When called on by the SADC to discuss trade issues such as EPAs, it also does not send experts from the various member NGOs and more knowledgeable regional partners such as the EJN, but staff from the Secretariat who know very little of the issues.[75] According to one of the SADC representatives:

> if they would have been more organized, they could have come here and literally pushed [for change . . .] They just want to come and speak to Summit meetings [. . . and] do not demand space in a strategic way in policy-making processes, sending proposals pertaining issues they are interested in.[76]

SADC-CNGO partly agrees with the criticism that its advocacy is rather weak and not that evidence-based, even though this is improving.[77] For regional civil society at large, '[s]ome of the [. . .] policy demands tend to be overly general and predictable and of little practical value for regional policy formulation' (SADC-CNGO 2010c: 11).

SAPSN also struggles to be taken seriously by the SADC due to lack of issue substance. SAPSN struggles to provide viable alternatives to the current regional agenda, based on evidence-based facts, alongside delivering criticism.[78] This is related to a general lack of knowledge of current development processes in the region. Therefore, comments on a new regionalist agenda presented in various SAPSN statements, such as People's Declarations, are rather sweeping, and no concrete programs for this people-driven regionalism are presented.[79] SAPSN itself agrees that 'making noise' at People's Summits in terms of demonstrations and marching must be matched with serious proposals for change, worked out between meetings, which is currently lacking.[80]

The weak knowledge foundations of SADC-CNGO and SAPSN stand in sharp contrast to research NGOs such as Trades Centre and SEATINI. Those possess well-researched information, often evidence based, that is sought after by the SADC. This is vital for their involvement in regional governance, which in the end strengthens their regional profiles. Of course, it must be noted again that the kind of knowledge they offer is in line with the SADC's problem-solving agenda, which is another important reason for their inclusion.

Other CSOs involved in this study share the tendency to focus their activities and agendas around the SADC. SATUCC, for example, is driven by an urge to report on economic, political and labour conditions in the quest to influence SADC policies and the 'regional SADC agenda' more generally (SATUCC n.d.). Furthermore, for ASCCI, one of the core interventions is to 'influence the trade agenda of SADC' (2012: 21), and SPSF aims to present joint positions on labour and employment issues at SADC meetings and liaise with SADC institutions (2010). Similarly, the central objectives of Trades Centre are to assist the SADC and COMESA to harmonize and deepen regional trade policies and to participate in the design and implementation of fair multi-lateral trading regimes (Trades Centre 2010: 4).

A common strategy to influence the SADC agenda is to monitor regional and national policy-makers' implementation of certain agreed-upon policies. For example, in 2013 SATUCC launched a regional campaign for the national ratification of the SADC Employment and Labour Protocol (SATUCC 2015). Also SADC-CNGO tries to push the SADC to practice what it preaches. In the latest SADC-CNGO Strategic Plan it is stated that 'one of the key roles of civil society organizations is to monitor the performance of SADC Secretariat [. . .] towards achieving [. . .] regional development commitments including basic human rights' (SADC-CNGO 2009a: 16). For example, SADC-CNGO is concerned about the fact that many SADC members still have protectionist trade policies. Therefore SADC-CNGO takes on lobbying the SADC to collectively address issues that go against deeper regional economic integration in order to live up to the Trade Protocol and RISDP (SADC-CNGO 2009a: 37–38).

This is further emphasized in the 2010 Forum Statement where SADC-CNGO and partners call upon member states to 'address key challenges to intra-regional trade and regional economic integration [. . . and] to speak with one voice and enhance cooperation and coordination when engaging trading partners' (SADC-CNGO 2010a). Furthermore, the forum is concerned about the difficulties faced by SADC citizens in moving around in the region due to restrictive and disparate labour migration policies and urges SADC member states to ratify the Protocol on the Facilitation of the Movements of Persons (SADC-CNGO 2010a). In a similar vein, satisfied with the slow implementation of the RPRF the forum in 2013 urged SADC to 'appropriately fund the regional and national poverty observatories' and establish a SADC Poverty Eradication & Development Fund (SADC-CNGO 2013: 10). It is obvious that SADC-CNGO and partners are careful not to harm their precious relationship with the SADC by exposing particular member states or using strong language even if this is beginning to change considering the increasingly critical position discussed above.

Last, it should be underlined that the SADC Civil Society Forum does not play a big role in terms of spurring on more concrete regional action connected to the meeting. The forum can be criticized for merely being a forum for debates, habitually releasing Civil Society Statements, indeed creating a sense of regionalization of development issues, but without resulting in more immediate regional advocacy action. The opposite is true of SAPSN. In this case, the construction of the SADC as a target for civil society advocacy is taking more radical forms, and shaming the SADC is done on more moral grounds. The SADC is viewed as an enemy which should be resisted, both because of its fundamental democratic deficit and its anti-development agenda. The SADC is portrayed as only engaging in rhetorical declarations about development cooperation and integration, without any serious action, and in fact is blamed for causing poverty and unemployment in the region when advancing a neo-liberal market-driven agenda (SAPSN 2008). Various SAPSN statements also charge that

> SADC leaders are using the SADC as a self-serving "old boys' club" for mutual support whenever the interests and power of the ruling elites come into conflict with the human rights, and the democratic and development aspirations of their own populations.
> (Godsäter and Söderbaum 2011: 13)

These perceptions of the SADC plant an urge among forum participants to take action. In this way, the People's Summit becomes an important venue for putting strong words and feelings into practice. According to the SAPSN coordinator, 'the People's summits are easy to mobilize people because there is a clear target in SADC, which calls for direct action'.[81] Hence, resistance of the SADC is translated into direct action using various contentious strategies such as popular marches, where the SAPSN activists shout various slogans demanding trade justice, no to EPAs and radical change of the SADC structure. In the words of one commentator, 'instead of engaging with SADC they will have a banner saying do away with SADC and they are very confrontational with the government'.[82]

The construction of the SADC as an enemy has indeed consolidated the SAPSN movement and created a regional advocacy momentum, but it should be noted that the demands often fall on deaf ears. This partly has to do with the anti-capitalist message but also the choice of methods for delivering it. In fact, it can be argued that SAPSN's version of shaming has been taken too far and become counter-productive. It is a thin line between making political leaders accountable and taking responsibility for development in the region on moral grounds, appealing to universal values of justice, gender equality and human rights and alienating the same leaders by using provocative language. This applies to SAPSN. The radical slogans used during SAPSN marches connected to the People's Summit and the ridiculing of political leaders in seminars scare off SADC officials. Regardless of what they have to say, SAPSN is easily brushed away because, according to one SADC representative,

> they are insulting [. . .] If you come to insult the Heads of State in the meeting, do you think they are going to listen? [. . .] Ultimately there is an individual who wants respect sitting at the table [. . .] They need to refine their tactics.[83]

However, SAPSN itself does not relate exclusion from the SADC to their mode of communication being too radical, arguing that it is the democratic right of people to deliver their opinions in the ways they see fit.[84]

CSOs and identity-making

On the whole, regional identity-making is not an important dimension of the regionalization of civil society dealing with trade-related issues, but for some regional networks the conscious construction of a clear 'we', that is a positive identity, plays a role in 'going regional'. This applies to EJN, SAPSN and SAT-UCC, which will be discussed later in this section. As was argued in the theoretical chapter, the creation of structural relationships among the members of a certain network in order to speak with one 'voice' greatly determines the strength of the network. Such unified 'voice' is in turn dependent on the extent to which members represent a specific constituency based on a common social trait or adherence to some specific values or principles. Regional research NGOs and business associations, on the other hand, do not appear to foster clear regional identities in either of these ways.

For networks other than those mentioned, it is questionable if regional identity-making plays a role for regional consolidation. For example, SADC-CNGO and member NGO coalitions do not seem to represent a particular social constituency. In its strategic plan for 2010–2014, it is vaguely stated that SADC-CNGO '[r]epresents NGO interests and perspectives on SADC institutions' (2009a: 13) but what kind of interests or perspectives and which constituencies are represented by these NGOs is not further explained. According to one prominent scholar, referring to the SADC-CNGO leadership, 'as far as I am concerned they only represent themselves'.[85] In fact, this criticism is not denied by SADC-CNGO itself. For example, the director of Botswana Council of Non-Governmental Organisations (BOCONGO), a member of SADC-CNGO, claims that the Civil Society Forums 'are not representative enough of people's views in their respective countries, it has always been delegations of the councils coming to the summits, only representing their councils'.[86] The SADC-CNGO Secretariat is also worried about exclusive tendencies and agrees that representation has not been as effective as it has wanted.[87] Furthermore, the principles and values guiding the activities of SADC-CNGO are also rather vague. Highly general formulations of 'equality and equity', 'respect for human rights and dignity' and 'people centred sustainable development approaches' (SADC-CNGO 2009a: 15) are not further clarified. One negative consequence of such lack of network identity, as will be discussed in the concluding chapter, is that the Secretariat struggles to hold the network together. In the absence of a unifying social trait or clearly stated shared values and principles, members tend to be preoccupied with particular, national interests.

Equally, regional research NGOs and business associations are not so explicitly value-driven and generally have a weak identity. For example, ASCCI claims to represent chambers of commerce and industry, trade associations and employer organizations and is '[m]andated to be the voice of the private sector' (ASCCI 2012: 8), without going into depth about which particular constituencies and interests are represented. Indeed, the 'private sector' in the broad sense of the term is very diverse, incorporating a range of different actors, including medium-sized business, transnational corporations and informal traders. It is also not clear what the underlying values that guide ASCCI are, except for sweeping comments about 'business development' and creating 'a unified private sector' (ASCCI 2012: 8). One slight exception to this is SEATINI. Claiming to be a 'people-centred non-profit seeking organization' (SEATINI 2011: 2), it is unclear who are the 'people' it represents. However, lacking a clear constituency, it nevertheless seems to be more values-driven in terms of commitment to a rights-based approach to development, a search for alternatives to the contemporary neo-liberal model of globalization and regionalization and regional and continental unity, which are elaborated upon at length in various documents (e.g. SEATINI 2011: 2–3).

In contrast, some RCSOs have constructed a clear regional positive identity based on certain values, experiences and/or social traits, even if they are in a minority. SAPSN is very active in manufacturing a regional SAPSN-identity based on shared values, world-views and lifestyles, even though it does not have a clear constituency, unlike for example SATUCC and SACBTA. The SAPSN Secretariat urges its members to have an SAPSN banner visible during local and national meetings in their home countries, to mention SAPSN and what it stands for in all publications by members and to speak on behalf of SAPSN at press conferences. According to the coordinator, these things bring a sense of belonging to a 'SAPSN-family'.[88] One important dimension of the SAPSN identity is a shared feeling of belonging to a common Southern African colonial past, transformed into a neo-colonial situation. This implies a link between the past colonialism and freedom struggle in Southern Africa and present-day popular mobilization and resistance to neo-liberal oppression by Western powers. In the words of the director of ZIMCODD,

> the contemporary common struggles in the region go back to the common struggles for liberation in the past. Guerrilla fighters were trained in various countries in the region, governments supporting each other and colonized people elsewhere in the region.[89]

Arguing along the same lines, according to the SAPSN coordinator it is not enough to have formal political independence from former colonizers. People still need to be involved in regional struggles, this time in terms of influencing processes where neo-liberal policies manufactured in the West are today affecting the region: '[S]uffering from certain policies from the IMF, the WB, WTO [. . .] we are now fighting another war together'.[90] In this war, SAPSN is to a large extent value driven,[91] manifested by sentiments related to social and economic justice, rejection of privatization, anti-neo-liberalism, an alternative approach towards development and 'regional solidarity'. On the whole, this brings the members together.[92]

Constructing a sense of regional solidarity is specifically important for popular mobilization within SAPSN and intimately linked to its identity. According to one interviewee, the act of showing solidarity is in fact the most important factor that binds the social movements and trade unions within SAPSN together.[93] According to the director of ZIMCODD:

> [n]ow when the colonization is gone, we should continue with the solidarity at the level of the people since the problems have not ended [. . .] The problems in South Africa are also problems for me in Zimbabwe and the social and economic and political problems are also problems for the region. Therefore, we want to give our solidarity to comrades in the region and also receive that solidarity. So we also go and assist other people in their struggle.[94]

Regional meetings, where NGO members and social movements' activists physically meet, play a major role in the construction of regional solidarity and identity-making, which in the end spurs regionalization of the more critical parts of civil society. SAPSN People's Summits and Southern African Social Forums (SASF)[95] are good examples of this. At the beginning of every People's Summit SAPSN reminds attendees about their historical regional connections and how they used to support each other's liberation struggles and urges the participants to continue such support today and revive past solidarity: 'People then often start telling stories on how they collected cloth and money to send to liberation movements in other countries'.[96] Together such stories about common struggles for freedom from colonial oppression in the past form an important part of the construction of contemporary struggles and regional solidarity. This implies evoking strong feelings of regional togetherness and the importance of helping people in need throughout the region. At the People's Summit in Namibia in 2010, for example, the meeting was characterized by 'lively cultural presentations and energized by the participants singing and chanting, receiving solidarity greetings from all fellow citizens of SADC and brief reports on their respective areas of work and the key concerns in their national terrains' (SAPSN 2010: 3). Furthermore, the coming together of activists from all around the region at SASF, sharing experiences of local and national struggles, creates a sense of regional comradeship which spurs regional action. For example, the SASF in Zimbabwe in 2005 was seen as an important manifestation of regional solidarity with the democratic forces in Zimbabwe, and the SASF in Swaziland in 2008 was an example of showing solidarity with the suppressed people of Swaziland, contesting the initial banning of the forum by the king.[97] At these SASF events people from all around the region are brought together, issues and community struggles are presented and linkages are forged. All in all, 'people celebrate what they are doing. They see other community people celebrating the same thing and they celebrate together. Then they go back home and say that we are more than this community'.[98] Thus, the forum acts as a springboard for the formation of a regional consciousness linked to solidarity among SAPSN activists and their perceived comrades throughout the region.

To move on, the construction of a transnational/regional identity on non-territorial terms, based on a perception of shared social traits, has a profound impact on the regionalization of some other CSOs. The regional consolidation of EJN is linked to a Christian church identity, which constitutes a strong theological base for its various regional activities.[99] According to the director of one EJN member in Mozambique, Conselho Cristão de Moçambique (CCM), the strong church foundation is a powerful uniting force for the network. He underlines that the churches, which make up the member council of churches, are very organized and manage to represent a Christian constituency in the region. The Christian identity is in turn based on Christian values – humanism, morality, dignity, respect, honesty, participation, justice and equality – which are shared by all EJN members in the region. This creates a powerful common platform that consolidates EJN.[100] In the words of one of EJN's funders, NCA, because of the common church identity, 'that oneness is there [. . . despite] language barriers'.[101]

Regional conferences and workshops are important venues for consolidating a regional church-based identity. Here, EJN staff actively try to make theological connections to the often technically inclined issues such as EPA and ICBT and present a Christian biblical rationale for engagement in these.[102] This has a unifying effect on the members of EJN, constructing a sense of regional belonging based on Christian values and identities. One concrete example is the Summit of Religious Leaders in Southern Africa in 2009, where religious leaders, representing NGOs and church communities throughout Southern Africa, including several members of EJN, met to discuss what role faith communities can play in seeking a sustainable future in terms of creating socio-economic justice, environmental sustainability, food security and poverty alleviation. The meeting was hosted by South African Faith Communities' Environment Institute (SAFCEI), an organization loosely linked to EJN. In the declaration from the summit, it is stated that

> [w]e, the members of faith communities from across Southern Africa [. . .] acknowledge that while we are of diverse faith traditions with varying beliefs and practices, we are united through our common commitment to a just care of the earth and all of God's creation.
>
> (SAFCEI 2009)

SATUCC is a good example of the cultivation of a borderless, non-territorial working-class identity. SATUCC seems to have a clear constituency in terms of trade unions, which in turn represent workers in the region. According to the former secretary general, the trade union members have got a clear understanding of their identity, rooted in the working class. In his words:

> [i]f you come from that [working class] background, you carry that with you throughout your lifetime [. . .] It is there, it is in us, we are working-class. So whatever we say, we have that background, that push [. . .] This gives us the identity and strength to articulate what we want to articulate because we know what we are.[103]

In other words, one important force that holds SATUCC together seems to be the identity of being a worker. In various SATUCC regional meetings and conferences, such as the annual SATUCC Congress, representatives of SATUCC members meet and share similar experiences of being 'workers' and of being denied social and economic rights, which adds to the consolidation of this identity.

Notes

1 Kuzvinzwa, interview, 11 December 2009.
2 Katchima, interview, 8 December 2008.
3 ICM is the old name of the current Sectoral and Cluster Ministerial Committee, but the functions are the same. The committee consists of ministers from each SADC member state and is responsible for overseeing the activities of the core areas of integration, monitoring and controlling the implementation of the RISDP, as well as providing policy advice to the council.
4 Horn, e-mail communication, 24 July 2012.
5 Pressand, interview, 27 November 2008.

6 Vilakazi, interview, 15 December 2009.
7 A memorandum of understanding (MoU) is a *document* describing a *bilateral* or *multilateral* agreement between two or more parties. It expresses a convergence of will between the parties, indicating an intended common line of action. It is often used in cases where parties do not imply a legal commitment.
8 Valy, interview, 21 November 2008.
9 Valy, interview, 21 November 2008.
10 Chigwada, interview, 3 December 2009.
11 Machemedze, interview, 4 December 2009.
12 Muchabaiwa, interview, 7 December 2009.
13 Simane, interview, 5 December 2008.
14 Uthui, interview, 24 November 2008.
15 Muchabaiwa, interview, 7 December 2009.
16 Katchima, interview, 8 December 2008.
17 Katchima, interview, 8 December 2008.
18 Ncube, interview, 8 December 2008.
19 le Pere, interview, 27 November 2008.
20 Muchabaiwa, interview, December 2009.
21 le Pere, interview, 27 November 2008.
22 le Pere, interview, 27 November 2008.
23 McKinley, interview, 1 December 2008.
24 Katchima, interview, 8 December 2008.
25 Katchima, interview, 8 December 2008.
26 Damon, interview, 15 December 2009.
27 Kuzvinzwa, interview, 11 December 2009.
28 le Pere, interview, 27 November 2008.
29 Damon, e-mail communication, 20 August 2012.
30 The Paris Declaration was the outcome of a High-Level Forum on Aid Effectiveness in Paris 2005 where ministers of developed and developing countries responsible for promoting development and heads of multilateral and bilateral development institutions met to discuss how to make development co-operation more efficient. The declaration strives to strengthen partner countries' national development strategies and operational frameworks; increase alignment of aid with partner countries' priorities, systems and procedures; enhance donors' and partner countries' accountability to their citizens and parliaments; eliminate duplication of efforts and rationalize donor activities; reform and simplify donor policies and procedures; and define measures and standards of performance and accountability of partner country systems (OECD 2005).
31 Damon, interview, 15 December 2009.
32 Vale, interview, 2 March 2005.
33 Gabriel, interview, 2 December 2008.
34 Ally, interview, 26 November 2009.
35 Muchena, interview, 1 December 2008.
36 le Pere, interview, 27 November 2008.
37 Chiriga, interview, 2 December 2009.
38 Kasiamhuru, interview, 2 December 2009.
39 Chidaushe, interview, 29 November 2009.
40 Sucá, interview, 24 November 2008.
41 Muchena, interview, 1 December 2008.
42 Damon, interview, 15 December 2009.
43 Ally, interview, 26 November 2009.
44 Gentle, interview, 17 December 2009.
45 Matanga, interview, December 2009.

46 McKinley, interview, 1 December 2008.
47 Gentle, interview, 17 December 2009.
48 Machemedze, interview, 4 December 2009.
49 Valy, interview, 21 November 2008.
50 Chigwada, interview, 3 December 2009.
51 Matanga, interview, 4 December 2009.
52 Barnard, interview, 26 November 2008; Mati, interview, 27 November 2009.
53 Pressand, interview, 27 November 2008.
54 Osei-Hwedie, interview, 5 December, 2008.
55 le Pere, interview, 27 November 2008.
56 E.g. Muchabaiwa, interview, 7 December 2009; Kasiamhuru, interview, 2 December 2009; Chidaushe, interview, 29 November 2009.
57 Mhlongo and Chiriga, interview, 2 December 2008.
58 Mhlongo and Chiriga, interview, 2 December 2008.
59 le Pere, interview, 27 November 2008.
60 Kasiamhuru, interview, 2 December 2009.
61 Muchabaiwa, interview, 7 December 2009.
62 Gabriel, interview, 2 December 2008.
63 Chiriga, interview, December 2009.
64 Kasiamhuru, interview, 2 December 2009.
65 Chiriga, interview, 2 December 2009.
66 Katchima, interview, 8 December 2008.
67 Katchima, interview, 8 December 2008.
68 Vilakazi, interview, 15 December 2009.
69 Vilakazi, interview, 15 December 2009.
70 Law, interview, 15 December 2009.
71 Simane, interview, 5 December 2008.
72 Muchabaiwa, interview, 7 December, 2009.
73 Gabriel, interview, 2 December 2008.
74 Mati, interview, 27 November 2009.
75 Pressand, interview, 27 November 2008.
76 Ncube, interview, 8 December 2008.
77 Muchabaiwa, interview, 7 December, 2009.
78 Ncube, interview, 8 December 2008.
79 Bond, interview, 14 December 2008.
80 Matanga, interview, 4 December 2009.
81 Kasiamhuru, interview, 2 December 2009.
82 Chiriga, interview, 2 December 2008.
83 Ncube, interview, 8 December 2008.
84 Kasiamhuru, interview, 2 December 2009.
85 le Pere, interview, 27 November 2008.
86 Simane, interview, 5 December 2008.
87 Muchabaiwa, interview, 7 December 2009.
88 Kasiamhuru, interview, 2 December 2009.
89 Matanga, interview, 4 December 2009.
90 Kasiamhuru, interview, 2 December 2009.
91 Chiriga, interview, 2 December 2009.
92 Pressand, interview, 27 November 2008.
93 Chiriga, interview, 2 December 2009.
94 Matanga, interview, 4 December 2009.
95 SASF is a continuation of the Africa Social Forum (ASF) that has taken place annually since Bamako in 2002 as a prelude to the World Social Forum (WSF) that was initiated

in Porto Alegre (Brazil) in 2001. The latter is an annual event that is deliberately organized to coincide with the World Economic Forum in Davos. The social forum process is generally constituted by members of the so-called alter-globalization or global justice movement who come together to coordinate campaigns, share and refine organizing strategies and debate and inform each other about various issues related to the fight against neo-liberalism (SASF 2013). In terms of SASF, the chief aim is to create regional solidarity against neo-liberal policies and to facilitate regional networking to strengthen solidarity among the peoples of southern Africa (PAAR 2011).

96 Kasiamhuru, interview, 2 December 2009.
97 Gentle, interview, 17 December 2009.
98 Peek, interview, 12 December 2008.
99 Damon, interview, 15 December 2009; Chidaushe, interview, 29 November 2009.
100 Moiana, interview, 17 November 2008.
101 Chidaushe, interview, 29 November 2009.
102 Damon, interview, 15 December 2009.
103 Katchima, interview, 8 December 2008.

Chapter 5
Civil society regionalization in the HIV/AIDS sector in Southern Africa

Key RCSOs

The five regional NGOs and networks related to HIV/AIDS that are the focus in this chapter will now be shortly described.

Africa Capacity Alliance (ACA) (formerly Regional AIDS Training Network, RATN) is a network of 37 NGOs, management institutions and university departments involved in HIV/AIDS work in Eastern and Southern Africa, based in Nairobi, Kenya. ACA strengthens the management and technical capacities of members, facilitates the exchange of ideas and experiences between members and lobbies RIGOs such as EAC, COMESA and the SADC to support its capacity-development agenda. More specifically, ACA training revolves around HIV prevention, treatment and care, impact mitigation and institutional strengthening (ACA 2015). In terms of the analytical distinction between different types of NGOs discussed in Chapter 1, ACA is primarily a facilitating network but with an element of advocacy.

The Southern African Aids Trust (SAT) is based in Johannesburg, South Africa, with six country offices in Malawi, Tanzania, Zimbabwe, Mozambique, Zambia and Botswana. SAT is an independent regional NGO that supports community responses to HIV and AIDS through the capacity strengthening of partners in prevention, care, treatment and support, impact mitigation, advocacy, information exchange and networking, including provision of micro grants. SAT is currently working in partnership with 130 community-based organizations and national advocacy and networking partners in six SADC countries. At the regional level, SAT hosts the Regional African AIDS NGOs (RAANGO), an informal network for regional HIV/AIDS service organizations in Southern Africa (SAT 2015). SAT is a good example of a service-providing NGO.

The Southern Africa HIV and AIDS Information Dissemination Service (SAfAIDS) is a regional NGO based in Harare, Zimbabwe, with four country offices in South Africa, Swaziland, Zambia and Mozambique. Its mission is to promote effective and ethical development responses to the AIDS epidemic and its impact. This is done through the capacity development of 150 local partner CSOs in nine countries, information production, collection and dissemination, networking and building partnerships and leadership in promoting dialogue on issues related to HIV and AIDS. SAfAIDS currently implements its programmes in ten countries in Southern Africa (SAfAIDS 2015). SAfAIDS is another example of a service-providing NGO.

The AIDS and Rights Alliance for Southern Africa (ARASA) is a regional partnership of 53 NGOs from all 15 SADC member states working together to promote a human rights approach to HIV/AIDS and TB. With a head office in Windhoek, Namibia, ARASA supports partners to monitor the efforts of national governments to protect, respect and uphold human rights in the context of national responses to AIDS and TB, as well as build the capacity of partners to promote a human rights-based response to TB, HIV and AIDS. ARASA directly lobbies the SADC on HIV/AIDS and rights issues (ARASA 2015). ARASA is a combination of an advocacy and service-providing network.

The Network of African People Living with HIV for Southern African region (NAPSAR) is a regional network of national CSOs for people living with HIV and AIDS (PLWHA) in 10 countries in Southern Africa. The regional secretariat is situated in Johannesburg, South Africa. NAPSAR seeks to improve the quality of life of people living with or affected by HIV/AIDS and to make sure they have equal access to social services related to prevention, treatment and care. It also wants to ensure that the voices of PLWHA are heard in policy-making related to HIV/AIDS on all levels. This is done through lobbying policy-makers, including the SADC, providing technical support and training to strengthen partner organizations and facilitating regional networking (NAPSAR 2015). In terms of the analytical distinction between different types of networks, NAPSAR is a good example of a combination of a facilitating and advocacy network.

Relations between the SADC and CSOs

Equivalent to the previous chapter, this section will discuss how the statist-capitalist informed social relations between the SADC institutions and various RCSOs influence civil society regionalization in the HIV/AIDS sector in three different ways. First, the overall low priority of HIV/AIDS compared with, for example, trade, which HIV/AIDS-related issues are prioritized in the SADC agenda and how this affects the regional work of CSOs will be discussed. Second, the focus is put on the direct and indirect creation of regional platforms for CSO collaboration. Third, and intimately related to the SADC's issue preferences, the inclusion of certain CSOs and exclusion of others in various SADC institutions will be analyzed in terms of how this affects civil society regionalization.

SADC issue preferences

SADC has designed a quite impressive regional governance infrastructure in the health field. Through the Protocol on Health, SADC has developed and harmonized a range of policies, frameworks and guidelines for HIV and AIDS, tuberculosis and malaria (SADC 2013). Also, a specific SADC Health Program was adopted by

SADC in 1997 and regularly updated, in line with global and regional health declarations and targets. The main cooperation instrument is the SADC Health Policy Framework, which aims to raise the regional standard of health for all citizens to an acceptable level by promoting, coordinating, and supporting efforts of member states to improve access to high-impact health interventions. It has designed proposed policies, strategies and priority areas such as health research and surveillance, health information systems, health promotion and education and sexually transmitted diseases such as HIV/AIDS. Marking the significance put on the latter, HIV and AIDS is addressed as a stand-alone cross-cutting issue which should permeate all SADC activities (SADC 2015a). Also, and most important here, it should be noted that policy-making and implementation of regional programs related to health, HIV/AIDS and other social issues involve collaboration with civil society.

Combating HIV/AIDS in the region is one of the main objectives in the amended SADC Treaty, alongside promoting sustainable and equitable economic growth and development and regional consolidation of democracy (SADC 2001). Similarly, HIV/AIDS is emphasized as one priority intervention area in the RISDP.

With regard to HIV/AIDS, SADC member states started to become more active in the early 2000s, realizing that HIV/AIDS had become a real threat to widespread development. An HIV/AIDS Unit was formed at the SADC Secretariat in 2003, and this unit has become responsible for implementing a special programme on HIV/AIDS (see what follows), mainstreaming HIV/AIDS and supporting other departments at the Secretariat in their HIV/AIDS work and overall HIV/AIDS policy development and harmonization within SADC (Oosthuizen 2006). The SADC Declaration on HIV/AIDS adopted in 2003 outlines a number of priority areas for dealing with the pandemic, that is prevention, improved care and treatment, accelerating mitigation, intensifying resource mobilization and strengthening institutional mechanisms, and urges member states to develop strategies and promote programmes (SADC 2003c). In the declaration it is stated that non-state actors are needed to stem the pandemic, and SADC–civil society collaboration is called for.

The main policy framework for dealing with the HIV/AIDS challenge on a regional level is the SADC HIV and AIDS Strategic Framework. The framework outlines a number of measures to address the impact of the HIV and AIDS pandemic in a comprehensive and complementary way. The plan has been updated and the latest version spans from 2010 to 2015 (SADC 2009). The goal of the framework is to

> Decrease the number of people living with and affected by HIV and AIDS in the SADC region, so as to ensure that HIV and AIDS is no longer a threat to public health and to the sustained socio-economic development of Member States.
>
> (SADC 2015c)

The measures and activities outlined in the framework relate to facilitation of best practices, programme delivery, research and policy development, capacity building and development of standards (SADC 2015a). For example, the Communicable Diseases Project facilitates development and harmonization of policies, frameworks and guidelines for HIV and AIDS, tuberculosis and malaria. In the area of disease surveillance, SADC has facilitated the development of supranational laboratories for HIV and AIDS and TB. In terms of capacity-building, a number of so-called focal persons for mainstreaming HIV and AIDS and human rights have been trained. Furthermore, SADC has initiated so-called mobile population clinics at borders in six member states providing voluntary counselling and testing, treatment of sexually transmitted infections such as HIV/AIDS and condom distribution services. The Secretariat also track and report progress on regional, continental and global HIV and AIDS commitments through the SADC HIV and AIDS Epidemic Reports (SADC 2013).

One important implementation instrument for the realization of the Strategic Framework is the SADC HIV/AIDS Special Fund. For the first round of funding, 13 projects amounting to a total amount of US$6,206,282 were approved up until 2013 and are currently under implementation in various SADC member states. The fund is to be used for small projects and activities that enhance the impact of existing HIV and AIDS programmes in member states, and CSOs are encouraged to apply (SADC 2015b).

SADC's work in the field of HIV/AIDS is closely linked to human rights. The SADC Declaration on HIV/AIDS states that

> the upholding of human rights and fundamental freedoms for all [. . .] is a necessary element in our regional response to the HIV and AIDS pandemic, [. . .] which would encompass access . . . to education, inheritance, employment, health care, social and health services, prevention, support, treatment, legal protection.
> (Kolla om SADC 2003a)

Besides the declaration mentioned above, there are a couple of other regional policy documents that address human rights issues in particular HIV-related areas. For example, the SADC Code on HIV/AIDS and Employment from 1997 urges member states to develop and harmonize standards for dealing with HIV/AIDS in workplaces (SADC 1997). One CSO claims that the code has been one of the most influential documents on HIV/AIDS and human rights in the region (ARASA 2009). Another human rights-related document is the SADC Policy Framework on Population Mobility and Communicable Diseases from 2009, which provides guidance on protecting the health of cross-border mobile populations with regard to communicable diseases such as HIV/AIDS (IOM 2010b: 34). Furthermore, the Protocol on Gender and Development from 2008 should also be mentioned. The Protocol aims to provide for the empowerment of women, eliminate discrimination and achieve gender equality in the region through gender-responsive legislation and programmes (SADC 2008). One section specifically deals with gender and HIV/AIDS and commits states to expand access to prevention, treatment and support for women who are infected and affected by HIV (ARASA 2009: 16). Last, the Model Law on HIV in Southern Africa, initiated by the SADC but formally linked to the SADC Parliamentary Forum (SADC-PF),[1] is a rather progressive regional document 'which say all the right things'.[2] The aims of the Model Law are to provide a legal framework for the review and reform of national legislation related to HIV/AIDS, to promote the implementation of effective social services, to ensure that the human rights of people affected by HIV/AIDS are protected and to stimulate specific measures to address the needs of social groups that are marginalized (SADC PF 2008).

However, in practice it is clear that some aspects of the HIV/AIDS agenda are considered more important for SADC than others, which affects interaction with CSOs. Human rights is generally not high up the agenda of most member states,[3] since realization of political and socio-economic rights threatens the power base of the ruling elite and, in the end, the regional state-centric, capitalist order. Human rights issues in terms of safeguarding the rights of people infected and affected by HIV to various AIDS services, as well as the particular rights of vulnerable social groups such as sexual minorities, are marginalized in the SADC agenda. In this vein, one interviewee draws attention to the fact that there is no specific official and legally binding regional policy on HIV/AIDS and human rights. The quite progressive Model Law has not yet been adopted as an official SADC document, nor has it been implemented by any member state.[4] Instead, service-delivery issues are prioritized by the SADC.[5] Mitigation, prevention, treatment and care are emphasized, but instead of pushing member states to deliver various AIDS services, the SADC drives an agenda in which such services are outsourced to CSOs, in line with the general neo-liberal trend discussed in Chapter 3. Hence, as will be discussed later, collaboration with service-providing CSOs who can assist the SADC in programme implementation is prioritized by the SADC.

In the SADC's practical work, human rights issues are downplayed in terms of action plans and implementation instruments. The director of ARASA concludes that

> [t]here are many countries that say all the right things in terms of we acknowledge that HR is essential to an effective response to HIV but when it comes to translating that into practice it does not work [. . .] SADC countries do not walk the talk [. . .] HR is not an issue that they readily jump to.[6]

For example, the SADC HIV and AIDS Strategic Framework is weak on human rights. The main objectives include that member states should deliver universal access to prevention and treatment, that the impact of HIV and AIDS on the socio-economic development of the region should be reduced, that sufficient resources should be mobilized and that institutional capacity should be enhanced. However, there are no clear obligations put on member states in terms of actual service delivery, and monitoring mechanisms are conspicuous by their absence. Human rights are also only mentioned as a cross-cutting issue and not as a priority area in and of themselves. Member states are recommended to deal with the promotion, protection and respect for human rights of people who are infected and affected by HIV/AIDS, but this is not concretized, and no further guidance is delivered. For example, there are no specific objectives in the framework related to protection of the human rights of vulnerable social groups (SADC 2009). Furthermore, even if the SADC HIV and AIDS Work Plan drawn from the Strategic Framework, of which the latest version found is for 2012 to 2013, is more concrete in terms of social service–provision targets in the areas of prevention, care and treatment, it puts no real obligations on member states to actually deliver. It is also weak on human rights issues, for example in terms of the protection of vulnerable social groups such as sexual minorities (SADC 2011c). Hence, the inclusion of human rights–related HIV/AIDS issues in policy documents is rather rhetorical. Also, in terms of the Special Fund, no reference is made to advocacy activities related to, for example, protection of human rights or to monitoring member states' provision of AIDS services in the priority areas for funding. Instead, only projects dealing with direct service-delivery activities related to, for example, prevention, organizational development, research and production of medicines are eligible for funds (SADC 2015b). In practice, therefore, most funds go to service-providing activities which yield faster and more visible results, in line with the demands of the market-oriented regional order.

Last, with or without progressive regional policy documents on HIV and human rights, due to the state-centric and neo-liberal nature of the SADC most important state decisions affecting the overall HIV/AIDS situation in the region are taken by member states on a national level. Therefore, the realization of an effective regional framework for protection of the rights of AIDS sufferers relies on the willingness of member states to implement various regional policy instruments and to allocate resources for project implementation. It is argued here that the lack of effective regional policy instruments and programmes dealing with HIV/AIDS and human rights boils down to the fact that SADC leaders and officials hide behind 'sovereignty principles', as discussed earlier, when progressive human rights resolutions are to be developed and implemented and when member states who fail to deliver are being pushed to do so. Lacking supra-national powers, the SADC is not an important actor in terms of promoting HIV/AIDS rights in the region. For example, the SADC has no power to enforce harmonization of human rights laws in the region and can only adopt protocols that *recommend* that member states align their laws and policies in the human rights field. Therefore, emphasizing human rights issues risks putting the SADC Secretariat on a collision course with member states.[7] Supporting the rights of sexual minorities, for example in terms of access to AIDS services, is particularly sensitive to the SADC, and there are very few interventions in this field.[8]

SADC focal point creation

Like for the trade sector, the SADC facilitates CSO regional co-operation, both directly and indirectly. This implies that it is creating regional platforms and acting as a regional focal point for regional civil society campaigns to evolve, which will be discussed in this section.

In the SADC HIV and AIDS Strategic Framework it is clearly stated that meaningful citizen participation, via civil society, 'is imperative in policy development and programme delivery' (SADC 2009: 33). Therefore, one important task for the SADC is to'[i]dentify and mobilize technical resources at regional and MS [member state] level, in order to strengthen and leverage expertise and knowledge within the region' (SADC 2009: 39). The SADC Secretariat has taken this task seriously and tries to coordinate regional activities on HIV/AIDS and set up various consultative and decision-making mechanisms for this. Most importantly, an HIV and AIDS Technical Advisory Committee (TAC), Working Groups and a SADC Partnership Forum (PF) have been established for enhanced participation of CSOs and the private sector in SADC policy-making, project implementation and delivery of technical expertise (SADC 2009: 20–21).

It is clear that the SADC Secretariat wants to stimulate regional civil society collaboration on HIV/AIDS issues and enhance involvement in the SADC's work. According to interviewees, the creation of regional platforms for engaging with civil society is viewed very positively and seen as important for regional coordination of HIV/AIDS CSOs.[9] The PF brings together all major players in the HIV/AIDS sector, including CSOs, and convenes twice a year. The PF is an important opportunity for regional civil society networking. During the meetings, CSOs, donors and the SADC discuss the strategic planning of the Secretariat, and CSOs give more concrete technical support to the unit.[10] The latter is done collectively through RAANGO. In fact, giving such responsibly to RAANGO and not to individual CSOs is in itself a way of facilitating and enhancing broader civil society collaboration in the HIV/AIDS sector, since the RAANGO members have to agree on common standpoints *vis-à-vis* the SADC. All in all, in this way the SADC acts as a facilitator of the consolidation of regional civil society cooperation and adds to the regionalization of that part of civil society dealing with HIV/AIDS.

Bilateral donors have also played a big role in pushing the SADC Secretariat to open the door to CSOs in the HIV/AIDS sector. Partly thanks to donors' efforts, CSOs such as SAT and NAPSAR have gained an entry point to the HIV/AIDS Unit and are part of regional project implementation and policy-making, boosting regionalization. Several donors are part of this process. Of most importance is the joint support provided to the SADC HIV/AIDS Unit by RNE, Irish Aid and SIDA, discussed further in the section titled Relations between donors and CSOs, in terms of capacity-building and financing the operationalization of the Unit. In this support, one important element has been to sensitize and push the SADC to open up for engagement with civil society and to actively link CSOs up with the SADC Secretariat in areas where the two have things in common.[11] UNAIDS's Regional Support Team in Johannesburg has also pushed for improved partnership between the SADC and civil society and has actively facilitated this process.[12] One concrete example is the PF, discussed earlier, which the donors have been instrumental in creating and maintaining. Because of donor financial support and engagement with the SADC HIV/AIDS Unit, according to SIDA, the unit now increasingly interacts with CSOs (SIDA 2009).

Furthermore, regional advocacy campaigns revolving around the SADC can be powerful instruments for regional consolidation. Perhaps the best example is the process leading up to the ratification of the SADC Gender Protocol in 2008. The Gender Protocol Alliance was formed in 2005 by 26 CSOs dealing with gender and HIV/AIDS issues in the region and launched a regional campaign for the SADC to adopt such a protocol. Every thematic area in the proposed new protocol had a lead organization, which was in charge of formulating that part. SAfAIDS led the sexual and reproductive health cluster. Overall coordination was done by Gender Links, a regional NGO based in Johannesburg, South Africa, that deals with gender and development issues, and SAfAIDS. These two CSOs worked closely together with the Gender Unit in the drafting of the Protocol (Gender Links 2009).

CSO inclusion in the SADC

The statist and capitalist social structure greatly affects civil society regionalization in the HIV/AIDS sector in terms of both facilitating and obstructing regional networking. Focal point creation was touched on already, and discussion now turns to inclusion and exclusion in regional governance. Compared to the trade sector, where many CSOs have a hard time engaging the SADC, in the HIV/AIDS sector the SADC is more open to interaction with civil society and has engaged with a broad range of CSOs, at least on a Secretariat level. Ultimately this strengthens regional CSOs. Most interviewed RCSOs feel welcomed at the SADC Secretariat, which has a positive effect on their work. Yet, as will be discussed further, CSO participation in other SADC institutions, such as the summit and COM, is much weaker.

The relationship between civil society and the SADC Secretariat in relation to HIV/AIDS has improved in recent years, and many interviewees claim that the SADC and CSOs work well together.[13] As already indicated, the HIV/AIDS Unit is the main SADC contact point for civil society in the HIV/AIDS sector. According to the unit representative, it has taken time to develop a relationship with civil society that is considered today to be 'very good'. In general there are no tensions or conflicts of interest between the unit and CSOs, regardless of the latter's approach to HIV/AIDS work. In contrast to her colleague in TIFI, the representative claims that the unit is open to collaboration with different types of CSOs. To her mind, technical NGOs are experts in their respective fields and provide policy advice to the SADC; membership-based NGOs bring the voices of their grassroots constituencies to the SADC; and the more activist-oriented social movements are important to scaling up HIV/AIDS work and pushing for more radical policy change.[14] One of the key civil society players in the PF, SAfAIDS, agrees with the unit representative's positive picture of SADC–civil society collaboration. According to its director, the HIV/AIDS Unit 'accommodates the diversity of civil society'.[15] Even if more critical actors such as ARASA have to be persistent and 'pushy' to get the Secretariat's attention, they do not feel excluded because of the fact that they advance a human rights agenda.[16] The same applies to NAPSAR, which claims that '[w]e work together with SADC and we are a key partner'.[17]

Furthermore, the unit representative claims that CSOs generally have great influence in regional policy-making and project implementation in the HIV/AIDS area. According to her, CSOs 'are very much involved and they do influence a lot of decisions and a lot of things that we implement as a region. [. . . They] should feel that their contributions are taken on board and valued'.[18] For example, after pressure from CSOs at the PF in 2008, the unit revised its strategic plan to include engagement with the media and private sector in the SADC's HIV/AIDS activities.[19] The DFID representative agrees with this picture. According to her, the official consultation mechanisms with civil society in the HIV/AIDS field work quite well: 'The HIV/AIDS Unit has come quite far in understanding its relationship with civil society and structures this relationship in a constructive way'.[20]

Many CSOs in this study are formally recognized by the SADC Secretariat and are invited to various regional meetings arranged by the SADC, such as the PF, as well as granted a seat in various policy-making forums, such as the TAC. The TAC is considered quite influential, since all plans, agendas and documents have to be scrutinized and evaluated by this committee before being sent to the COM for decision-making. The main institutionalized collaboration between the SADC and civil society occurs through RAANGO, and the principal venue is the PF. RAANGO is given two hours in every meeting to voice the concerns of its members and address pertinent issues in the region.[21] RAANGO members are also given a chance to make inputs to various policy documents such as strategic plans. In 2008, for example, RAANGO was extensively consulted on the new Strategic Framework for HIV/AIDS 2010–2015, addressed earlier, and was used as the main civil society referral body in the process.[22] In this vein, CSOs have taken on the role of monitoring the SADC and making it accountable for its HIV/AIDS-related activities. Hence, at the PF the unit accounts for its activities in terms of progress and failures during the past year and the extent to which it has dealt with issues brought up at the last meeting.[23] The formal recognition of CSOs has strengthened ties between the SADC and RCSOs and expanded the space for CSOs to influence SADC policy-making (which will be discussed in what follows), which in the end enhances regional work.

In terms of specific RCSOs, SAT aims to assist SADC in policy-making and improve national and regional project implementation (SAT 2008: 16). SAT is primarily collaborating with the SADC HIV Unit, and there are regular meetings between the two (SAT 2014a). SAT is a member of the SADC working group on HIV Prevention, while SADC's HIV/AIDS Unit is represented in SAT's board (SAT 2014b). Moreover, SAT conducts joint research with SADC. For instance, it took part in a regional study on the needs of HIV–positive adolescents in the region, which was funded by the HIV and AIDS Unit (SAT 2014a and b). All in all, the former SAT representative believes that SAT is taken seriously by the SADC and claims that the relationship between SAT and the unit is close.[24]

ACA continuously lobbies RIGOs such as EAC, COMESA and the SADC to support its HIV capacity-development agenda and to give high priority to training in regional policy-making and project implementation (ACA 2009, 2011a). According to ACA, 'with strengthened partnerships with regional and national bodies and participation in key and strategic regional activities, ACA's presence in regional fora has increased over time' (ACA 2013: 33). For example, ACA has a formal partnership with the SADC Secretariat (ACA 2011a). In this capacity, ACA has co-hosted various regional HIV/AIDS conferences with SADC, for example the HIV Capacity Building Partners Summit in Eastern and Southern Africa held in Nairobi, Kenya, in 2011 and a joint arrangement among RCSOs such as ACA, SAT, NAPSAR and SAfAIDS as well as the SADC. The summit brought together CSOs dealing with capacity-building linked to HIV/AIDS-related work, as well as governments, RIGOs and donors, to assess progress, to share achievements and best practices and to identify gaps in capacity-building in Eastern and Southern Africa (ACA 2011b). Furthermore, ACA provides training on HIV/AIDS to the SADC Secretariat and SADC member states (ACA 2009). ACA also participates in various working groups and technical committees, such as the steering committee for the development of the so-called SADC HIV Capacity Building Framework, which gives technical HIV/AIDS support to member states. ACA provided SADC with technical support in the implementation of this framework (ACA 2011a: 9).

NAPSAR claims to work closely with the unit. According to the director of NAPSAR, the SADC quickly recognized the network as the main body for representing PLWHA in the region.[25] The partnership between NAPSAR and the SADC is formalized within the SADC PLWHA Framework from 2008. In its capacity of representing PLWHA in the region, NAPSAR is also a member of the HIV/AIDS TAC (NAPSAR 2015). Furthermore, the collaboration with the SADC has resulted in its participation in the design and review of a number of SADC policy documents. For example, NAPSAR was influential in the development of the Population Mobility Framework as well as the model law and made inputs to the latest SADC Business Plan. NAPSAR has also provided the SADC with policy-relevant research on issues related to HIV and human rights. For example, together with SAT it conducted a study on the needs of young people who live with HIV/AIDS, which also highlighted gaps in the current provision of health services to young people in the region. The project was financed by the SADC through the Special Fund, discussed earlier. NAPSAR is currently pushing the SADC to adopt a Regional Treatment Protocol (NAPSAR 2011: 5, 7, 11, 19).

ARASA's main goal is to promote a human rights approach to HIV/AIDS and TB in the SADC region (ARASA 2013a). ARASA is a formal member of the TAC, and its director serves as an expert on HIV and human rights. ARASA has also provided technical inputs to various HIV/AIDS treatment and prevention policy documents (ARASA 2010: 25–26). For example, ARASA was consulted by the

Regionalization in the HIV/AIDS sector 109

SADC Secretariat in the creation of a model law, together with SADC-PF.[26] According to the director of ARASA, it has a substantial say in the design of various policy documents.[27] ARASA has been engaged in various regional advocacy campaigns that target the SADC and its member states. For example, in 2010 ARASA teamed up with a range of trade unions, researchers and ex-mineworker organizations in Swaziland and Lesotho to urge the SADC Secretariat and the South African government to improve the local and cross-border management of HIV–infected mineworkers in the region (ARASA 2010: 16). Furthermore, in 2014 ARASA supported strategic litigation relating to TB on the mines in South Africa, Lesotho, Swaziland and Mozambique in order to promote and protect the rights of mineworkers vulnerable to lung disease (ARASA 2014). Related to this, ARASA demands a Code of Conduct to operationalize the SADC Declaration on TB & Mines and Code of Good Practice (ARASA 2013b). According to an external evaluation of ARASA's work, it is deemed important by policy-makers, including the SADC, and by civil society in making sure that the voice of human rights–related CSOs is heard at the regional level. On the whole, ARASA is considered a key link between civil society and the SADC (Singizi Consulting 2012: 46, 57).

Last, in terms of influencing SADC policy-making, SAfAIDS, mainly acts through RAANGO.[28] It is uncertain to what extent SAfAIDS sits on the TAC and participates in the various working groups. SAfAIDS's main contribution to policy influence is more indirect, disseminating information which is used by various CSOs in their advocacy work at national and regional levels.[29] For example, it distributes various information materials related to treatment and supports partners to develop and implement effective HIV interventions at workplaces (SAfAIDS 2006). As one of the leading CSOs in the Gender Protocol Alliance, SAfAIDS also provided alliance members with information and research around gender, HIV/AIDS and health which was used in advocating for and designing the Gender Protocol. In the process, SAfAIDS was selected to represent regional CSOs in the SADC Task Force, put together by the Gender Unit, and was responsible for providing guidance on the protocol sections dealing with HIV/AIDS (SAfAIDS 2006: 12). Acknowledging the policy influence of SAfAIDS and Gender Links, according to one SADC representative the Gender Protocol was as much the product of the Alliance as the SADC.[30] Furthermore, SAfAIDS provides training services to SADC officials and governmental institutions dealing with HIV/AIDS. For example, it arranged a training course in 2008 about documentation and the sharing of Best Practices in HIV and AIDS programming in the Southern African region (SAfAIDS 2012).

The fact that SADC–civil society collaboration is endorsed by both parties and generally considered to be well functioning, as argued, is intimately linked to a shared (problem-solving) approach to HIV/AIDS work. As already indicated, many of the CSOs involved in SADC-led HIV/AIDS regional governance, such as SAT, ACA and SAfAIDS, in many respects want to contribute to the SADC's HIV/AIDS agenda, as outlined for example in the Declaration and Strategic Framework 2010–2015. These actors view governments and RIGOs as partners in a common endeavour to provide AIDS-related services to various target groups. This is manifested, for example, in the Summit Communique from the HIV Capacity Building Partners Summit in Nairobi mentioned earlier. The communiqué calls upon 'civil society organisations, regional economic communities, private sectors and institutions [. . .] to commit themselves [. . .] and play their role as *partners* in the implementation of effective HIV capacity building initiatives towards achieving universal access' (ACA 2011b, my emphasis).

This partnership approach is clearly displayed by SAT, which is

> further committed to contributing to universal access to prevention, treatment, care and support for people of the SADC region, and to mitigation of the impact of AIDS communities and its members, through an expanded, comprehensive and sustained response, in line with SADC's HIV and AIDS Business Plan.
> (SAT 2008: 4–5)

More particularly, SAT wants to contribute to the area of capacity development of community responses to HIV/AIDS in the plan (SAT 2008: 4), which is in fact one of the SADC's core areas in its HIV/AIDS work. SAT therefore supports local and national partners in a range of activities such as HIV prevention, care and support, impact mitigation and ART literacy (SAT 2011: 6). Similarly, ACA wants to contribute to the SADC's goal of enhanced institutional HIV/AIDS capacity in the region through delivering capacity-building and training to various institutions, state as well as non-state, that are involved in prevention, care, support and mitigation (ACA 2009: 16). Last, SAfAIDS's production and dissemination of information to and facilitation of collaboration between various stakeholders in the region resonates well with the SADC's aim to identify and mobilize technical resources and share expertise and best practices in the region. All in all, these examples imply that CSOs in this study take an active role in delivering AIDS-related services and thereby participate in the reproduction of the capitalist social order in which responsibility for social service provision is increasingly outsourced to non-state actors in line with the neo-liberal demand.

CSO exclusion in the SADC

As in the case of the CSO involvement in regional governance in the trade sector, the equivalent role played by CSOs related to HIV/AIDS has to be problematized. It is true that CSOs are involved in service delivery and some policy-making, but this involvement is generally conditional and takes place on the SADC's terms. To start with, it is argued that CSOs are primarily called upon when the SADC needs them on various matters related to HIV/AIDS, and not due to some overall commitment to facilitate civil society participation in regional integration. One major reason for the participation of CSOs in SADC-led regional HIV/AIDS governance is the fact that the SADC lacks sufficient knowledge and expertise in many

HIV/AIDS areas to implement the Strategic Plan. Therefore, the SADC is in great need of NGOs' competence. In many regards, CSOs are seen as important partners because of their expertise and ability to provide services. According to the director of SAfAIDS, even though the SADC's capacity to do HIV/AIDS work has been strengthened because the unit's organizational capacity has been improved, the unit is still rather weak and relies quite a lot on civil society. For example, the SADC needs the technical expertise of CSOs to design regional policy documents.[31]

Another important reason for the SADC's positive attitude towards civil society is its willingness to outsource service-delivery activities related to prevention, mitigation, care and treatment to civil society actors such as ACA, SAfAIDS and SAT, in line with the overall neo-liberal regional governance agenda. One instrument for this is the Special Fund which, as discussed, mainly supports activities related to service provision. According to the representative of the unit, '[i]n the HIV/AIDS-sector CSOs are key actors and SADC cannot have a meaningful response without them'.[32] The PF is particularly important for the SADC to involve CSOs in the implementation of the HIV/AIDS agenda. If the Secretariat is tasked to work on a particular issue as set out in the Strategic Framework, for example in terms of providing certain services, but lacks resources or knowledge, the unit tries to find a partner in the forum who is willing to assist and take responsibility for that task.[33]

In the HIV/AIDS sector more broadly, service-providing NGOs are generally in a great majority, at the expense of more critically inclined human rights advocacy organizations which question the structural causes behind, for example, lack of AIDS treatment (SIDA 2009). Taking a historical perspective, the initial HIV/AIDS CSOs that came about were service organizations focusing on mitigating the immediate effects of the pandemic through counselling, home-based care and other services. In fact, 'there have always been few organizations that focus on HR and a right based response to HIV . . . and this has perpetuated through time'.[34] Therefore, there are also few human rights CSOs working on a regional level (Singizi Consulting 2012). AIDS and human rights is a contested area for many CSOs, governments and donors, and it is only during the last 5 years that human rights have started to be acknowledged in the HIV/AIDS sector (Singizi Consulting 2012).

Advancing a human rights agenda, critical CSOs such as NAPSAR and ARASA have a different, more advocacy-oriented approach to SADC-led regional HIV/AIDS governance when compared with more service-oriented CSOs. In their view, the SADC and member states have the prime responsibility to deliver AIDS services, not civil society, and need to be pushed to live up to their commitments. According to ARASA, despite political commitments to promote a human rights–based response to HIV, many countries have not fulfilled the commitments they have made on paper. Therefore, ARASA claim to have an important function to perform in monitoring policy, legislative and programmatic responses to HIV, TB and sexual and reproductive health and human rights in the region and address both rights abuses and delays in fulfilling basic social and economic rights (ARASA 2013a). In a similar vein, NAPSAR claim that denying PLWHA access to services in relation to treatment, care and prevention is considered a human rights abuse.

Therefore, NAPSAR advocates the SADC and member states to scale up AIDS treatment. According to the director of NAPSAR, 'our logic behind treatment and prevention is more controversial than distributing condoms'.[35] However, contesting national and regional politics around HIV/AIDS makes these CSOs quite controversial in the eyes of most governments. Therefore, NAPSAR members that work on LGBT (lesbian, gay, bisexual and transsexual) rights and HIV/AIDS are excluded in many ways in their respective states.[36] ARASA takes this critical approach one step further and calls for deeper law reform. Hence, even if one important task is still to monitor the implementation of various existing legal and policy frameworks connected to treatment and prevention, in line with the work of NAPSAR, another important challenge is to 'move beyond a narrow focus on protecting the rights of PLWHA to a broader equality agenda' (ARASA 2009: 96). This entails not only strengthening existing rights but also fundamental reform of discriminatory laws, policies, practises and beliefs against marginalized groups in society in conservative judicial areas, such as criminalization of same-sex relations and transmission of HIV (ARASA 2009: 94, 96).

Even if they are involved in policy dialogues with the SADC Secretariat, for example through the TAC, and are deemed important partners by the unit, on a deeper decision-making level critical CSOs such as NAPSAR and ARASA are generally not interesting to the SADC and its member states, since they challenge the dominant problem-solving HIV/AIDS approach in the region that is related to the neo-liberal discourse. In that way, these CSOs go against the workings of the capitalist system. In fact, despite the quite impressive SADC-CSO interaction accounted for earlier, according to one commentator, 'if [the Secretariat] is the high point of civil society interaction [with] SADC it is very sad'.[37] Because of the entrenched statism in the SADC, member states want to retain decision-making power in all issue areas, including HIV/AIDS. The SADC decides what levels in the SADC hierarchy CSOs are allowed to have influence at. Therefore, the bulk of SADC cooperation with CSOs in the HIV/AIDS sector in terms of policy-making takes place at lower levels at the Secretariat, for example through the unit, TAC, PF and various working groups. The most important policy decisions, governing the overall HIV/AIDS agenda, are taken by member states in COM and summit meetings. CSOs are excluded in these forums. In addition, without any monitoring and enforcement mechanisms, these decisions are then left to be implemented through the members' goodwill.[38] SADC member states shy away from advancing a human rights agenda, and the summit and COM devote little attention to human rights and AIDS issues. Hence, since much important decision-making is taking place elsewhere, CSOs such as ARASA which seek to reform the overall HIV/AIDS agenda in the region are very reluctant to strengthen interaction with the Secretariat. In the words of the director of ARASA, 'we rarely go [to the PF] because it is just a room full of a huge amount of different people listening to an update from SADC which is not all that interesting'.[39] In terms of the unit, which is supposed to lead the region in terms of HIV/AIDS intervention, it is not performing in the way that some CSOs expect. The unit is considered very constrained in terms of what it can do, lacking power and resources and not being important in terms of policy development.[40] This is related to the prevailing sovereignty-boosting and neo-liberal regional governance in which member states refuse to transfer supranational power to the Secretariat and prioritize trade over social issues. In line with the overall tendency to put most resources into trade, unsurprisingly the Trade Directorate is stronger and more resourced and the people working there are more effective in putting their issues on the SADC agenda.[41]

Relations between donors and CSOs

This section will discuss how the statist-capitalist informed social relations between donors and RCSOs influence civil society regionalization in the HIV/AIDS sector in two different ways. First, the role of donor funds in facilitating civil society regionalization and the dependency this creates on behalf of CSOs will be analyzed and, second, the ways in which donor agendas shape the nature of this process. However, the first task is to list the most important donors involved in this sector.

Key donors

Irish Aid has a Regional Programme on HIV/AIDS for Southern and Eastern Africa, with the purpose being to promote and strengthen the regional response to prevent the spread of HIV/AIDS and reduce its impact in Eastern and Southern Africa (Irish Aid 2008). This is coordinated by a Regional Advisor and based at the Pretoria office in South Africa. In essence, the regional programme complements the national level by addressing the cross-border dimensions of HIV/AIDS issues, for example in terms of the linkage between migration and the spread of HIV, and through strengthening the exchange of information between national actors. In the regional programme, Irish Aid supports a range of organizations, including intergovernmental organizations and regional NGOs (Irish Aid 2008).

The Swedish International Development Co-operation Agency's (SIDA) funds to regional HIV/AIDS activities are channelled through the Swedish-Norwegian Regional HIV/AIDS Team for Africa (referred to as the Team). The Team is a joint programme of the governments of Sweden and Norway which was started in 2000, covers Sub-Saharan Africa and is based at the Swedish embassy in Lusaka, Zambia. The Team's main functions are to provide financial support and dialogue with regional partners for a strengthened regional response to the HIV/AIDS pandemic and to give technical assistance to the Swedish and Norwegian embassies in the region in their national HIV/AIDS work (SIDA 2011). The Team provides regional platforms for networking, interaction and exchange of information between various state and non-state organizations involved in HIV/AIDS work and to build the capacity of both RIGOs and regional NGOs and networks. Moreover, the Team finances key regional forums such as the PF and RAANGO (SIDA 2009).

The UK Department for International Development (DFID) also has a specific regional programme in Southern Africa, alongside the national activities in various countries. The regional programme is administered from the regional DFID office in South Africa. In comparison with SIDA and Irish Aid, DFID's regional programme is broader than HIV/AIDS and includes other areas of engagement. Within the HIV/AIDS theme, DFID has partners from both civil society and the state. In terms of the latter, DFID supports the implementation of the SADC HIV/AIDS Business Plan, and technical and financial support has also been given to RCSOs within RAANGO (DFID 2006).

The Royal Netherland Embassy (RNE) has a regional programme which solely deals with HIV/AIDS issues, which is managed by their office in South Africa. The overall objective of the programme is to 'accelerate the response to the AIDS pandemic, through regional cross-border approaches, which complement/strengthen country-level efforts, leading to more efficient/effective country-level prevention and mitigation efforts' (RNE 2009: 2). Apart from support to the SADC HIV/AIDS Unit, RNE gives financial and technical support to several regional NGOs and networks (RNE 2009: 2). One core aspect of the regional programme is to facilitate linkages between state and non-state actors on a regional level, for example through the PF.[42]

Besides bilateral development co-operation with a number of countries in Africa, the Canadian International Development Agency (CIDA) also has a Regional Programme for Southern and Eastern Africa that has two components: economic growth and children and youth. The latter focuses on reducing the spread of HIV/AIDS in the region. The overall goal of the programme is to build the capacity of regional institutions, organizations and networks, including regional HIV/AIDS CSOs, to more effectively stimulate sustainable economic growth and secure a future for children and youth (CIDA 2012).

Besides these bilateral donors, a few private foundations, trusts and INGOs are involved in supporting the regionalization of civil society in the HIV/AIDS sector. The most important one is the Dutch-based Humanist Institute for Development Cooperation (HIVOS), which has an HIV/AIDS Sector within its Civil Choices Programme, administrated by its regional office for Southern Africa based in Harare. The HIV/AIDS Sector involves providing support to national and regional CSOs in terms of project financing, organizational development and networking, strengthening of advocacy and promoting participation of CSOs in international forums. HIVOS recognizes the overriding importance of the participation of and co-operation among CSOs of PLWHA and women in advocacy and campaigns (HIVOS 2009: 16–17).

Dependency on donor funds

The constellation of donors involved in the regionalization of civil society in the HIV/AIDS sector is a bit different when compared with the trade sector. Private foundations, trusts and INGOs are more involved in trade-related support than HIV/AIDS, and the opposite is true for bilateral donors. In the HIV/AIDS sector, bilateral donors run the show, and as we have seen the most prominent ones are RNE, Irish Aid, SIDA, CIDA and DFID. These donors have embarked on regional programmes supporting RCSOs doing regional work, for example SAfAIDS, SAT and ACA, and RIGOs such as the SADC. However, the regional work of these donors is far from being as important as the national. In fact, regional support is more or less questioned by most donors in terms of the added value, which makes funding for regional civil society very uncertain in the long run.

For most bilateral donors, it seems that supporting the regionalization of civil society is not an obvious thing to do and is a source of great debate. According to the RNE representative,

> here is this catch-22 situation whereas if you purely work on the regional level, what are the outcomes; [. . .] meetings, papers, networks and when there is such an urgency in fighting the epidemic people are saying, you know, this is useless [. . .] we have enough of that, we need implementation on the ground. So it is a constant endeavour to justify that you are actually adding something that will make country processes work better.[43]

Every year, then, RNE asks itself if it should spend its money on bilateral programmes instead because it sees better results on the national than the regional level.[44] Even if RNE has a regional programme within the HIV/AIDS sector, it has encountered many challenges in implementing it due to the widespread national bias in Dutch development co-operation. Regardless of the regional programme, in practice the attention of Dutch staff in Southern Africa is primarily on the national level: 'Regional initiatives are at best a lower order priority and at worse a distraction. There is very few staff in the region or in the Hague whose work has an explicit regional focus' (NRE 2009: 20). It is claimed that regional programming is an unusual aid modality and that most staff engaging with the regional programme have little understanding of the regional level (NRE 2009: 20).

In terms of DFID, similarly the country-based approach takes primacy in enhancing development in Southern Africa. Regional and continental initiatives are only undertaken where they can add value to the country-based approach (DFID 2006). Even the regional activities of the Team are much less in volume than bilateral Swedish and Norwegian support to individual countries.[45] Furthermore, according to Irish Aid, its regional programme on HIV/AIDS in principle functions as a complement to the national level. In fact, one important element of the regional work is to support Irish authorities in various countries to exchange information in order to develop the national response in various countries (Irish Aid 2008). It should also be noted that what often is called a 'regional' programme by bilateral donors is in fact a multi-country approach where the same thing is done in many countries, without coordination of these activities or targeting of regional actors such as the SADC.[46]

The RCSOs in this study are concerned about the overall national priorities of bilateral donors and claim that few of these appreciate and understand what regional CSOs really do. According to the director of ARASA, it has taken some effort to persuade donors, particularly the bilateral ones, that regional work is important.

ARASA is still sometimes approached by donors such as Irish Aid and SIDA, who want to discuss what the value added of the regional level really is.[47] In the same vein, the director of SAfAIDS claims that donors want projects that are easily monitored, and regional activities do not always lend themselves to that.[48]

It is obvious that donors play an important role for civil society regionalization, making financial resources available for regional HIV/AIDS activities. However, this has to be problematized. First of all, even if there are indeed bilateral donor funds available for regional civil society work in the HIV/AIDS sector, as shown, due to their national inclinations, donors constantly question this type of support. This creates a rather vulnerable financial situation for most RCSOs, at least in a long-term perspective. The availability of donor funds can also create regional 'briefcase' CSOs in which financial resources are used by staff members for personal enrichment rather than broader development objectives. In fact, there is a lot of self-interest and territory-marking in the HIV/AIDS sector, including at the regional level. According to one CSO leader,

> I have been astonished many times by the attitudes of civil society organizations which sometimes have stopped representing the interests of their own constituencies and started representing their own interests [. . .] civil society is not a saint. I have been disappointed many times.[49]

According to another commentator,

> why people move from government to NGOs is because [. . .] they have realized that you can get a lot of money [. . .] It is more of an income generating activity. This is almost like charity work, that is why they call it non-profit, but it pays more than any other work really [. . .] It is really, really, really good business. You have nice offices, you have nice cars, you have high salaries [. . .] Everyone wants to get as much money as possible as organizations and you want to be seen as doing the work that is expected. If you look at which people have the best houses in town, they work at NGOs such as SAT and SANASO.[50]

However, such rent-seeking is a risky business and jeopardizes the existence of CSOs, since financial mismanagement, of course, is generally not tolerated in the donor community. As in the trade sector as exemplified by SADC-CNGO and SAPSN, donor dependency makes RCSOs very vulnerable, and changing donor preferences can terminate their activities, for example in cases of economic fraud.

One telling example of the latter is the former SANASO, which was one of the most important regional players in the HIV/AIDS field for many years. SANASO was a regional network of 10 national CSOs involved in HIV/AIDS work in Southern Africa, facilitating contact among members around the region, and promoting cooperation between civil society for mutual learning and to better utilize each other's resources to create a common position on issues in the HIV/AIDS response in the region. SANASO engaged the SADC extensively and was highly involved in various policy forums at the Secretariat (SANASO 2011). However, in 2008 and 2009 donors on several occasions complained that funds intended for certain HIV/AIDS activities were instead allocated to the operation of the office. For example, funds were used to buy a second office car without the consent of the donors, which was used for the director's private business. The director also increased her salary by 50%, which was not endorsed by the donors, and even used some funds for various personal expenses.[51] In an audit of SANASO commissioned by the lead donor, SIDA, in 2008, it was concluded that 'the outcome [. . .] has been dismal [. . . There is] suspect misappropriation of project funds' (Ramstedt 2008). In effect, SIDA and other donors later decided to withdraw their funds, and SANASO ceased to exist in 2009.[52] This is a very good example of how doing regional HIV/AIDS work for personal enrichment jeopardizes an organization's existence.

Donor influence on the CSO agenda

Discussing the role of donors more broadly, the availability of regional funds seems to be greater for service-delivery activities when compared with rights-based work. One CSO is concerned with the '[u]nwillingness or reticence of some funders to support advocacy and training work on human rights' (ARASA 2007: 15). According to the Trust study, mentioned earlier, this has partly to do with the fact that many donors consider CSOs responsible for basic service delivery to marginalized people in light of the reduction of the welfare state. In addition, service delivery gives donors 'good press at home', as Western taxpayers would 'rather support poor street children than advocacy groups' (Southern Africa Trust 2010b: 16). This should not be underestimated in a time of economic recession and given the overall trend towards a results-based approach and demands for efficiency within the donor community.[53] Bilateral donor aversion to supporting advocacy-based human rights work also has another, more political dimension. Just as SADC member states refrain from collaboration with human rights-related CSOs, many donors, especially bilateral ones, also find supporting human rights work controversial.[54] One concrete reason is that this can harm foreign relations between the donor agency and recipient country. One example is the previous Dutch support to Treatment Action Campaign (TAC) in South Africa, which put pressure on the South African government to scale up the delivery of AIDS medicines. However, collaboration with TAC, which was criticizing the government, was tricky because it could harm foreign relations between Holland and South Africa and was eventually terminated.[55]

As discussed in the last section, operating in a capitalist structural framework where development activities are increasingly carried out according to the market logics of supply and demand and accumulation of capital, CSOs in the HIV/AIDS sector are increasingly run like businesses. Therefore, when looking for potential funders they tend to go where the money is. As indicated, many donors increasingly prefer to fund HIV/AIDS projects that are easily measured. The consequence of this is that many NGOs in the sector, on local, national as well as regional levels, seem to go for service provision because the results there are more tangible and measurable.[56] This stands in sharp contrast to rights-based work, where it is difficult to see immediate results because the impact of advocacy for AIDS rights, for example in terms of networking, research and monitoring, is hard to measure:[57] 'Log frames don't really work with HR [. . .] but you can count how many people you have put on treatment. It is easier to show results, whereas with HR it is difficult'.[58] As it is a rather non-profitable development activity, many CSOs refrain from doing advocacy work related to human rights. According to one commentator: 'NGO-staff do not want to lose their jobs and therefore they play safe and apply for money related to service provision, and not for example pushing governments to find better treatment'.[59] In general, then, it is easier to get donor money for service delivery than for human rights work, which also applies at the regional level. This has made a fundamental imprint on civil society regionalization in the HIV/AIDS sector, which is highly problem solving in character.

Donors involved in supporting the regionalization of civil society in the HIV/AIDS sector generally have great influence over the type of work carried out by their recipients. This relates to donors supporting service provision as well as advocacy related to human rights. In the words of the representative of RNE,

> there are those NGOs who do advocacy and act as watch dogs vis-à-vis governmental actors, and those who collaborate hand in hand with government in delivering services [. . .] If you as a donor are aware of who is doing what you can influence the level playing field.[60]

Since service-providing activities are privileged, this is what most CSOs such as SAT, ACA and SAfAIDS put their focus on. Consequently, few bilateral donors work with regional advocacy organizations. The latter get the bulk of their funds from private funders and trusts. For example, NAPSAR is funded by Trust Africa, an African foundation based in Senegal and the UK National Lottery, as well as SIDA (NAPSAR 2012). In the same vein, the main donors of ARASA are SIDA, OSISA and the Ford Foundation.[61] Hence, the exception to the rule among bilateral donors is SIDA, which in fact questions the general focus on service delivery. It explains its support to advocacy and human rights in the following way: '[I]n an era when many of the NGOs are mainly acting primarily as service providers, an organization such as ARASA is supported to lift other organizations to the level of providing more critical engagement' (SIDA 2009: 64). This quote shows that more critically inclined donors have a vested interest in steering their recipients in a certain strategy and issue direction. Hence, ARASA is used by SIDA to infuse a more advocacy-oriented agenda in the HIV/AIDS sector, in line with the agenda of some critical private funders in the trade sector, as shown in Chapter 4.

Donor influence is often manifested in more direct interventions in the work of their recipients. The representative of Irish Aid, for example, claims that her agency has a great influence on the work of its civil society partners, being involved throughout the process of project management in terms of giving technical input to strategic planning, for example. According to her, this is normal in the donor community, since donors always have their own agendas: 'We can't help, you know, that we tell partners once in a while that it would be good if you could include this [. . .] For example Irish Aid is always happy when issues of children are included'.[62] The director of SAT agrees that donor dependency affects its strategic planning. Donors often want to discuss what issues and projects should be prioritized.[63]

Relations between CSOs

The relationships between CSOs in the HIV/AIDS sector on a regional level seem to be rather harmonious, unlike the trade sector. Due to the dominance of the service-providing agenda, reproduced by SADC influence and donor funding, most HIV/AIDS CSOs share the same problem-solving approach and perform similar activities, even though different emphasis is put on prevention, treatment, care or mitigation. According to one commentator, CSOs in the HIV/AIDS sector more broadly agree on the content of the issues, for example in terms of the nature of the HIV/AIDS problems and the strategies needed for dealing with them, when compared with CSOs in other sectors.[64] This implies that relations between mainstream service-providing CSOs and the minority of CSOs doing human rights are rather smooth. This is exemplified by CSO co-operation within RAANGO. According to the SAT representative, she has not experienced any tensions between the members of the network,[65] and the director of ARASA claims that '[w]e have a very good working relationship with other regional organizations, mainly through the forum of RAANGO [. . .] even though we focus on different things'.[66] Compared with the trade sector, where ideological rivalry risks fragmenting civil society on the regional level, the harmonious relations between HIV/AIDS CSOs could strengthen civil society regionalization in the long term, benefitting coordination between CSOs in different fields and broad coalition-building.

CSOs and issue-framing

In this and the next section, the focus will be on the agency of RCSOs in the HIV/AIDS sector, albeit within the context of the statist and capitalist regional order. Hence, as will be clear in the coming two sections, while partly an autonomous process, the internal motivations of RCSOs to 'go regional' are influenced by external actors such as the SADC and donors. Relations between the SADC and CSOs in particular affect how regional NGOs and networks frame issues and construct identities. The section will start by discussing two dimensions of civil society regionalization related to issue-framing: regional issue-framing and construction of regional target groups. Then the role of regional identity-making for civil society regionalization will be investigated.

Regional issue-framing

Regional issue-framing plays an important role for regional consolidation of RCSOs in the HIV/AIDS sector. The perception of HIV/AIDS issues as having a regional 'Southern African' character is widespread among regional organizations in this study.[67] For example, according to the director of SAfAIDS:

> HIV/AIDS crosses borders, it is an issue that affects the whole region and not just nationally. There are many examples of HIV/AIDS issues in terms of prevention, treatment etc. that have a regional scope, for example an infected person living in Zimbabwe who needs access to treatment in South Africa. Such situations and more generally flows of people [...] need to be addressed on a regional level, you can't have one country with certain protocols and another country with nothing.[68]

Such regional understanding of HIV/AIDS has spurred SAfAIDS's involvement in the Gender Protocol Alliance, discussed previously, in regional information dissemination and in other regional activities.[69] In the same vein, SAT argues that the key drivers of the pandemic are similar within the region, including concurrent partnership by men and women with low consistent use of protection, which affects local communities throughout the region in a similar fashion. Another general feature of the pandemic throughout the region is also the fact that women and children are hardest hit (SAT 2008: 4–5). Due to these regional similarities, SAT believes it can use similar empowering techniques to develop the capacity of communities in various countries in the region to deal with the pandemic (SAT 2011: 14).

The director of NAPSAR suggests that HIV/AIDS issues related to human rights are regional. There are a number of similarities between rights-related issues in the countries in the region, for example the marginalization of certain social groups such as sexual minorities. Therefore, NAPSAR pushes the SADC and member states to standardize and harmonize policies and laws related to human rights and AIDS between countries in the region.[70] ARASA also believes that rights-related issues are very similar in the region, for example criminalization of same-sex relations and poor access to AIDS treatment in prisons. Therefore, '[i]t makes sense to work on a regional level'[71] in terms of networking and sharing of information and best practices between ARASA partners in order to enhance national advocacy as well as work regionally to push the SADC to adopt regional resolutions.[72]

Furthermore, when national CSOs physically meet in regional conferences, forums and advocacy campaigns, this has a heavy impact on the regional constitution of the networks and NGOs they are linked to. Regional issue-framing plays an important role here. SAT, for example, regularly arranges regional meetings for its partners to discuss various HIV/AIDS issues, and some kind of regional consensus is often reached on how to best deal with these. According to the director of SAT, in these meetings 'we share knowledge in order to create one voice from Southern

Africa based on what is happening in several countries'.[73] She specifically mentions one regional seminar in 2009 where 60 to 70 partners in the region participated. Through intense discussions, the participants agreed on the best methods for working with HIV/AIDS problems in Southern Africa, resulting in a publication that claims to deliver the voice of civil society in HIV/AIDS prevention in the region.[74] Such regional issue-framing helps in uniting the different partners of SAT and thereby strengthens the regional consolidation of the organization. According to the SAT director, because of the many regional meetings they arrange, a feeling of regional connectedness among the partners is created, based on similar perceptions of the work they do. In these meetings, partners often state that they 'are part of the SAT-family',[75] which, it should be underlined, is not based on shared social traits or values and therefore not linked to a deeper sense of belonging and identity.

Another good example of regional issue-framing at regional meetings is a pan-African civil society meeting in 2009 organized by the African Council of Aids Service Organizations (AFRICASO) to discuss a certain UN report. Several RCSOs from Southern Africa participated, for example SAfAIDS. Among the Southern African CSOs an understanding of the specificity of the issues in this part of Africa developed during the meeting. For example, when relating to other African civil society groups, the Southern African CSOs identified particular key drivers for the spread of HIV in Southern Africa as a region. Hence, the regional issue-framing within the Southern Africa group depended on the 'othering' of other African regions such as East Africa, which was perceived as constituting a different social context, harbouring other types of factors for the spread of HIV. In fact, certain HIV issues 'might have different names in different countries and played out differently but in essence is the same thing'.[76]

Furthermore, in the communiqué developed at the end of the HIV Capacity Building Partners Summit in 2011 discussed previously, participants reached consensus about key challenges and proposed actions for future HIV/AIDS work in the ESA region. In the communiqué it is stated that, since there are many common challenges in the region, such as the capacity-building needs of women, children and other key populations at risk, methodologies and practices should be replicated and harmonized across the region (ACA 2011b: 56–57). As one of the organizers, ACA provided leadership in the discussions during the summit and was highly involved in building such consensus. This, it is claimed, strengthened ACA's profile in the region (ACA 2011a: 9). Hence, regional meetings such as the summit, which provide platforms for CSOs and other stakeholders to reach agreement on common problems and ways of dealing with them, are a powerful example of regional issue-framing, which ultimately strengthens the regionalization of CSOs.

For ARASA, regional meetings are also important to stimulate partners to reach consensus about key regional concerns.[77] The annual Partnership Forum is the biggest platform for ARASA partners to share their accomplishments and identify advocacy priorities (ARASA 2012). At the forum in 2011, the partners agreed on four themes to prioritize in their national and regional advocacy during 2012, including expanded access to prevention services and preventing criminalization of HIV transmission and exposure.[78] According to its director, 'ARASA has managed through the partnership forum to raise awareness of issues that are more regional'.[79] This has strengthened the ARASA regional partnership.

Construction of regional target groups

As in the case of the trade sector, for many RCSOs involved in HIV/AIDS work regional issue-framing is strongly linked to the SADC. The SADC is an important international target for CSOs in the HIV/AIDS field, such as SAfAIDS, which actively supports the SADC agenda.[80] Furthermore, SAT clearly states that the geographical location of its programmes is the 'SADC region', and the SADC is framed as an important regional actor in terms of overall regional coordination of the HIV/AIDS sector and setting necessary priorities (SAT 2008: 4, 22). Therefore, as already indicated, one important driving force behind SAT's regional work is contributing to the SADC's Business Plan for HIV/AIDS. Similarly, a lot of NAPSAR's regional work centres on the SADC, which is deemed an important actor for the harmonization of human rights laws and policies in the region and for pushing member states to improve AIDS services for PLWHA. Therefore, NAPSAR is currently pushing the SADC to adopt a Regional Treatment Protocol (NAPSAR 2011: 19). According to the director of NAPSAR, the actual establishment of the network also depended a lot on the SADC's formal recognition.[81] In the same vein, according to ARASA the SADC is perceived as an important regional actor in ensuring that human rights remain a central concern of the national response to HIV/AIDS by member states. Since legal and policy frameworks for protecting the rights of PLWHA against unfair discrimination are partly in place, one focus for ARASA and its partners is to monitor the SADC and member states to increase implementation, which to a large extent lags behind. ARASA tries to expose those member states that fail to materialize the adopted laws and policies (ARASA 2009: 97).

In terms of regional campaigns such as the Gender Protocol Campaign, the centre of gravity is often the SADC. The Protocol Campaign is a good example of a successful SADC advocacy campaign based on evidence-based knowledge and which used shaming as an important instrument to achieve its objectives, as discussed in the theoretical chapter. In recognition for the campaign, the African Union bestowed an award on GL, SAfAIDS and partners for being outstanding CSOs promoting the rights of African women (Gender Links 2014). Gender Links and SAfAIDS were instrumental in building up knowledge in various areas within the Protocol Campaign, a key factor behind pushing the SADC member states to sign the Gender Protocol. The Alliance managed to create a knowledge bank of gender and HIV/AIDS issues in the region, built on members' experiences of working with those issues in different countries, as well as processing and compiling this information for the SADC and the media. This included technical expertise in various areas, such as statistics on the situation of women in the region and knowledge about various regional policy frameworks, policies and programmes on gender equality and human rights in Southern Africa and globally. Furthermore, the advocacy pursued by the Alliance was evidence based in the sense that the policy claims were rooted in the voices and perspectives of grassroots women in the region, obtained by various studies conducted by members of the Alliance (Gender Links 2009). For example, the Regional Audit of Sexual and Reproductive Rights carried out by SAfAIDS measured the performance of SADC countries against the poor commitment to various international policy frameworks such as the African Charter on Human Rights, for example in terms of the linkage between HIV/AIDS and gender inequalities (SAfAIDS 2006: 10–11).

Most importantly, one essential factor behind the Alliance's ability to convince the SADC leaders of the importance of a regional Gender Protocol was also the use of this knowledge in a strategic way, shaming the SADC for not practicing what it preaches. For example, the Alliance showed the difference between member states' existing gender policies and their bad record of working towards gender equality in reality: 'It was known that most governments in the region paid lip service to women's issues while the practices were different' (Gender Links 2009: 42). The Protocol was seen as an important regional legal instrument to push governments to deliver according to their promises in terms of advancing gender equality. According to the Gender Links representative, 'we say [. . .] this is something our governments are committed to do, as civil society we take on to hold that government accountable [. . . .] Civil society organizations exist to be watch dogs'.[82] In the advocacy campaign, the Alliance therefore invoked various initiatives that the SADC had previously taken towards the realization of the protocol but which had so far failed to materialize. For example, a COM meeting in 1997 urged the SADC to establish a policy framework for mainstreaming gender in all its activities, the SADC Treaty called for a protocol on Gender and Development in 1992 and RISDP identified gender as one of the most important crosscutting issues. Therefore, 'the Alliance's knowledge [. . .] provided the moral and political tools needed to push through a half-open door' (Gender Links 2009: 34). The Alliance also tries to push the SADC members to implement the Gender Protocol through GL's Gender Barometer project (Gender Links 2015).

One difference between SAPSN's contentious advocacy style, discussed in the last chapter, and the Alliance's more pragmatic approach is the different use of language. Instead of mocking SADC leaders for not delivering on gender issues, in line with the SAPSN style, the Alliance learned how to talk to senior policymakers in COM and other SADC decision-making bodies during the drafting process in ways that made them listen and take many of the policy demands on board. For example, the Alliance was careful not to use language that was too prescriptive and managed to frame gender and HIV/AIDS issues in a way that was accepted by government representatives. This of course required compromises, since demanding a comprehensive, detailed document on all gender equality and women's rights would scare off government officials. However, the inclusion of a number of clear targets in the Protocol was a huge gain for the members of the Alliance, who then had a platform for measuring governments' performance.

Regional issue-framing linked to regional advocacy campaigns is a powerful tool for regional consolidation. The Protocol Campaign is a good example of this, successfully using the shaming strategy to influence a regional target, which spurred regional CSO coalition-building and raised the regional profile of CSOs such as SAfAIDS and Gender Links, among others. The campaign had a positive effect on CSOs' influence on the SADC, which in turn further strengthened the Alliance members. According to one commentator, belonging to the same campaign (such as the Protocol Campaign) generally creates and at the same time builds on a sense of regional belonging among CSOs,[83] which leads to the question of identity-making, discussed in the next section.

CSOs and identity-making

Identity-making is generally a weak dimension of civil society regionalization in the HIV/AIDS sector. Not representing a particular constituency, CSOs such as SAT, SAfAIDS, ACA and, to a certain extent, ARASA display a weak sense of a regional 'we'. Shared values, principles, past experiences or sharing a common social trait can create a deeper sense of regional belonging, but more often this is not the case. This also applies to the afore-mentioned HIV/AIDS organizations.

SAT is very clear about not being membership based,[84] and its work is not geared towards a common social constituency. Instead, it views its local partners in the region more as clients, supporting their capacity to deal with the pandemic. Even though SAT's work is underpinned by some universal values, such as the protection and promotion of human rights, gender equality and public health principles, the overriding belief is that communities 'are best placed to define their own needs' in a spirit of diversity and respect for ethnic, religious, political and other types of social differences between communities (SAT 2008: 12–13). Hence, unlike ARASA and NAPSAR, SAT does not actively foster regional consolidation of local communities, laying the foundation for a regional identity within the organization. Not being membership based nor guided by universal values such as participation, human rights and transparency, which play against regionalization of identity, also applies to SAfAIDS (SAfAIDS 2006: 2). Contrary to the above CSOs, ACA is a membership organization, but the member institutions are highly diverse, with no common denominators other than delivering AIDS capacity-building services. The members are everything from medical foundations, management institutes, local government institutions and university departments to religious organizations and NGOs. Studying the latest ACA Strategic Plan and Annual Report it is also not clear what the underlying values or principles are, other than sweeping comments about RBA and gender equality (ACA 2009, 2011a). All in all, studying the CSOs, there are no signs of fostering a regional sense of identity and belonging among partners and members.

On the other hand, NAPSAR has a clear constituency, that is HIV-positive people. Through their organizations, regardless of ethnic, religious, class and national differences, the people involved in NAPSAR share the same experience of living with HIV/AIDS. This common social trait transcends national borders and creates a regional sense of community. In fact, according to the director of NAPSAR, the HIV/AIDS identity is what ultimately builds up the organizational character and is also the greatest strength of the network. For the members, this identity is the reason they are actually part of the network:[85]

> We as people living with HIV/AIDS are different compared with organizations that are representing people living with HIV/AIDS [such as SAT, SAfAIDS and ACA...] NAPSAR's identity, NAPSAR's uniqueness and NAPSAR's competitive advantage [...] is that HIV/AIDS is about ourselves, about our lives.[86]

In fact, PLWHA make up the bulk of NAPSAR's organizational structure, from local and provincial members of the country organizations to the regional board. The latter is made up of the chairpersons of the member organizations, who are all HIV positive. The common HIV-positive identity lays the foundation for a strong sense of regional solidarity between member organizations, which results in an urge to support each other's national struggles in a common effort to improve the protection of human rights of people infected and affected by HIV/AIDS in the region. Regional meetings are important for the regional community-building within NAPSAR. Interacting with each other during these regional meetings and reaching consensus on which specific issues to focus on, the members of NAPSAR reproduce and strengthen a common identity of being HIV positive,[87] which further consolidates the NAPSAR network.

Even if not as strong as in the case of NAPSAR, regional solidarity also plays a certain role in the regional consolidation of ARASA. The ARASA partners do not have a similar distinct common identity of being HIV positive, even if some are, but do share similar experiences of fighting injustices related to discrimination against people affected by HIV/AIDS. Being largely value driven, the partners share a common cause of improving the human rights for PLWHA through the region, which creates a sense of 'we', even if it is not as pronounced as for NAPSAR. According to the director of ARASA,

> [i]ncreasingly there is a feeling among ARASA partners that they are part of this big family. If one is wronged, then others will stand up [...] It did not used to be as cohesive as it is now [...] ARASA is today an increasing critical mass of indigenous NGOs who are standing up for issues in the region.[88]

One important manifestation of and instrument for regional community-building within ARASA is its Declaration of Principles, in which the partners formally commit themselves to certain values and principles. For ARASA, '[t]he basis of the partnership is solidarity and shared responsibility in the struggle to advance social justice in the region [. . .] supporting each other in addressing human rights violations in our respective countries' (ARASA n.d.: 1). The declaration is in itself an important vehicle for fostering a sense of togetherness within ARASA and is in fact unique for CSOs in this study. Hence, it is clear that the construction of feelings of togetherness, for example through the declaration and discussions at the forum, play an important role in regional consolidation of ARASA. This can be contrasted with SAT, which rather than strengthening ties between local partners, for example through building consensus on key challenges and facilitating a formal adherence to common values, seems to cultivate a spirit of social, ethnic and religious difference between and uniqueness of communities.

Notes

1. SADC PF is a forum for regional political party co-operation in Southern Africa, based in Windhoek, but it does not officially belong to the SADC. It aims to strengthen the SADC's implementation capacity by involving parliamentarians, their parties and also NGOs in SADC activities and to promote the principles of human rights and democracy. Among its activities, SADC PF makes recommendations to the SADC on how to improve its operations, gives policy advice and scrutinizes the SADC budget (Oosthuizen 2006).
2. Clayton, interview, 16 February 2012.
3. Clayton, interview, 16 February 2012.
4. Clayton, interview, 16 February 2012.
5. Clayton, interview, 16 February 2012.
6. Clayton, interview, 16 February 2012.
7. Msosa, interview, April 2012; Clayton, interview, 16 February 2012.
8. Mxotshwa, interview, 27 March 2012; Msosa, interview, 23 April 2012.
9. Page, interview, 24 November 2009; Mxotshwa, interview, 27 March 2012.
10. Sandström, interview, 27 November 2009.
11. Anamela, interview, 26 November 2009; van Tol, interview, 30 November 2009.
12. Sandström, interview, 27 November 2009.
13. van Tol, interview, 30 November 2009; Yates, interview, 14 December 2009; Page, interview, 24 November 2009; Sandström, interview, 27 November 2009.
14. Sanje, interview, 11 December 2009.
15. Page, interview, 24 November 2009.
16. Clayton, interview, 16 February 2012.
17. Mxotshwa, interview, 27 March 2012.
18. Sanje, interview, 11 December 2009.
19. Sanje, interview, 11 December 2009.
20. Yates, interview, 14 December 2009.
21. Sandström, interview, 27 November 2009.
22. Page, interview, 24 November; Sandström, interview, 27 November 2009.
23. Page, interview, 24 November; Sandström, interview, 27 November 2009.
24. Sandström, interview, 27 November 2009.
25. Mxotshwa, interview, 27 March 2012.
26. Clayton, interview, 16 February 2012.
27. Clayton, interview, 16 February 2012.
28. Page, interview, 24 November 2009.
29. Page, interview, 24 November 2009.

30 Ncube, interview, 8 December 2008.
31 Page, interview, 24 November 2009.
32 Sanje, interview, 11 December 2009.
33 Sanje, interview, 11 December 2009.
34 Clayton, interview, 16 February 2012.
35 Clayton, interview, 16 February 2012.
36 Mxotshwa, interview, 27 March 2012.
37 Clayton, interview, 16 February 2012.
38 Gender Links 2009; Clayton, interview, 16 February 2012.
39 Clayton, interview, 16 February 2012.
40 Msosa, interview, 23 April 2012; Clayton, interview, 16 February 2012.
41 Msosa, interview, 23 April 2012.
42 van Tol, interview, 30 November 2009.
43 van Tol, interview, 30 November 2009.
44 van Tol, interview, 30 November 2009.
45 Sandström and Thiis, interview, 7 March 2005.
46 Schoeman, interview, 19 November 2009.
47 Clayton, interview, 16 February 2012.
48 Page, interview, 24 November 2009.
49 Kujinga, interview, 1 December 2009.
50 Msosa, interview, 23 April 2012.
51 Msosa, interview, 23 April 2012.
52 Msosa, interview, 23 April 2012.
53 van Tol, interview, 30 November 2009.
54 Msosa, interview, 23 April 2012.
55 van Tol, interview, 30 November 2009.
56 Msosa, interview, 23 April 2012; Clayton, interview, 16 February 2012.
57 van Tol-RNE, interview, 30 November 2009.
58 Clayton, interview, 16 February 2012.
59 Msosa, interview, 23 April 2012.
60 van Tol, interview, 30 November 2009.
61 Clayton, e-mail communication, 3 August 2012.
62 Anamela, interview, 26 November 2009.
63 Sandström, interview, 27 November 2009.
64 Barnard, interview, 26 November 2008.
65 Sandström, interview, 27 November 2009.
66 Clayton, interview, 16 February 2012.
67 Sandström, interview, 27 November 200;, Clayton, interview, 16 February 2012; Mxotshwa, interview, 27 March 2012; Page, interview, 24 November 2009.
68 Page, interview, 24 November 2009.
69 Page, interview, 24 November 2009.
70 Mxotshwa, interview, 27 March 2012.
71 Clayton, interview, 16 February 2012.
72 Clayton, interview, 16 February 2012.
73 Sandström, interview, 27 November 2009.
74 Sandström, interview, 27 November 2009.
75 Sandström, interview, 27 November 2009.
76 Page, interview, 24 November 2009.
77 Clayton, interview, 16 February 2012.
78 Clayton, interview, 16 February 2012.
79 Clayton, interview, 16 February 2012.
80 Page, interview, 24 November 2009.
81 Mxotshwa, interview, 27 March 2012.

82 Tolmay, interview, 27 November 2009.
83 Kujinga, interview, 1 December 2012.
84 Sandström, interview, 27 November 2009.
85 Mxotshwa, interview, 27 March 2012.
86 Mxotshwa, interview, 27 March 2012.
87 Mxotshwa, interview, 27 March 2012.
88 Clayton, interview, 16 February 2012.

Chapter 6
Conclusion

The concluding chapter will start by comparing the dynamics of civil society regionalization in the trade and HIV/AIDS cases and make some more general conclusions, which will make up the bulk of the chapter. Some words about how 'regional' the CSOs involved in this study are will also be said. It will be argued that in terms of the sample of CSOs in this study and the specific five ways in which CSOs can be considered 'regional', civil society regionalization is quite a strong process. However, there are still many problems related to 'going regional', that is lack of policy influence, a weak sense of regional identity, weak legitimacy, donor dependency and intra-civil society fragmentation, which is discussed in the third section. Last, some remaining research problems related to civil society regionalization will be considered.

Dynamics of civil society regionalization

Relations between RIGOs and CSOs

One major conclusion of this book is that CSOs, across and beyond the trade and HIV/AIDS sectors, generally struggle to participate in formal, SADC-led regionalism, due to the deeply rooted statism in Southern Africa. States want to be in sole control of regional integration, regardless of lofty statements in various declarations about the importance of civil society in this process, and as a consequence the SADC and its various institutions are rather closed to the involvement of CSOs. Olivet and Brennan reach a similar conclusion when comparing the involvement of civil society in regional processes in Latin America, Southeast Asia and Southern Africa. They argue that civil society has generally met with institutional barriers and has largely been marginalized in MERCOSUR, ASEAN and SADC respectively (Olivet and Brennan 2010). However, contrary to the conclusions of much previous research on civil society regionalization in Southern Africa (e.g. Matlosa and Lotshwao 2010; Peters-Berries 2010; Pressend 2010; Landsberg 2012), all CSOs are not equally marginalized in the SADC, and civil society cannot be generalized as playing an insignificant role on the regional level. SADC–CSO relations in Southern Africa are much more complex than that and some CSOs, from both cases, are indeed increasingly involved in regional governance, which will be shown later in this section. Igarashi (2011) notes the same positive trend in

Southeast Asia, where the prominence of (some) transnational CSOs in relation to ASEAN has been growing. Similarly, despite state domination in Caribbean regionalism, CARICOM member states are slowly realizing that solutions to regional social and economic challenges require collaboration with a range of CSOs (Anyanwu 2014). In the case of HIV/AIDS, CSOs are generally more included in the SADC, since this area is not seen as important compared to trade, and less is at stake for the member states in terms of policy-making. The SADC can therefore afford to open more doors to civil society inclusion in policy-making. Additionally, as already indicated, in providing AIDS services to vulnerable social groups at the margins of the market-oriented regional order, CSOs are needed to make the regional neo-liberal project work. In the trade sector, on the other hand, member states carefully guard their (national) interests and are more reluctant to include CSOs, especially the more critical ones, in line with the entrenched statism in the region. Nevertheless, some CSOs are indeed involved in trade-related regional governance.

Another important conclusion is that where CSOs have, in one way or another, managed to engage the SADC, that organization has greatly shaped civil society regionalization. In these cases, a lot of regional CSO activities revolve around the SADC, sometimes in tandem with and in other cases in reaction against the SADC agenda. First, the SADC sets and dominates the regional trade and HIV agendas, which in turn sets the stage for which CSOs are included and excluded in SADC-led regional governance. In the present neo-liberal, market-oriented regional order, trade is considered the most important aspect of regional integration, at the expense of social issue-areas such as HIV/AIDS, which receive less attention. Therefore the regional FTA is considered the flagship of the SADC. A lot is at stake for SADC members in terms of implementation of the trade integration scheme, seeking to control policy-making in the field, which makes them highly dominant in the interaction with civil society. The SADC emphasizes certain types of trade issues in line with neo-liberal regional governance (i.e. trade liberalization, facilitation of the movement of goods, private-sector support and the EPA) at the expense of others (i.e. ICBT, labour rights and the movement of workers).

HIV/AIDS is generally not given as much attention as trade in policy-making and project implementation in the SADC, which is evident from the heavy financial emphasis put on the latter. Additionally, when HIV/AIDS is targeted in regional governance, this is strongly geared towards problem-solving activities in terms of service delivery related to care, prevention, mitigation and capacity-building. The link among trade integration, development and HIV/AIDS is made explicit in many SADC policy documents in terms of the latter being an obstacle for regional trade and development and the operation of a regional market. In line with the neo-liberal trend of outsourcing provision of social services to private actors, a lot of responsibility for delivery of AIDS services is put on CSOs, on a national and regional level, in place of the member states. This implies that, despite (rhetorical) statements in various policy documents, the human rights component of the SADC HIV/AIDS agenda, in terms of safeguarding the right to AIDS services and the political rights of people infected and affected by HIV, especially vulnerable groups such as sexual minorities, is weakly implemented. Efforts to harmonize laws in relation to AIDS and human rights and to push member states to provide AIDS-related services shine by their absence, partly because such political interventions go against the free-market logic.

The SADC has great influence on civil society regionalization by setting the overall regional agenda within which CSOs perform regional governance functions, for example in terms of providing research and capacity building, monitoring implementation, assisting in policy development and provoking critical advocacy for policy reform. The same applies to donors, who push CSOs in certain directions, as discussed in what follows. This not only affects the type of work CSOs do but also, indirectly, determines which CSOs can be eligible as partners to the SADC and which are marginalized. CSOs such as regional business, research and HIV/AIDS NGOs working within the parameters of the current neo-liberal regional order, possessing knowledge and expertise that the SADC is missing and providing services and policy advice, are involved in various regional institutions. In fact, these CSOs are needed for the SADC to implement the various regional governance schemes. On the other hand, other CSOs are excluded from SADC when they contest the current neo-liberal regional integration: for example by demanding that ICBT should be incorporated in the SADC agenda and by pushing for regional harmonization of human rights laws connected to HIV/AIDS. This resembles the processes in which CSOs engage with regional environmental governance in East Africa, where the EAC and its various regional institutions have shown collaboration interest only in those sections within civil society that are compliant with and uncritical of their business and deliver various services related to, for example, resources management (Godsäter 2013).

The inclusion/exclusion dynamics is particularly evident in the trade arena, for example in relation to trade negotiations within the SADC, including EPA. Due to the prevalent statism in the region, such negotiations tend to be constructed in such a way that CSOs are excluded and therefore have a hard time gaining influence. The same trend can be discerned in Latin America, where CSO access to and influence on trade-based negotiations related to the FTAA and MERCOSUR are extremely limited (Grugel 2006). Such exclusion can also spur a radicalization of civil society engaged with trade issues in Southern Africa, with the critical trade agenda of EJN and SAPSN a good example of this. Yet, in line with these facts, CSOs such as SPSF, SEATINI and Trades Center that provide the SADC and COMESA with technical expertise and policy advice, albeit within the prevalent neo-liberal trade agenda, are engaged in policy discussions and even included in formal trade negotiations. This is reminiscent of CSO involvement in ASEAN in Southeast Asia, where those actors driving a market-oriented agenda are favoured at the expense of more critical voices trying to advance alternative regionalism (Igarashi 2011).

Through its inclusion and exclusion of different CSOs in regional governance, the SADC plays a big role in fostering – or hindering – civil society regionalization.

By creating space for participation in trade and HIV/AIDS-related regional governance and by giving CSOs an active role in the implementation of the SADC agenda through participation in various technical committees, partnership forums, and trade negotiations, the SADC spurs and strengthens the regional operation of included CSOs. In fact, many CSOs such as SADC-CNGO, SATUCC, NAPSAR and SAT are so tied to the SADC agenda that interaction with the Secretariat in particular, but also other regional institutions, is an important reason for their existence. However, at the same time, especially in the trade sector, many of those CSOs that work hard to be included in regional policy-making struggle in vain and are somehow excluded due to their more critical agenda. Being rather dependent on acceptance by the SADC, exclusion negatively affects their regional status, which works against regionalization. However for a few CSOs, such as SAPSN, exclusion can in fact make them stronger. In fact, as will be discussed, SAPSN partly thrives on its outside identity. Exclusion from the SADC can spur the regionalization of civil society for those CSOs with a critical and anti-SADC agenda in the sense that they consolidate regionally around a common enemy.

Last, civil society regionalization in Southern Africa is also more directly influenced by the SADC in that the RIGO facilitates regional networking and coalition-building, creating concrete platforms for state–civil society interaction. The best examples are the HIV/AIDS PF and the RPO framework. Donors also play an important role in this process, financially supporting regional forums as well as pushing the SADC to create space for interaction with civil society. On a more indirect level, as with the rise of regional summitry in East Asia, with several regional networks emerging as a result of response to international summits (Gilson 2011a), the SADC has spurred regional coalition-building in terms of acting as a focal point around which CSOs consolidate regionally. The Civil Society Forum and People's Summit are a case in point, as well as the campaign for a regional Gender Protocol. In this way the SADC plays a major role for civil society regionalization.

Relations between donors and CSOs

Without donor funds, there would probably be scant regionalization of civil society. This is one of the most important conclusions that emerges from comparing the trade and HIV/AIDS cases. The availability of donor funds for regional activities is a major force behind CSOs 'going regional'. CSOs are generally greatly dependent on donor funds for regionalization, lacking other means of resource mobilization. It should be noted, though, that some regional research NGOs, such as Trades Centre and SEATINI, have managed to generate some alternative income based on consultancy work, which has eased the level of dependency somewhat. In fact, donor dependency has created many challenges for CSOs active on the regional level.

First of all, donor dependency has put CSOs in a very vulnerable financial situation, especially in the HIV/AIDS sector, where many of the donors (mostly bilateral) tend to regularly change their funding preferences. At the moment they question the value added of the regional level and might withdraw from supporting regional work. But in the trade sector also, regional networks such as SADC-CNGO, ASCCI, SATUCC and SAPSN have suffered from inactivity due to periods of shallow donor interest. This partly has to do with the fact that donors, especially the bilateral ones, influenced by the statist social structure, tend to prioritize support to RIGOs such as the SADC and its work in the trade arena, at the cost of financing CSOs. Few regional activities would take place without regional donor funds and, coupled with the donor influence on CSOs' regional agendas discussed in what follows, civil society regionalization is not only donor dependent but also donor driven. Latin American CSOs working on the regional level face similar challenges. Being heavily dependent on a limited number of financial sources, funding difficulties constrain their capacity to participate consistently in regional policy-shaping processes (Korzeniewicz and Smith 2005). One scholar concludes that 'the momentum for transnational campaigning is difficult to sustain over time, with the result that activism ebbs and flows, picking up in moments when opportunities open up and scaling back at other times' (Grugel 2006: 214). Furthermore, the vulnerability inherent in regional work is related to the strong nationalist undercurrent in civil society regionalization. Regional issue-framing and to a lesser extent regional identity are indeed important forces for civil society regionalization, but on the whole regional consciousness is still in a rather embryonic form and would not in itself be enough of an incentive for CSOs to regionalize. This will be discussed further in the third section.

Second, marked by the capitalist world order, donor–CSO relations tend to foster rent-seeking and profit-making tendencies within civil society, also on a regional level. This has also been observed in East Asia, where the realm of transnational civil society is penetrated by the dominant neo-liberal discourse (Igarashi 2011: 24). In fact, donor money can corrupt CSOs in both the trade and HIV/AIDS sectors in the sense that regional activities are somehow motivated by an urge to fulfil (sometimes personal) material needs and not by the desire to benefit needy people. One tragic example is SANASO, which developed into a regional briefcase NGO when it became a private project for the director to enrich herself, resulting in the eventual termination of the organization due to mismanagement of donor funds. However, this should not be seen as an isolated example but rather as an important negative aspect of donor dependency. Due to the capitalist social structure, donor funding fosters a market orientation within civil society which encourages CSOs such as SANASO, which are increasingly driven by a quest to make money. There could well be more SANASOs out there on the regional level. In the end, donor dependency creates a very vulnerable civil society regionalization which can easily lose pace if donor funds are suddenly withdrawn or if the CSOs implode due to economic greed.

Third, donors have great influence over the regional agendas of CSOs, which in the end affects the ways that CSOs regionalize. Hence, influenced by the overarching capitalist world order, donors indirectly use their CSO partners in Southern Africa to either reproduce or contest the prevailing order. The study shows how most donors, mainly bilateral, foster a problem-solving way of thinking within regional civil society, especially in the HIV/AIDS sector, where CSOs are supported to deliver services to mitigate the negative effects of the neo-liberal project for poor people. Those few CSOs in the HIV/AIDS case which pursue a human rights agenda, such as ARASA and NAPSAR, mainly attract private donors. In these two cases, as for many of the CSOs in the trade sector, donors such as OSISA, NCA and Diakonia view their recipients as partners in a common quest for structural transformation of the neo-liberal world order. All this ultimately affects what issues are dealt with and what types of strategies are used by CSOs in their regional work. The point here is that donors play an important role not only in terms of financial facilitation but also by shaping the nature of civil society regionalization, which, together with the inclusion of certain CSOs and the exclusion of others in SADC-led regional governance, creates a quite heterogeneous regional civil society (especially in the trade sector).

Relations between CSOs

The statist-capitalist regional order ultimately creates a heterogeneous civil society regionalization, even though this is more pronounced in the trade than the HIV/AIDS sector. In fact, one major contribution of this book is to show that the regionalization of civil society in Southern Africa is a highly diverse process, contrary to what other studies have noted (e.g. Saguier 2007; Olivet and Brennan 2010; Igarashi 2011). As noted in Chapter 1, one important exception is Iheduru, who notes the 'multiscalarity' of regional civil society engagement in West Africa (2014: 155) in terms of CSOs gravitating from one role to the other depending on the issues, circumstances and available resources. This view is in line with the overall critical understanding of civil society in Africa as complex and even contradictory. Hence, in the same vein, RCSOs in this study interpret and relate differently to the overall statist-capitalist world order, are funded by different donors supporting different agendas and engage the SADC in dissimilar ways. One way of portraying the heterogeneity of regional civil society is to categorize the CSOs involved in this study[1] based on the types of strategies used, the issue focus and the relationship to regional governance institutions. Four categories of CSO – commercial CSOs, partner CSOs, critical reformist CSOs and resistance CSOs – are discussed in what follows and summarized in Table 6.1.[2]

Commercial CSOs are only found in the trade sector. They support the SADC's neo-liberal trade agenda, which implies that their focus lies on trade liberalization, facilitation of regional trade and the movement of goods, as well as private-sector development in the region. Many regional activities centre on the SADC, such as providing research on the named issues, lobbying for a better business climate in the region and arranging regional conferences for business and policy-makers in the trade arena. The SADC is recognized for its emphasis on business and trade and is perceived as a partner in advancing regional trade integration. Therefore, in most cases commercial CSOs are included in SADC-led regional trade governance. In fact, the SADC considers commercial CSOs to be key partners in advancing regional trade integration. Examples of this category are SPSF and ASCCI.

Table 6.1 Categorization of 16 regional CSOs in the trade and HIV/AIDS sectors in Southern Africa

	Regional activities	Issue focus	Inclusion/ exclusion in the SADC	Examples
Commercial CSOs	Lobbying, policy advice, research	Trade facilitation and liberalization, private-sector development	Inclusion	SPSF, ASCCI
Partner CSOs	Research, policy advice, monitoring, lobbying, information dissemination,	RPO, regional trade integration, HIV-info dissemination, HIV capacity	Inclusion/partly exclusion	Trades Centre, SARDC, SEATINI, SAT, ACA, SAfAIDS, SADC-CNGO
Critical reformist CSOs	Advocacy, research	ICBT, AIDS-rights, ANSA	Partly inclusion/ exclusion	ARASA, NAPSAR, EJN, SATUCC, CBTA/ SACBTA
Resistance CSOs	Advocacy, popular mobilization	Trade justice, people-driven regionalism	Exclusion	SAPSN

Partner CSOs share the neo-liberal and market-oriented world-view of commercial CSOs and the SADC but want to strengthen the development, social, HIV/AIDS and poverty-alleviation dimensions of the SADC regional agenda. This approach implies supporting those social groups that are marginalized and negatively affected by the neo-liberal project. Besides focusing on regional trade facilitation and EPA, therefore, important regional issues are the RPO, HIV capacity-building and the dissemination of HIV-related information. For partner CSOs, regional policy frameworks related to trade liberalization, poverty alleviation and HIV/AIDS are in place, but the SADC and member states need to be monitored in order to accelerate implementation. Partner CSOs provide various services, technical expertise and policy assistance to regional policy-makers in the SADC and also COMESA, related to these issues, as well as supporting local and national state, business and civil society actors in various ways. Partner CSOs are included in SADC-led regional governance or at least strive to be, since the SADC is considered an important partner in a common quest for regional development. Examples of partner CSOs are SADC-CNGO, SAfAIDS, SAT, ACA, Trades Centre, SEATINI and SARDC.

Critical reformist CSOs also emphasize the development, social and poverty dimensions of regional integration but are more critical towards the current neo-liberal trend in the region and therefore focus on different sets of issues compared with the partner CSOs. In essence, these CSOs have a more rights-based approach, dealing with ICBT, labour and AIDS rights and propose alternative regional policy frameworks. Contrary to commercial and partner CSOs, critical reformist CSOs are not, as the name indicates, content with current regional governance and want fundamental reform of the present policy frameworks related to trade and HIV/AIDS. This includes giving voice to marginalized social groups in society, such as informal traders and HIV-positive people. The critical reformist CSOs believe in engagement with regional policymakers, and the SADC is considered important for regional integration, but these associations consider regional policy frameworks to be in great need of reform. These groups engage with SADC in a more critical way and advocate for policy reform to benefit various marginalized groups. Critical reformist CSOs are largely excluded from formal regional governance structures due to their critical agendas. Examples of this category are ARASA, NAPSAR, EJN, SATUCC and CBTA/SACBTA.

Resistance CSOs emphasize structural transformation of the current neo-liberal regional order and strongly oppose SADC-led regional governance. These groups put forward still stronger and more radical demands for trade justice, people-driven regional integration and EPA resistance. They also tend to use more contentious methods such as demonstrations and civil disobedience. In essence, this category of CSO believes that service provision merely reproduces a highly unjust society and the prevailing capitalist order. Instead, the patterns of unsustainable development must be identified and transformed, and this can only be done through popular mobilization. Interaction with state actors is therefore contentious. The SADC is considered to be a regional enemy, causing regional disintegration and poverty due to its neo-liberal agenda, and should therefore be resisted. However, since many regional activities centre around the SADC, resistance CSOs still 'engage' the SADC, if only indirectly. Due to their critical agendas and contentious methods, they are highly excluded from the SADC. The only example of a resistance CSO covered in this research is SAPSN.

The civil society regionalization process shows somewhat different patterns in the two cases, and the heterogeneity is not equally pronounced in both of them. For example, ideological rivalry is clearer in the trade than the HIV/AIDS sector. The trade sector is marked by ideological tensions among CSOs, manifested in diverging ideas about EPA, in different emphasis put on trade issues and in dissimilar perceptions of regional integration, as well as different choices of work strategies, that is social mobilization and advocacy from the 'outside', or service provision, policy assistance and lobbying from the 'inside'. The existence of two mutually exclusive civil society platforms for SADC engagement – namely the People's Summit, driven by SAPSN and social movements, and which resists the SADC agenda; and the Civil Society Forum, driven by SADC-CNGO and NGO partners, which wants to engage and support it – is an important illustration. In the HIV/AIDS sector, these ideological differences are less pronounced, which stems from the fact that most CSOs support the SADC agenda, including CSOs that are to some extent also more critical and human rights oriented, such as NAPSAR and ARASA, and want to be included in policy discussions at the SADC Secretariat and contribute towards the implementation of SADC-led HIV/AIDS programs through delivering various services. Moreover, the HIV/AIDS sector is generally dominated by bilateral donors, which are on the whole inclined towards problem-solving agendas, in contrast to the trade sector where private donors are in a majority, pursuing a more critical agenda. Hence, most CSOs in the HIV/AIDS sector are engaged in measurable and less politically sensitive service-delivery activities such as HIV capacity-building, information dissemination, community support and distribution of AIDS drugs. However, resource-based competition seems to be strong in both cases. Geared towards a market orientation and enticed by donor money, CSOs have become competitors in the donor market. This also creates quarrels about who should be entitled to 'lead' in specific issue areas. All in all, the ideological and resource-based tensions in the trade sector, and to a lesser extent in the HIV/AIDS sector, can possibly hamper overall regionalization in terms of making it difficult for broader regional civil society co-operation to occur across ideological divides.

A similar feature of regional intra-civil society relations in the trade and HIV/AIDS sectors is the general domination of South African CSOs over those from other countries, which tends to fragment civil society regionalization. This tendency is in line with the overall capitalist power dynamics in the region, in which South Africa and its businesses dominate regional processes. Half of the 16 CSOs investigated in this study have, in different ways, a heavy South African influence. Six CSOs, that is SPSF, SAT, SAfAIDS, ARASA, NAPSAR and EJN, are based in South Africa. SATUCC is in practice led by COSATU from South Africa, notwithstanding that the regional secretariat is in Gaborone.[3] SAPSN was founded in South Africa and was coordinated by AIDC for the first five years (SAPSN n.d.a), which made a big imprint on the further development of the network. South African CSOs are often more resourced, better staffed and more successful in lobbying, service provision and popular mobilization. South African dominance is felt by CSOs from across the region and is often manifested in various regional forums. According to one commentator, 'everything in the region goes through South Africa and the most logical city to have a meeting is Johannesburg'.[4] For non-South African CSOs, often lacking sufficient resources, it is expensive to travel outside the country in order to attend regional meetings, which are mostly in South Africa. According to the Mozambican Debt Group (MDG), an SAPSN member, 'in some meetings there can be 50 people from South Africa and one from Mozambique and one from Angola'.[5] Additionally, being in such a great minority, one negative result of this is the fact that many of the Portuguese-speaking participants from Mozambique and Angola have a hard time communicating their ideas, according to another CSO from Mozambique, CCM.[6]

Furthermore, since the 'node of resistance is South Africa',[7] the South African domination and marginalization of CSOs from other countries in the region is particularly strong in the critical section of regional civil society. The great majority of the critical reformist and resistance CSOs in this study from both sectors are from South Africa. In regional forums such as the SASF and the People's Summit,

South African CSOs often take the lead and tend to dominate participants from other countries.[8] As indicated in Chapter 3, the strong and rather autonomous civil society in South Africa has allowed the cultivation of an arena for more radical groups. This spills over to the regional level and, hence, South African CSOs are often the most vocal and militant ones at regional forums.[9] Compared with the more critical stance of South African CSOs, the general approach towards government actors including the SADC in, for example, Mozambique is more diplomatic and pragmatic.[10] Due to their dominating and radical attitude, one scholar concludes that 'it is hard to interact with the South African CSOs'.[11] The power dynamics between CSOs from South Africa and other parts of the region tend to further increase regional intra-civil society tensions. According to one commentator, this can hamper the overall fight for social justice and development in the region.[12] In contrast to South African domination, CSOs from Tanzania seem to be bystanders in regional processes, poorly involved in regional work. According to this project's database survey, in the HIV/AIDS and Environment sectors, only 0.6% and 1%, respectively, show some sort of regional engagement. As might be recalled, the corresponding numbers for South Africa are 15% for HIV/AIDS and 25% for Environment. All in all, there are indications that regional civil society activities are geographically asymmetrical.

CSOs and issue-framing

The internal motivations of CSOs to 'go regional' play less of a role for civil society regionalization than forces related to SADC–CSO and donor–CSO relations, especially identity-making. Nevertheless, issue-framing is an important dimension of civil society regionalization and worthy of more discussion. Even though regional issue-framing is partly an autonomous process stemming from within CSOs and facilitating the development of a regional consciousness, this process must also be understood in connection with the overall statist–capitalist regional order. In essence, the ways trade and HIV/AIDS issues are framed regionally are intimately related to SADC–CSO and donor–CSO relations.

All CSOs in the study, across both cases, show a rather strong propensity to frame their issues as 'regional', which greatly affects their potential and willingness to 'go regional'. Most networks, but also NGOs, have fostered an idea of 'Southern Africa' as an unified region among their members and partners, where trade and HIV/AIDS-related issues are seen as common, affecting and concerning people throughout the region in similar ways. Hence, deficient access to AIDS services occurs in most countries in the region; the way HIV is transmitted is specific to Southern Africa compared with other African sub-regions; the situation of poor people, including informal traders, is similar throughout the region; and EPA affects regional integration in Southern Africa. In addition, regional issue-framing is coupled with a widespread view within most RCSOs that their members and partners have a shared responsibility for improving the HIV/AIDS, development and trade situations, which necessitates regional collaboration, spurring regionalization.

Such unified perceptions of trade and HIV/AIDS issues are rather absent among regional networks in the Baltic region, according to one of few studies that analyze the role of ideas and identity-making in civil society regionalization. There, the lack of commonly perceived causes to rally around has made it difficult for network members to create a solid ground for co-operation (Reuter 2007: 257).

That said, CSOs in Southern Africa do not put equal emphasis on the regional level in their perception of trade and HIV/AIDS. Of the studied CSOs, regional NGOs, particularly research NGOs such as SEATINI, Trades and SARDC, make the strongest claims about issue regionalization and most forcefully stress the interlinkage among the local, national and regional arenas. A considerably portion of their research output and information dissemination concerns regional issues, and their policy proposals are often directed towards regional policy-makers such as the SADC and COMESA. On the other hand, even though regional issue-framing does play a big role for many of the regional networks, their regional work is generally not grounded among their members, whose main concerns often lie on the national level. Hence, regional networks such as SADC-CNGO, ACA and SAT-UCC are quite contradictory since the regional secretariats, regional boards and various policy documents emphasize regional commonalities and regional action at the same time as members, to varying degrees, focus on national and local work. In fact, one important mandate of these and other networks is to support the work of national members, whereby these networks occasionally become drawn into national issues and agendas. In the end, this risks taking focus away from the regional arena and diluting the regional aspect of their work. In essence, this has to do with a weak regional identity, discussed in the next section. Most importantly, to a certain extent engaging with 'regional' issues is partly instrumental for these organizations in order to obtain regional donor funds.

Furthermore, as indicated, regional issue-framing among the CSOs in this study is generally linked to the SADC agenda, as well as affected by donor dependency. Hence, this aspect of being motivated to 'go regional' has to be understood in relation to the statist-capitalist regional order. For those CSOs which relate to and even align their regional work with various SADC documents, the SADC plays a big role in their (regional) understanding of trade and HIV/AIDS issues. Additionally, being part of formal neo-liberal regional governance, CSOs such as SADC-CNGO, SPSF and SAT are influenced to view trade and HIV/AIDS issues from a problem-solving standpoint, which has great influence over their inclination to deliver services and assist in policy development. Hence, a regional understanding of trade and HIV/AIDS issues is coupled with an SADC–Induced problem-solving approach, which has been exemplified throughout this chapter.

On the other hand, as mentioned, some CSOs relate differently to the statist-capitalist world order and are more critical of neo-liberal regional governance and hence tend to be marginalized in the SADC institutional framework. These CSOs frame trade and HIV/AIDS issues differently, albeit still in relation to the SADC agenda. Critical reform of and even resistance to the SADC agenda is advocated. For example, viewed as a regional issue concerning informal traders from different countries in similar ways, these associations have pushed for inclusion of the 'informal' aspect of trade integration on the SADC agenda. Similarly, the SADC is pushed to enforce harmonization of AIDS rights policies in the region in order to give people affected and infected by HIV equal treatment wherever they live. Last, these groups blame the SADC for causing regional disintegration and advancing a regional agenda that causes regional trade injustice and social marginalization.

In all of these cases, the SADC is constructed as a regional target for engagement in terms of either collaboration or contestation, which stimulates regional action of various sorts.

CSOs and identity-making

Comparing the trade and HIV/AIDS cases in terms of regional identity-making it can be concluded that this dimension of civil society regionalization is the weakest. For most regional NGOs and networks, in both cases, lacking a clear social constituency and strong values, principles and common experiences of, for example, oppression and poverty, identity-making plays a minor role for regional consolidation. Reuter (2007: 256) makes a similar observation in the Baltic region, claiming that ideas about regional identity, constructed by the region-building discourse, are far from realization among NGO networks. In terms of Southern Africa, the general lack of identity-making is despite the fact that issues are often framed regionally, which shows that identity-making and issue-framing are not necessarily connected, even if there are contact points. Hence, issues can be framed regionally and linked to the SADC agenda without cultivating regional community-building.

Combining evidence from the two cases, it is argued that even if the staff and board members of regional NGOs and networks advance a regional agenda, at the same time they often identify themselves with the national level and do not link up with a broader regional community of, for example, activists, workers, informal traders, Christians or HIV-positive people. Hence, as indicated, for regional NGOs in particular, regional issue-framing and regional work have a dose of instrumentality in the sense of being used as a way of getting an entry point to the SADC or attracting regional donor funds. On the other hand, for CSOs that represent a specific social group, transnational social markers such as working-class identity, as in the case of SATUCC, and being HIV positive, as in the case of NAPSAR, inform the construction of regional identity and a sense of belonging to a common community that transcends national borders. In these cases, regional identity-making is an important force behind 'going regional', forming regional coalitions of people with similar challenges due to their common social background. Regional solidarity campaigns such as the regional trade union support to oppressed workers and other people in Zimbabwe and the mutual support of NGOs working with human rights abuses of sexual minorities are good examples.

Regional meeting places such as the ARASA and NAPSAR annual partnership forums, the SATUCC Congress and the SAPSN People's Summit are particularly important for the construction of regional identities, as well as for regional issue-framing. In these meeting places people with similar social backgrounds and experiences or sharing certain values and principles physically coalesce. At these meetings, regional consolidation is often actively supported by the staff and board members of the arranging organization, which facilitates the construction of common identities, cross-country solidarity and a regional understanding of trade and HIV/AIDS issues. Hence, an 'NAPSAR identity' based on common experiences of being HIV positive and being denied access to AIDS services; a 'workers identity' within SATUCC based on common working-class experiences of social marginalization; a 'Christian' identity within EJN, based on Christian ethics and values; and an 'SAPSN identity' based on feelings of regional solidarity with oppressed people in the region and perceptions of shared experiences of colonialism and neo-colonialism, are essential for holding together and strengthening these networks. In terms of the latter, other scholars have also come to the conclusion that a common commitment to regional solidarity is important for drawing the members of (critical) regional networks, such as SAPSN, together (Olivet and Brennan 2010: 121). The regional network identities are further consolidated through public communication, often in relation to regional conferences, in which organizational banners are presented, press releases are given and common statements are delivered.

A few more words should be said about the regional identity of resisting CSOs such as SAPSN, which should partly also be seen in terms of opposition to the current neo-liberal regionalism. This identity thrives on a social construction of an 'evil other', considered responsible for various forms of oppression and injustice. If this 'other' is a regional target, often the SADC, it spurs advocacy and popular mobilization on the regional level. Hence, the SAPSN identity not only comes from within the network, based on internal mechanisms, but also centres on external actors such as SADC and is a good example of an exclusive identity or 'outside' identity. Ignoring the demands made by SAPSN activists, the SADC further fuels this identity-making process. In this case, strengthening the SAPSN identity in terms of being an outsider, the marginalization of SAPSN in SADC-led regional governance strengthens the regional status of the network. Moreover, the existence of two parallel civil society forums around the SADC adds to this process, since activists at the People's Summit often construct their colleagues in the Civil Society Forum as 'others' who are being co-opted by the SADC.

How 'regional' is civil society in Southern Africa?

As indicated throughout this book, academic researchers often consider civil society on the regional level in Southern Africa to be weak and even insignificant.[13] Such statements are highly problematic, since civil society regionalization is a very complex and even paradoxical process in which, as we have seen, a number of CSOs in Southern Africa do engage regionally in a variety of ways and are quite successful in what they are doing. In essence, as will be shown, civil society on the regional level cannot be ruled out as either weak or insignificant, even though it is true that CSOs are confronted with many challenges in their regional work. However, while being heavily influenced by external actors such as the SADC and foreign donors, regional CSOs are not necessarily passive and powerless. The dismissal of regional civil society in Southern Africa, almost becoming a truism, will be challenged in this section.

In order to discuss the regional presence of CSOs and perhaps come to the conclusion that civil society regionalization is an insignificant process (as most scholars do), we first have to define what it is that is considered weak or strong and why. This involves being clear about, first, which part of civil society is being considered, given that civil society is very diverse and is engaged in a number of different issue areas, as well as, second, the particular aspect of civil society regionalization that is being examined, for example regional identity-making or engagement with the SADC. Without defining what part or dimension of civil society regionalization is being assessed, scholars such as Landsberg (2012), Peters-Berries (2010), Matlosa and Lotshwao (2010) and Pressend (2010) come to the premature and generalized conclusion that civil society in Southern Africa is weak on the regional level.

The book has earlier highlighted five things that make CSOs 'regional': namely, creating regional organizational forms, framing issues regionally, engaging with formal regional governance, using regional donor funds and constructing regional identities. If these points are used as criteria against which the regional presence of CSOs is measured, the 16 CSOs in this study are not necessarily weak in terms of the first four. In fact, quite the contrary is true.

To start with, CSOs in this study have a developed regional organizational infrastructure in Southern Africa, which gives them a strong regional presence. Regional NGOs reside in one particular country where the head office is located, but activities are undertaken in several countries in the region, often via a great number of partner organizations coordinated by field offices. Regional networks either have a separate regional secretariat or are hosted by one of the members. Often the national members of the network span the whole region. In both cases, the staffs of the secretariat and board members are recruited regionally and represent several countries. Regional meetings, such as annual partnership forums, bring the various stakeholders together on a regular basis. Furthermore, the headquarters of several of the regional NGOs and networks, such as SEATINI, Trades Centre, SAT and ACA have developed great capacity on trade and HIV/AIDS-related issues, which often surpasses that of the SADC Secretariat. Therefore, their expertise is strongly requested by the SADC, which in turn gives them an opportunity to influence regional policy-making.

Second, as shown in the previous section, CSOs in this study show a strong regional engagement in terms of issue-framing. It should be noted that issue-framing can be seen as both a dimension of civil society regionalization, in terms of an intra-organizational mechanism behind 'going regional', and as a measure of CSOs' regional engagement. CSOs in this study generally put strong emphasis on the regional level in their perception of trade and HIV/AIDS issues, which spurs regional coalition-building, advocacy of regional target groups such as the SADC, research on regional issues, provision of services to regional actors and information dissemination in the region. Furthermore, the SADC informs the ways that trade and HIV/AIDS issues are regionally interpreted and therefore indirectly plays an important role for civil society regionalization, discussed further at the end of this chapter. CSOs' strong focus on the SADC in their understanding of trade and HIV/AIDS helps them develop a regional consciousness, which further strengthens the regional appearance.

Third, all CSOs in this study somehow, though in different ways, engage with regional governance frameworks, and many of them are quite successful in terms of providing various services to the SADC and COMESA and in assisting in policy development, even if this mostly applies to those actors who buy into the SADC's neo-liberal agenda. Some CSOs – for example regional research NGOs such as Trades Centre and SEATINI – are important partners to the SADC and also COMESA, giving policy advice in trade negotiations and providing policy-makers with policy-relevant research on various trade-related issues. Such partnership is also seen in the HIV/AIDS field, where the interaction between CSOs and the SADC Secretariat, particularly the HIV/AIDS Unit, is strong. CSOs such as SAT, ACA and NAPSAR are very active in various SADC technical committees, the PF and other policy forums and have made important contributions to various regional policy frameworks. Furthermore, some CSOs such as SAfAIDS have conducted successful advocacy campaigns. Through the Gender Protocol Alliance, SAfAIDS has managed to push the SADC to adopt a Protocol on Gender and Development. Additionally, the SADC has recently started to show a growing interest in the ICBT sector and has adopted some new policy instruments, partly thanks to growing pressure from CSOs such as SATUCC.

Fourth, CSOs in this study are 'regional' in terms of attracting regional donor funds, which is essential for their regional operation. As was discussed in the previous section, donor funds for regional activities are increasingly available to CSOs in the trade and HIV/AIDS sectors, even though they are not very sustainable, and CSOs to a varying degree manage to make use of these funds. CSOs are also good at using donor funds in a range of different ways to suit their particular needs. Some examples are organizational and administrative support in terms of capacity building of regional secretariats; more general financial support and grant-making; more specific regional projects, such as EJN's EPA Watch programme, and regional campaigns, such as the Gender Protocol Campaign; and regional networking and coalition building, including arranging and participating in regional forums. However, the flip side of using regional funds is donor dependency, which can jeopardize civil society regionalization in the long run, as discussed in the next section.

Fifth, as in the case of issue-framing, regional identity-making can be seen as a force behind civil society regionalization as well as a sign of how regional CSOs are. In terms of the latter, discussed here, regional identity-making is generally not very pronounced among CSOs in this study compared with the other ways of being regional. However, a few of the studied CSOs have managed to construct a strong sense of regional belonging among their partners and members, which has improved their status in the region. For example, the shared perception by SAPSN members of a common historical colonial experience, transformed into present-day struggle against global and regional neo-liberal powers, has informed the construction of a regional SAPSN identity. Additionally, belonging to a specific social group, sharing common social traits such as being a 'worker', 'Christian' or 'HIV/AIDS positive', constitutes the foundation of a quite strong non-territorial, Southern African identity for SATUCC, EJN and NAPSAR respectively. Regional identity-making also has to be problematized, which will be done in the next section.

Furthermore, it is often commonly perceived that the SADC has a tendency to dominate and to exclude parts of regional civil society in regional governance, which is also emphasized in this book. This is related to a more general criticism within academia that the SADC, in most facets, is 'weak'. For example, scholars have highlighted the organizational weakness of various SADC institutions, especially the Secretariat, in terms of their limited resources and low capacity (le Pere and Tjönneland 2005), and the reluctance of member states to transfer power to the supra-national level, making the SADC rather toothless (Matlosa and Lotshwao 2010; Afadameh-Adeyemi and Kalula 2011). This, in the end, plays against the inclusion of civil society in the SADC. Additionally, the SADC's commitment to strengthening political integration and establishing common political and democratic values is questioned (Mulaudzi 2006; Peters 2011), as well as the emphasis it puts on development in regional integration (Ajulu 2007; Blaauw 2007) and its willingness to support regional identity-making and citizenship (Williams 2006). Last, even the very heart of the SADC's regional governance agenda – trade liberalization and integration – is accused of being too slow (Peters 2011; TRALAC 2012). However, this book has shown that, regardless of the mentioned weaknesses, the SADC is in different (sometimes more indirect) ways very important for civil society regionalization to occur. In fact, one central conclusion of this book is the great importance of the SADC as a driving force and incentive for CSOs to 'go regional'. Hence, in terms of fostering bottom-up regional co-operation, the role SADC plays in regional integration is not necessarily 'weak', at least not in terms of the parts of civil society studied in this project.

Problematizing civil society regionalization

Despite the generally strong regional appearance among CSOs in this study, 'going regional' still has to be problematized on a number of points. First, picking up the thread from the end of the last section, one of these relates to the weak bottom-up nature of civil society regionalization. As indicated in Chapter 3, state-led regionalism in Africa and elsewhere tends to have 'largely developed without the citizens' (Fioramonti 2012: 159), excluding the diversity of voices and roles in broader society, serving the specific interests of the ruling elite and reflecting the neo-liberal agendas of the industrial and financial powers (Fioramonti 2012: 159). A similar critique can also be delivered about civil society regionalization, including the majority of the CSOs in my sample, since many CSOs active regionally are rather elitist and lack legitimacy among ordinary citizens.

Many regionally active CSOs, including the trade and HIV/AIDS sectors, show a weakness in the ways they are linked with and accountable to the groups whose voices they want to represent on the regional level and poorly reflect the interests of poor people and marginalized social groups (Southern Africa Trust 2009). This is linked to the fact that, due to donor dependency, many regionally engaged CSOs in the Southern and other parts of Africa tend to focus on upward accountability, whereby they spend significant energy to satisfy the requirements and needs of boards, councils of management and donors, at the expense of downward accountability in terms of responsibility to the constituencies they claim to work for (Trust Africa 2008). RCSOs are not only criticized for failing to maintain their relationship with the people they claim to represent but can also be accused of not even having a constituency, as in the example of SADC-CNGO, discussed earlier.

For regional networks such as SATUCC, SADC-CNGO, ARASA and ACA, it is more complicated to maintain legitimacy on a regional than national level, since it is unclear what the actual constituency is. For example, is it the national member organizations or their respective target groups? According to one scholar, it is hard to say how close the aforementioned regional networks are to ordinary people because they primarily represent national NGOs *per se*. Therefore, in order to evaluate the legitimacy of these networks, one has to find out how much their national members actually reach out to the grassroots level,[14] which is beyond the scope of this study. Hence, the legitimacy of regional networks cannot be determined through an aggregation of the legitimacy of their members. However, as indicated earlier, there are reasons to believe that many national NGOs and networks are driven by pecuniary considerations and not a genuine development interest and serve the interests of a limited number of people at the expense of broader grassroots communities. This of course complicates the legitimacy of regional networks and the NGOs to which they are related.

Some regional networks such as EJN, NAPSAR and SATUCC have a vast membership in Southern Africa in terms of churches, HIV/AIDS organizations and labour organizations in almost all of the SADC countries, representing Christians, HIV-positive people and workers on a broad scale. It might be the case that these regional networks, as membership-based organizations, gain what van Rooy calls 'automatic credibility' (2004: 64) because of the sheer number of affiliates. For example, according to the EJN director:

> we are not a grassroots organization but we represent organizations that work on a grassroots level [. . .] Our legitimacy comes from the fact that we are not a briefcase NGO, but have strong members in the countries who are committed to the grassroots.[15]

Yet if legitimacy is seen in terms of the quality of the linkage to the constituencies of these CSOs – for example regarding how much the CSOs are actually accountable to the people they claim to represent and how much their constituencies are involved in decision-making and project planning and implementation – then legitimacy has to be questioned. This can make the regionalization of civil society weak in terms of it not being grounded on a more grassroots level.

To link this argument to the question of issue-framing and identity-making, it is questionable if SATUCC, EJN, SADC-CNGO, ACA, ARASA and NAPSAR really represent a widespread sense of regional understanding and identity among their member organizations' constituencies, such as workers, HIV-positive people and church communities. It must be questioned if SATUCC's members, that is national coalitions of trade unions, and in turn their member organizations, cultivate the same feelings for a borderless, transnational/regional community of workers as the Secretariat and the regional board. Hence, to what extent is the transnational/regional working-class mentality relevant for and rooted among grassroots workers on the ground? All in all, the regional presence of regional networks and NGOs can be a rather elite-driven process not rooted among local and national members. This will be further discussed when 'regional' identity-making is scrutinized.

Furthermore, in terms of SAPSN, resisting regional governance and striving towards people-driven 'transformation' does not automatically make it a positive force in society or for democracy. Agents of civil society resisting regional governance have clearly managed to fill a vacuum created by the absence of real alternative state-led regionalisms. But in filling this gap, these agents are not necessarily 'people driven', and their frequently proclaimed links to the grassroots and to 'people's' need to be scrutinized and debated. Despite the participation of CBOs, which are locally based, in People's Summits, on a more general level the resistance sections within SAPSN are an elite-led process, dominated by a relatively small number of NGO representatives and activists. For example, contrary to SATUCC, most CSOs participating in SAPSN are not membership based. The number of participants and stakeholders involved is steadily increasing, but the agenda and output are dominated by a limited number of vocal activists. Their ability to deliver their message (their 'voice') and to finance their activities is also heavily dependent on how successful they are in attracting donor funding from INGOs, private trusts and foundations. These critical factors raise questions about legitimacy, accountability and representation. According to one commentator:

> SAPSN is more of a shadow membership-based network and should not be regarded as a representative network in the region [. . .] SAPSN is not a result of local grassroots mobilization that leads to some kind of regional network [and therefore] does not constitute any kind of genuine civil society collaboration in the region.[16]

Second, nationalism is still a strong undercurrent for many members of and partners to regional networks and NGOs, which are often nationally oriented and preoccupied with national issues. This is a well-established fact within the academic community and civil society in the region.[17] In the words of one commentator, 'among regional civil society structures, the inclination towards nationalism [. . .] has undermined [. . .] solidarity' (Pressend 2010). This is linked to the general nationalist tendencies among people in the region, in turn enforced by the deeper statist social structure in Southern Africa. The nationalist inclination is an inbuilt problem of networks such as SAPSN, ACA, SADC-CNGO and ASCCI, which partly exist to support the national work of their members. Hence, many regional networks suffer from their members' general inability and unwillingness to connect local and national issues with broader regional processes. According to a prominent Mozambican scholar, if CSOs do not make a regional political-economic analysis of development issues in Southern Africa, there are no incentives to engage regionally:

> The political economy of Mozambique is connected to and affected by the regional processes. The levels are integrated. The situation in Zimbabwe affects the whole region; you cannot run away from that. If you don't see these regional commonalities you don't see the point of engaging regionally.[18]

This is the case for many CSOs on a national level, including members of regional networks in this study.

It can be argued that the ultimate strength of regional networks is related to the ability of their national members to take regional issues forward to the national and local levels and to make the network active between regional meetings and campaigns, which is often not the case. Since national agendas and interests make big imprints on the activities of members, regional momentum tends to die out between regional events, and the regional work of the network then loses pace. Hence, partly because of members' preoccupation with 'national' issues, SAPSN has a very low profile between regional events such as the People's Summit. SAPSN is very diverse, with CBOs, women's groups, social movements, NGOs and other types of organizations focusing on their own particular local and national struggles, often without relating to the broader regional struggle.[19] This undermines the regional consolidation of the network. For example, one SAPSN member, MDG, claims that the debt issues they deal with are mainly seen in light of the national Mozambican agenda. MDG has therefore not taken the regional context seriously enough and struggles to relate national issues to regional processes, which results in a weak regional engagement within SAPSN and elsewhere.[20] The fact that the construction of regional identities depends a lot on regional gatherings, as discussed earlier, which are limited in time and scope, as well as the (weak) regional commitment of their members, makes the regional SAPSN identity superficial and vulnerable. The SAPSN representative confesses that not much happens in between summits and blames the members for not taking the regional and global issues discussed at the summit further in their respective countries.[21] There is a risk, then, that the regional solidarity and community-building created during regional events is not sustained in a long-term perspective.

SADC-CNGO faces similar challenges, claiming that 'members are not moving at the same pace as the Secretariat' (SADC-CNGO 2010d: 7). The fact that some members fail to take regional issues seriously can partly be attributed to the organizational structure of SADC-CNGO, which is constituted by national NGO coalitions, formed around national interests, and which possess the prime decision-making power at the expense of the quite weak secretariat. Therefore, some scholars argue that SADC-CNGO, similarly to SADC, 'may have fallen into the same trap of perceiving regional integration through statist [. . .] lenses' (Matlosa and Lotshwao 2010: 40). In terms of SATUCC, similarly, the regional presence and agendas are not evident to national members, and it is not clear to them why they should actually be part of SATUCC.[22] This is partly related to the fact that SATUCC is dominated by COSATU, which tends to prioritize support for national economic processes in South Africa.[23] Finally, ARASA blames its members for being too caught up with their national activities to maintain on-going engagement with the regional secretariat (ARASA 2007: 10). All in all, due to the nationalist preoccupation of many CSOs, deeply influenced by the statist social structure, for civil society 'Southern Africa as a region is under construction'.[24]

This raises serious questions about how rooted the regional issue-framing and regional identities of the regional NGOs and networks in this study are among the national and local partners and members, discussed earlier. This resonates with the wider problem of the cementation of national sentiments among people in the region, which spills over to CSOs. In the end, nationalistic tendencies can obstruct civil society regionalization. Another contributing factor, linked to the foregoing, is the organizational structure of many regional networks and NGOs. Primarily being of a facilitating, service-providing nature, especially in the case of HIV/AIDS, the focus lies on facilitating the work of national members and partners. Additionally, the aim of some of these CSOs, at least on paper, is also to influence regional policy-making, in line with the advocacy-type NGO and network, which can foster a regional consciousness and spur regionalization. Yet, as shown in the empirical chapters, influencing regional policy-making is a difficult endeavour, and many networks, such as SADC-CNGO, tend to resort to providing services to the national members. Regional CSOs face similar problems in Latin America, the Baltic region and East Asia. In terms of Latin America, most regional groups which engage regionally remain rooted in their national contexts and interpret regional integration with their particular national experiences (Grugel 2006: 225). Similar tendencies can be discerned in the Baltic region, where few regional networks have managed to organize around principles other than nationality (Reuter 2007: 256). In East Asia, in fact, regional networking and information sharing can be seen merely as another means of trying to influence national politics.

In the end, this implies that 'transnational networks implicitly affirm the legitimacy of state authority within regional governance' (Gilson 2011a: 144).

Furthermore, if civil society regionalization is not based on a widespread sense of belonging to a regional community among the actors involved, regional work can be quite vulnerable to external pressures, such as declining donor funds, which in the end can play against regionalization. At the same time, as shown in the end of the last section, there is evidence of a general increase in interest in regional issues and regional engagement among CSOs. These seemingly contradictory processes might be explained by the fact that, as already indicated, civil society regionalization can be rather short term, superficial and brittle, partly driven by material interests, and not reflecting more genuine, deeply rooted sentiments of regional community-building. When 'going regional', CSOs do this partly because of an urge to be associated with regional policy-makers, gaining (sometimes personal) power, and because there is money available for regional work. Hence, in many respects, civil society regionalization tends to be driven by SADC and donors.

Third, despite the success of CSOs in this study in attracting regional donor funds, these funds can also weaken them. In fact, civil society regionalization can be considered weak in the sense of RCSOs being dependent on donor funding for their existence. For many CSOs involved in this study, such dependency creates a very vulnerable financial situation where regional work can lose pace and even terminate if donor funds dry out. SANASO is a clear-cut example. Hence, if regionally active donors decide to concentrate on new issue areas and/or to focus more on other levels of engagement, that is local and national, this can severely harm civil society regionalization. The HIV/AIDS sector is particularly at risk here because of the high involvement of bilateral donors, which generally tend to question the value added of the regional level. In the trade sector, dominated by private donors, CSOs might be less at risk, since these donors have a more genuine commitment to the regional level.

Fourth, the fact is that civil society regionalization is a very heterogeneous process, and this heterogeneity can in itself play against further strengthening of regionalization. The ideological and resource-based competition among CSOs, stemming from the statist and capitalist regional order, creates a rather diverse and divided civil society regionalization, especially in the trade sector, which might be weakened if this competition increases. Additionally, and linked to this, civil society regionalization has its winners and losers, which implies that some pockets of regional civil society, that is regional NGOs and some networks with close links to SADC-led regional governance and donors, are quite strong. In contrast other, more critical sections of regional civil society, which challenge the mainstream neo-liberal discourse in the region, are generally more marginalized among RIGOs and (especially bilateral) donors and, hence, make less of an impact on the character of civil society regionalization. It must be concluded that critical reformist and resistance CSOs are less powerful on the regional scene than their commercial and partner colleagues.

Fifth, because of the strong statist undercurrent in Southern Africa, manifested in a general SADC domination over civil society discussed in Chapter 3, even though some of the CSOs involved in this study are formally involved in policy discussions at the SADC Secretariat, for example in relation to the HIV/AIDS PF, the TAC, TIFI meetings and the RPO, this does not make them influential on a deeper level. This especially relates to the more critically inclined CSOs. Hence, considering the fact that these meetings occur within the powerless and quite insignificant SADC

Secretariat, the real policy influence of civil society on the SADC is kept to a minimum. CSOs are only allowed to influence regional agenda setting and implementation on low policy levels. As also indicated in Chapter 3, member states are reluctant to circumvent national sovereignty or transmit any decision-making powers to supranational regional institutions such as the Secretariat and Tribunal. The decision making of more political weight takes place elsewhere, in summits and COM meetings, where member states are in control and CSOs are not welcome, except for some occasional posts in the policy debate by business NGOs. In these forums, dominated by the neo-liberal market-oriented trade agenda, human rights, improved service delivery, ICBT, regional citizenship and other issues pertinent to many critical CSOs are low on the agenda. Hence, on the whole, due to the inherent statism in the region, civil society is rather powerless in relation to the SADC and its member states. As already indicated, SADC–CSO relations greatly take place on the former's terms.

Future research areas

This study is an important contribution to the understanding of civil society regionalization, not only in Southern Africa but also in other world regions. Nevertheless, there are still many gaps in the study of civil society regionalization and what forces drive this process that call for further research in the field. First, one gap in the present study, as well as other studies related to civil society regionalization, is the exclusive targeting of 'regional' NGOs and networks, leaving out those local and national CSOs which also engage regionally. Even if their engagement is generally more occasional, these actors nevertheless play a role in civil society regionalization, in terms, for example, of engaging RIGOs, doing research on regional issues and building up regional networks and NGOs as members and partners. In addition, as we have seen, some of them play a big (negative) role in regional identity-making and community-building, diluting the regional consciousness of the networks they are part of by invigorating national interests and agendas, which needs to be further interrogated. Future research, then, has to involve a broader sample of CSOs involved in regional work, including not only local and national but also international/global NGOs and networks in order to present a more comprehensive picture of civil society regionalization. The linkage between regional and global processes is important. How does global civil society, for example through global forums such as World Social Forums, INGOs and TANs, impact civil society regionalization in various world regions?

Second, investigating mass media and ICT and the ways in which CSOs relate to them in the process of 'going regional' can greatly benefit understanding of civil society regionalization in Southern Africa and also other regions. In terms of mass media, the diffusion of ideas about the region, for example in terms of trade, HIV/AIDS and other types of development-related issues, through transnational communication and media circulation is important for regional integration to evolve

(Blaauw 2007: 58), including the regionalization of civil society. Mass media is a helpful source of information on regional issues for CSOs and an important vehicle to spread their agendas to the wider public in the region. Two examples from Southern Africa are the South African newspaper *Mail & Guardian*, with its coverage of regional development issues, and *SADC Today*, a regional bulletin about SADC regional processes published by the regional information centre SARDC. Being featured in these and other types of media, as well as becoming more knowledgeable about regional processes, can strengthen the regional profile of CSOs (Southern Africa Trust 2010a). Hence, media can possibly raise the regional awareness of CSOs and strengthen regional issue-framing and identity-making, which fuels civil society regionalization. These processes are important to study in future projects. Furthermore, the use of ICT can be important for civil society regionalization and another aspect of 'going regional'. For Sub-Saharan Africa as a whole, there has been a remarkable growth in ICT services in the past decade (MISA 2007). The SADC region in particular is quite well interconnected in terms of communication facilities. For example, all countries have established mobile telephone networks, and the number of Internet users is steadily rising (Peters-Berries 2010: 116). ICT can be a powerful force for regional integration, facilitating cross-border co-operation and transnational communication. In terms of civil society, ICT can strengthen co-operation among CSOs. In Zimbabwe, for example, through the Kubatana project[25] disparate CSOs have been able to work together and pool their resources in order to voice their concerns about human rights abuses in the country. This has involved the use of various communication technologies such as the Internet and e-mail. This is one example of the positive effect of the increased presence of ICT for coalition-building among CSOs in Southern Africa, which can also be used to break down geographical boundaries and spur trans-border coalition-building (Michelson 2006). It is without doubt that ICT plays an important role for CSOs on a regional level. Strategically using various communication channels for regional work can indeed strengthen regionalization. Hence, studying the use of media and ICT in regional collaboration would enhance understanding of the motivations for 'going regional'. This is an important task for future investigations.

Third, as indicated earlier in this chapter, there is a big debate around the legitimacy of CSOs. However, this debate primarily relates to so-called 'global civil society' and NGOs operating on a local-national level, not least in an African context. The legitimacy of CSOs operating regionally, in Africa and elsewhere, is largely under-researched and not particularly mentioned in the debate. While not explicitly focusing on this dimension of civil society regionalization, this research has shown that there are worrying signs of a general lack of legitimacy on behalf of regional NGOs and networks, which tend to be rather elitist. However, this question needs a lot more attention in future studies. This implies, for example, digging deeper into the extent to which CSOs on a regional level are representative of and accountable to various social groups in society and how much the grassroots people that CSOs often claim to safeguard and even represent are involved in decision-making, project planning and implementation. In other words, how grounded is civil society regionalization on a more grassroots level? This touches upon important overarching questions related to how 'democratic' regional CSOs are and what 'democracy' means on a regional civil society level. Democracy is a hot topic in the discussion of regional governance in terms of how democratic RIGOs are, not least in Southern Africa, where the democratic state of the SADC is called into question (e.g. Godsäter 2014). It is equally important to scrutinize how bottom-up the so-called bottom-up aspect of regionalization really is and put the democratic state of RCSOs in the spotlight.

Notes

1 Categorization of different organizations is common in the social sciences, including IR and political science, for example in terms of CSOs involved in global governance (Armstrong et al. 2004; Costoya 2007) and types of international organizations (Jacobson 1984; Archer 2001).
2 Note that this categorization is not mutually exclusive. The four 'categories' are not clear-cut and should be understood more as CSO positions in various areas.
Considering their often complex and sometimes contradictory positions, it is possible for CSOs in this study to 'belong' to more than one of the categories. Also, since the outlook of CSOs is not static, their positions change over time, and so does their placement in a certain category. The following categorization is foremost an attempt to conceptualize the heterogeneity of civil society on the regional level and will naturally change in line with the evolution of civil society regionalization.
3 Ngwane, interview, 3 December 2008.
4 Gentle, interview, 18 December 2009.
5 Nemete and Guileugue, interview, 20 November 2008.
6 Moiana, interview, 17 November 2008.
7 Bond, interview, 14 December 2008.
8 Ngwane, interview, 3 December 2008.
9 Ngwane, interview, 3 December 2008.
10 Nemete and Guileugue, interview 20 November 2008.
11 Castel-Branco, interview 24 November 2008.
12 Gentle, interview 18 December 2009.
13 The 'weakness' of regional civil society in this literature is both referred to how much (or rather how little) CSOs have 'gone regional', in other words their regional presence, as well as their power to influence regional policy-making and possession of material resources. This section will foremost discuss the former even though policy influence and resource possession will also be briefly discussed.
14 Osei-Hwedie, interview, 5 December 2008.
15 Damon, interview, 15 December 2009.
16 Gentle, interview, 18 December 2009.
17 Muchabaiwa, interview, December 2009; le Pere, interview, 27 November 2008; Mati, interview, 27 November 2009; Vale, interview, 2 March 2005.
18 Castel-Branco, interview, 24 November 2008.
19 Gentle, interview, 18 December 2009; Bond, interview, 14 December 2008.
20 Nemete and Guileugue, interview, 20 November 2008.
21 Kasiamhuru, interview, 2 December 2009.

22 Gabriel, interview, 2 December 2008.
23 Ngwane, interview, 3 December 2008.
24 Gabriel, interview, 2 December 2008.
25 The Kubatana Project, led by the Kubatana Trust of Zimbabwe, aims to strengthen the use of e-mail and Internet strategies for Zimbabwean NGOs and makes human rights and civic education information accessible to Zimbabwean civil society (Kubatana Trust 2013).

References

Literature

Acharya, A. 2003. Democratisation and the Prospects for Participatory Regionalism in Southeast Asia. *Third World Quarterly*, 24(2), 375–390.

Afadameh-Adeyemi, A. and Kalula, E. 2011. SADC at 30: Re-examining the Legal and Institutional Anatomy of the Southern African Development Community, in *Monitoring Regional Integration in Southern Africa Yearbook. Vol. 10*, edited by A. Bösl, A. du Pisani, G. Erasmus, T. Hartzenberg and R. Sandrey. Stellenbosch: Trade Law Centre for Southern Africa, 5–22.

Ajulu, R. 2005. The New EAC: Linking Subregional and Continental Integration Initiatives, in *The Making of a Region: The Revival of the East African Community*, edited by Rok Ajulu. Johannesburg: Institute for Global Dialogue, 17–28.

———. 2007. Open versus Developmental Integration – What Options for SADC?, in *Revisiting Regionalism in Southern Africa – Proceedings of the Fourth Southern African Forum on Trade (SAFT)*, Pretoria, South Africa, 3–4 September 2007. Johannesburg: IGD and Windhoek: Friedrich-Ebert-Stiftung, 25–39.

Ameli, S. R. 2011. The Organisation of the Islamic Conference: Accountability and Civil Society, in *Building Global Democracy? Civil Society and Accountable Global Governance*, edited by J. A. Scholte. Cambridge: Cambridge University Press, 146–162.

Anyanwu, C. D. 2014. Can Caribbean Civil Society Effectively Influence Regional Policy?: Overcoming National and Regional Challenges in CARICOM, in *Civil Society and World Regions*, edited by L. Fioramonti. Lanham, MD: Lexington, 63–75.

Archer, C. 2001. *International Organizations*. London: Routledge.

Armstrong, D. and Gilson, J. 2011. Introduction: Civil Society and International Governance, in *Civil Society and International Governance*, edited by D. Armstrong, V. Bello, J. Gilson and D. Spini. New York: Routledge, 1–12.

Armstrong, D., Lloyd L. and Redmond, J. 2004. *International Organisation in World Politics*. New York: Palgrave Basingstoke.

Ayers, A. J. 2008. Introduction, in *Gramsci, Political Economy, and International Relations Theory: Modern Princes and Naked Emperors*, edited by A. J. Ayers. Basingstoke: Palgrave, 1–25.

Bach, D. 2005. The Global Politics of Regionalism: Africa, in *Global Politics of Regionalism*, edited by M. Farrell, B. Hettne and L. Van Langenhove. London: Pluto Press, 171–186.

Baert, F., Scaramagli, T. and Söderbaum, F. 2014. Introduction: Intersecting Interregionalism, in *Intersecting Interregionalism*, edited by F. Baert, T. Scaramagli and F. Söderbaum. Dordrecht: Springer, 12–23.

Balule, B. T. 2009. The Legal Environment of SADC-Civil Society Interaction in Pursuance of Human Security, in *Furthering Southern African Regional Integration—Proceedings of the 2008 FOPRISA Annual Conference*, edited by J. M. Kaunda and F. Zizhou. Gaborone: BIDPA, 87–96.

Blaauw, L. 2007. *Transcending State-Centrism: New Regionalism and the Future of Southern African Regional Integration*, PhD-thesis, Grahamstown: Rhodes University. [Online]. Available at: http://eprints.ru.ac.za/1355/1/blaauwfinal dissertation.pdf [accessed: 25 October 2012].

Blee, K. M. and Taylor, V. 2002. Semi-Structured Interviewing, in *Social Movement Research, in Methods of Social Movements Research*, edited by B. Klandermans and S. Staggenborg. Minneapolis: University of Minnesota Press, 92–117.

Bøås, M. 2001. Regions and Regionalisation: A Heretic's View, in *Discussion Paper 11, Regionalism and Regional Integration in Africa: A Debate of Current Aspects and Issues*. Uppsala: Nordic Africa Institute.

Bøås, M. and Hveem, H. 2001. Regionalisms Compared: The African and Southeast Asian Experience, in *Comparing Regionalisms: Implications for Global Development*, edited by B. Hettne, A. Inotai, and O. Sunkel. Basingstoke: Palgrave, 93–131.

Bob, C. 2005. *The Marketing of Rebellion: Insurgents, Media, and International Activism*. Cambridge: Cambridge University Press.

Bobden, S. and Wyn Jones, R. 2005. Marxist Theories of International Relations, in *The Globalization of World Politics: An Introduction to International Relations*, edited by Baylis and S. Smith. Oxford: Oxford University Press, 225–249.

Boli, J. and Thomas, G. M. 1999. INGOs and the Organization of World Culture, in *Constructing World Culture: International Nongovernmental Organizations Since 1875*, edited by J. Boli and G. M. Thomas. Stanford, CA: Stanford University Press, 13–49.

Botto, M. 2014. Civil Society, Labour Movements, and the Challenge to Capitalist Regional Integration in Latin America, in *Civil Society and World Regions*, edited by L. Fioramonti. Lanham, MD: Lexington, 49–62.

Bowden, B. 2006. Civil Society, the State, and the Limits to Global Civil Society. *Global Society*, 20(2), 155–178.

Buckley, K. 2012. *Global Civil Society and Transversal Hegemony*, Paper to the Annual Convention of the International Studies Association, San Diego, USA, 31 March–3 April, 2012.

Buechler, S. M. 1993. Beyond Resource Mobilization? Emerging Trends in Social Movement Theory. *The Sociological Quarterly*, 34(2), 217–235.

———. 1995. New Social Movement Theories. *The Sociological Quarterly*, 36(3), 441–464.

Buzan, B. and Wæver, O. 2003. *Regions and Powers: The Structure of International Security*. Cambridge: Cambridge University Press.

Chandler, D. 2004. *Constructing Global Civil Society: Morality and Power in International Relations*. Basingstoke: Palgrave Macmillan.

Costoya, M. M. 2007. *Towards a Typology of Civil Society Actors: The Case of the Movement to Change International Trade Rules and Barriers*, UNRISD Civil Society and Social Movements Programme Paper Number 30, October 2007. Geneva: UNRISD.

Cox, R. W. 1981. Social Forces, States and World Orders: Beyond International Relations Theory. *Millennium: Journal of International Studies*, 10(2), 126–155.

———. 1983. Gramsci, Hegemony and International Relations: An Essay in Method. *Millennium: Journal of International Studies*, 12(2), 162–175.

———. 1987. *Production, Power, and World Order*. New York: Columbia University Press.

———. 1993. *Critical Political Economy*, paper presented at the UNU Lecture day, Oslo, August 17, 1993.

———. 1996. Gramsci, Hegemony, and International Relations: An Essay in Method, in *Approaches to World Order*, edited by R. W. Cox and T. J. Sinclair. Cambridge: Cambridge University Press, 124–143.

———. 1999. Civil society at the Turn of the Millennium: Prospects for an Alternative World Order. *Review of International Studies*, 25(1), 3–28.

Curley, M. 2007. The Role of Civil Society in East Asian Region Building, in *Advancing East Asian Regionalism*, edited by M. Curley and N. Thomas. New York: Routledge, 179–201.

Dagnino, E. 2011. Civil Society in Latin America, in *The Oxford Handbook of Civil Society*, edited by M. Edwards. Oxford: Oxford University Press, 122–133.

Damon, M. and Jeuring, K. 2010. *Informal Cross-border Trade as an Instrument in Alleviating Poverty*. Johannesburg: OSISA. [Online]. Available at: http://www.docstoc.com/docs/30196949/Informal-Cross-border-Trade-as-an-Instrument-in-Alleviating-Poverty [accessed: 30 August 2012].

Deen-Swarray, M. and Schade, K. 2006. Perception of Business People and Non-state Actors on Regional Integration: A SADC-wide Survey, in *Monitoring Regional Integration in Southern Africa Yearbook. Vol. 6*, edited by A. Bösl and W. Breytenbach Stellenbosch: Trade Law Centre for Southern Africa, 51–80.

Della Porta, D. and Diano, M. 2006. *Social Movements and Introduction*. Malden: Blackwell.

———. 2011. Social Movements, in *The Oxford Handbook of Civil Society*, edited by M. Edwards. Oxford: Oxford University Press, 68–79.

Dibie, R. A. 2008. Introduction: NGOs and Human Development in Africa: Theory and Model for Collaboration, in *Non-Governmental Organizations (NGOs) and Sustainable Development in Sub-Saharan Africa*, edited by R. A. Dibie. Lanham, MD: Lexington Books, 1–25.

Dicklitch, S. 1998. *The Elusive Promise of NGOs in Africa: Lessons from Uganda*. Basingstoke: MacMillan Press.

Dupuy, K. 2012. *States and NGOs: Regulatory Pressure and Organizational Response*, Paper to the Annual Conference of the International Studies Association, San Diego, USA, 31 March–3 April, 2012.

Edwards, M. 2009. *Civil Society*. Cambridge: Polity Press.

Fantasia, R. and Hirsch, E. L. 1995. Culture in Rebellion: The Appropriation and Transformation of the Veil in the Algerian Revolution, in *Social Movements and Culture*, edited by H. Johnston and B. Klandermans. Minneapolis: University of Minnesota Press, 144–159.

Farrell, M. 2005. The Global Politics of Regionalism: An Introduction, in *Global Politics of Regionalism*, edited by M. Farrell, B. Hettne and L. Van Langenhove. London: Pluto Press, 1–17.

Fawcett, L. 2005. Regionalism from a Historical Perspective, in *Global Politics of Regionalism*, edited by M. Farrell, B. Hettne and L. Van Langenhove et al. London: Pluto Press, 21–37.

Fawcett, L. and Hurrell, A. 1995. Introduction, in *Regionalism in World Politics*, edited by L. Fawcett and A. Hurrell. New York: Oxford University Press, 1–6.

FDC. 2007. *Mozambican Civil Society Within: Evaluation, Challenges, Opportunities and Action*. Maputo: FDC. [Online]. Available at: http://www.civicus.org/media/CSI_Mozambique_Country_Report.pdf [accessed: 25 October 2012].

Ferguson, J. 1995. From African Socialism to Scientific Capitalism: Reflections on the Legitimation Crisis in the IMF-ruled Africa, in *Debating Development Discourse: Institutional and Popular Perspectives*, edited by D. B. More and G. J. Schmitz. New York: St Martin's Press, 129–148.

Fine, B. 2010. From the Political Economy of Development to Development Economics, in *The Political Economy of Africa*, edited by V. Padayachee. London: Routledge, 60–82.

Fine, G. A. 1995. Public Narration and Group Culture: Discerning Discourse in Social Movements, in *Social Movements and Culture*, edited by H. Johnston and B. Klandermans. Minneapolis: University of Minnesota Press, 127–143.

Finnemore, M. and Sikkink, K. 2001. Taking Stock: The Constructivist Research Program in. International Relations and Comparative Politics. *Annual Review of Political Science*, 4, 391–416.

Fioramonti, L. 2012. Conclusion – Building Regions from Below: Has the Time Come for Regionalism 2.0? *The International Spectator: Italian Journal of International Affairs*, 1(47), 151–160.

Florini, A. M. 2000. Lessons Learned, in *The Third Force: The Rise of Transnational Civil Society*, edited by A. M. Florini. Washington, DC: Carnegie Endowment for International Peace, 211–240.

Fowler, A. 2011. Development NGOs, in *The Oxford Handbook of Civil Society*, edited by M. Edwards. Oxford: Oxford University Press, 42–54.

Freund, B. 2010. The Social Context of African Economic Growth 1960–2008, in *The Political Economy of Africa*, edited by V. Padayachee. London: Routledge, 39–59.

Gale, F. 1998. Cave 'Cave! Hic dragons': A Neo-Gramscian Deconstruction and Reconstruction of International Regime Theory. *Review of International Political Economy*, 5(2), 252–283.

Gamson, W. A. 1995. Constructing Social Protest, in *Social Movements and Culture*, edited by H. Johnston and B. Klandermans. Minneapolis: University of Minnesota Press, 85–106.

George, A. L. and Bennett, A. 2005. *Case Studies and Theory Development in the Social Sciences*. London: MIT Press.

Gill, S. 2008. *Power and Resistance in the New World Order*. Basingstoke: Palgrave.

Gilpin, R. 1987. *Political Economy of International Relations*. Princeton: Princeton University Press.

Gilson, J. 2011a. Governance and Non-governmental Organizations in East Asia, in *Civil Society and International Governance*, edited by D. Armstrong, V. Bello, J. Gilson and D. Spini. New York: Routledge, 129–147.

———. 2011b. Structuring Accountability: Civil Society and the ASIA-Europe Meeting, in *Building Global Democracy? Civil Society and Accountable Global Governance*, edited by J. A. Scholte. Cambridge: Cambridge University Press, 206–224.

Giuffrida, L. and Müller-Glodde, H. 2008. Strengthening SADC Institutional Structures. Capacity Development is the Key to the SADC Secretariat's Effectiveness, in *Monitoring Regional Integration in Southern Africa Yearbook. Vol. 8*, edited by A. Bösl, W. Breytenbach, T. Hartzenberg, C. McCarthy and K. Schade. Stellenbosch: Trade Law Centre for Southern Africa, 120–148.

Godsäter, A. 2013. Regional Environmental Governance in the Lake Victoria Region: The Role of Civil Society. *African Studies*, 72(1), 64–85.

———. 2014. The Democratization of the Southern Africa Development Community, in *The Democratization of International Institutions. First International Democracy Report*, edited by L. Levio, G. Finizio and Nicola Vallinoto. New York: Routledge, 242–257.

Godsäter, A. and Söderbaum, F. 2011. Civil Society in Regional Governance in Eastern and Southern Africa, in *Civil Society and International Governance*, edited by D. Armstrong, V. Bello, J. Gilson and D. Spini. New York: Routledge, 148–165.

Grant, J. A. and Söderbaum, F. 2003. Introduction: The New Regionalism in Africa, in *The New Regionalism in Africa*, edited by J. Grant and F. Söderbaum. Aldershot: Ashgate, 1–17.

Grovogui, S. N. and Leonard, L. 2008. Uncivil Society: Interrogations at the Margins of Neo-Gramscian Theory, in *Gramsci, Political Economy, and International Relations Theory: Modern Princes and Naked Emperors*, edited by A. J. Ayers. Basingstoke: Palgrave, 217–237.

Grugel, J. 2004. State Power and Transnational Activism, in *Transnational Activism in Asia: Problems of Power and Democracy*, edited by N. Piper and A. Uhlin. London: Routledge, 26–42.

———. 2006. Regionalist Governance and Transnational Collective Action in Latin America. *Economy and Society*, 35(2), 209–231.

Harrison, G. 2010. *Neo-liberal Africa.* London: Zed Books.

Hawthorn, G. 2000. Running the World Through Windows. *New Left Review*, 5 Sep–Oct 2000, 101–110.

Hearn, Julie. 2007. African NGOs: The New Compradors? *Development and Change*, 38(6), 1095–1110.

Heinrich, V. F. 2004. Assessing and Strengthening Civil Society Worldwide. *CIVICUS Civil Society Index Paper Series*, 2(1).

Hettne, B. 1999. Globalization and the New Regionalism: The Second Great Transformation, in *Globalism and the New Regionalism*, edited by B. Hettne, A. Inotai and O. Sunkel. New York: Macmillan, 1–24.

———. 2005. Beyond the 'New' Regionalism. *New Political Economy*, 10(4), 543–571.

Heywood, A. 2011. *Global Politics.* Basingstoke: Palgrave.

Higgott, R. A., Underhill, G. R. D. and Bieler, A. 1999. Introduction: Globalisation and Non-state Actors, in Non-state Actors and Authority in the Global System, edited by R. A. Higgott, G. R. D. Underhill and A. Bieler. London; New York: Routledge, 1–12.

Hinds, K. 2008. *Civil Society Regionalisation and Access to Policy Space: The Case of CARICOM*, International Studies Association's 49th Annual Convention, San Francisco, USA, 26–29 March 2008. [Online]. Available at: http://citation.allacademic.com/meta/p_mla_apa_research_citation/2/5/2/5/0/pages252509/p252509-1.php [accessed: 25 October 2012].

Hurrell, A. 1995. Regionalism in Theoretical Perspective, in *Regionalism in World Politics: Regional Organization and International Order*, edited by L. Fawcett and A. Hurrell. London: Pluto Press, 37–73.

Igarashi, S. 2011. The New Regional Order and Transnational Civil Society in Southeast Asia: Focusing on Alternative Regionalism from below in the Process of Building the ASEAN Community. *World Political Science Review*, 1(7), 1–31.

Iheduru, O. C. 2014. Civil Society and Regional Integration in West Africa: Partners, Legitimizers, and Counter-hegemonic Actors, in *Civil Society and World Regions*, edited by L. Fioramonti. Lanham, MD: Lexington, 137–160.

Inayatullah, N. and Blaney, D. L. 2004. *International Relations and the Problem of Difference.* London: Routledge.

IOM. 2010a. *Informal Cross-border Trade Sector Report*, February 2010, Geneva: IOM. [Online]. Available at: http://iom.org.za/web/images/publications/icbt.pdf [accessed: 25 October 2012].

———. 2010b. *Regional Needs on HIV-prevention Needs of Migrants and Mobile Populations in Southern Africa.* Geneva: IOM. [Online]. Available at: http://reliefweb.int/sites/reliefweb.int/files/resources/D15308ABA5BB167F492576E3001F88CD-Full_Report.pdf [accessed: 25 October 2012].

Jacobson, H. J. 1984. *Networks of Interdependence: International Organizations and the Global Political System.* New York: Alfred A. Knopf.

Jenkins, J. C. 1983. Resource Mobilization Theory and the Study of Social Movements. *Annual Review of Sociology*, 9, 527–553.

Johnston, H. 2002. Verification and Proof in Frame and Discourse Analysis, in *Social Movements and Culture*, edited by H. Johnston and B. Klandermans. Minneapolis: University of Minnesota Press, 62–91.

Johnston, H. and Klandermans, B. 1995. The Cultural Analysis of Social Movements, in *Social Movements and Culture*, edited by H. Johnston and B. Klandermans. Minneapolis: University of Minnesota Press, 3–24.

Jönsson, C., Sommerer, T., Sqatrito, T. and Tallberg, J. 2012. *TNA Access to International Organization: The Transnational Turn in Global Governance and its Normative Implications.* Paper Presented at the Annual Meeting of the International Studies Association, San Diego, 1–4 April 2012.

Kanyenze, G., Kondo, T., Martens, J. and Jauch, H. 2006. *The Search for Sustainable, Human Development in Southern Africa.* Harare: ANSA.

Kanyinga, K. and Mitullah, W. 2007. *The Non-Profit Sector in Kenya.* Nairobi: The Institute for Development Studies, University of Nairobi. [Online]. Available at: http://www.akdn.org/publications/civil_society_kenya_nonprofit2.pdf [accessed: 25 October 2012].

Katezenstein, P. J. 2005. *A World of Regions: Asia and Europe in the American Imperium.* Ithaca and London: Cornell University Press.

Katz, H. 2006. Gramsci, Hegemony, and Global Civil Society Networks. *Voluntas*, 17, 333–348.

Keck, M. E. and Sikkink, K. 1998. *Activists Beyond Borders: Advocacy Networks in International Politics.* Ithaca, NY: Cornell University Press.

Keck, M. E. and Sikkink, K. 1999. Transnational Advocacy Networks in International and Regional Politics. *International Social Science Journal*, 51(159), 89–101.

Kim, S. and Fiori, A. 2014. The Potential of Civil Society in Regional Governance in East Asia, in *Civil Society and World Regions*, edited by L. Fioramonti. Lanham, MD: Lexington, 77–90.

Kimani, N. 2007. *Reinvention of Environmental Governance in East Africa: Explanatory and Normative Dimensions.* PhD-thesis, Canberra: Australian National University. [Online]. Available at: http://regnet.anu.edu.au/sites/default/files/files/NicholasKimani_Thesis.pdf [accessed: 25 October 2012].

Klandermans, B. and Staggenborg, S. 2002. Introduction, in *Methods of Social Movements. Research*, edited by B. Klandermans and S. Staggenborg. Minneapolis: University of Minnesota Press, ix–xx.

Klandermans, B., Staggenborg, B. and Tarrow, S. 2002. Conclusion: Blending Methods and Building Theories in Social Movement Research, in *Methods of Social Movements Research*, edited by B. Klandermans and S. Staggenborg. Minneapolis: University of Minnesota Press, 314–349.

Koening-Archibugi, M. 2012. *Non-governmental Voters in Global Assemblies: Insights from the International Labour Organization*, Paper to the Annual

Convention of the International Studies Association, San Diego, USA, 31 March–4 April 2012.

Kornegay, F. 2006. *Pan-African Citizenship and Identity Formation in Southern Africa: An Overview of Problems, Prospects and Possibilities. Research Report 107*. Johannesburg: Centre for Policy Studies.

Korzeniewicz, R. P. and Smith, W. C. 2005. Transnational Civil Society Actors and Regional Governance in the Americas: Elite Projects and Collective Action from Below, in *Regionalism and Governance in the Americas: Continental Drift*, edited by M. Serrano and L. Fawcett. Basingstoke: Palgrave Macmillan, 135–157.

Krishna, S. 2009. *Globalization and Postcolonialism – Hegemony and Resistance in the Twenty-first Century*. Lanham, MD: Rowman & Littlefield.

Lamy, S. L. 2005. Contemporary Mainstream Approaches: Neo-realism and Neo-liberalism, in *The Globalization of World Politics: an Introduction to International Relations*, edited by J. Baylis and S. Smith. New York; Oxford: Oxford University Press, 205–224.

Landsberg, C. 2006. People to People Solidarity: Civil Society and Deep Integration in Southern Africa. *Transformation*, 61, 40–62.

———. 2012. The Southern African Development Community's Decision-making Architecture, in *Region-building in Southern Africa: Progress, Problems and Prospects*, edited by C. Saunders, G. A. Dzinesa and D. Nagar. London: Zed Books, 63–77.

Le Pere, G. and Tjönneland, E. N. 2005. *Occasional Paper No 50: Which Way SADC?* Johannesburg: IGD.

Leysens, A. 2001. Critical Theory, Robert Cox and Southern Africa, in *Theory, Change and Southern Africa's Future*, edited by P. Vale, L. A. Swatuk and B. Odén. Basingstoke: Palgrave, 219–236.

———. 2008. *The Critical Theory of Robert W. Cox. Fugitive or Guru?* Basingstoke: Palgrave.

Lorenz, U. 2011. *When "Not So Weak" Bargain with "Not So Strong". Transforming the Transformative Power of Europe in North-South Trade Negotiations?*, Paper at the KFG Workshop on Mapping Agency. Comparing Regionalisms in Africa, Centre for Area Studies, Freie Universität Berlin, 7–8 July 2011.

Lorenz-Carl, U. and Rempe, M. 2013. *Mapping Agency. Comparing Regionalisms in Africa*. Farnham: Ashgate.

Macdonald, L. 1994. Globalising Civil Society: Interpreting International NGOs in Central America. *Millennium: Journal of International Studies*, 23(2), 267–285.

Makanza, T. n.d. *Poverty Eradication and Sustainable Livelihoods: Making the Decent Work Agenda Work for the Region*. Gaborone: SATUCC.

Makombe, P. F. 2010. *Informal Cross Border Trade and SADC: The Search for Greater Recognition*. Johannesburg: OSISA. [Online]. Available at: http://www.trademarksa.org/sites/default/files/publications/Informal_Cross_Border_Trade_and_SADC_2011.pdf [accessed: 25 October 2012].

Mulaudzi, C. 2006. *Occasional Paper No 51: The Politics of Regionalism in Southern Africa*. Johannesburg: IGD.

Masango, R. and Haraldsson, M. 2010. *Across Southern African Borders with Informal Cross Border Traders*. Cape Town: EJN. [Online]. Available at: http://www.ejn.org.za/images/stories/Learning%20Centre/Trade%20Issues/1%20EJN%20Research/ICBT_Policy_Brief.pdf [accessed: 30 August 2012].

Matlosa, K. 2006. The Role of Political Parties in Regional Integration in the SADC Region, in *Monitoring Regional Integration in Southern Africa Yearbook. Vol. 6*, edited by A. Bösl, W. Breytenbach, T. Hartzenberg, C. McCarthy and K. Schade. Stellenbosch: Trade Law Centre for Southern Africa, 116–139.

Matlosa, K. and Lotshwao, K. 2010. *Political Integration and Democratisation in Southern Africa: Progress, Problems and Prospects*. Johannesburg: EISA.

McAdam, D., McCarthy, J. D. and Zald, M. N 1996. *Comparative Perspectives on Social Movements: Political Opportunities, Mobilizing Structures and Cultural Framings*. Cambridge: Cambridge University Press.

McCarthy, J. D. and Zald, M. N. 1977. Resource Mobilization and Social Movements: A Partial Theory. *American Journal of Sociology*, 82(6), 1212–1241.

Melucci, A. 1995. The Process of Collective Identity, in *Social Movements and Culture*, edited by H. Johnston and B. Klandermans. Minneapolis: University of Minnesota Press, 41–63.

Meyer, D. S. 2004. Protest and Political Opportunities. *Annual Review of Sociology*, 30, 125–145.

Michael, S. 2004. *Undermining Development: The Absence of Power among Local NGOs in Africa*. Oxford: James Currey.

Michelson, E. S. 2006. Clicking Toward Development: Understanding the Role of ICTs for Civil Society. *The Journal of Technology Studies*, 32(1), 53–63.

Mijere, N. J. N. 2009. *Informal Cross-Border Trade in the Southern African Development Community*. Addis Abeba: OSSREA.

MISA. 2007. *Access to Information: A Comparative Analysis of Zimbabwe's Media Laws with Other Jurisdictions*. Harare: MISA. [Online]. Available at: http://www.afdb.org/fileadmin/uploads/afdb/Documents/GenericDocuments/14.%20Zimbabwe%20Report_Chapter%2012.pdf [accessed: 26 January 2013].

Mittelman, J. 1999. Rethinking the 'New Regionalism' in the Context of Globalization, in *Globalism and the New Regionalism*, edited by B. Hettne, A. Inotai and O Sunkel. New York: Macmillan, 25–53.

Mittelman, J. H. and Chin, C.B.N. 2000. Conceptualizing Resistance to Globalization, in *The globalization syndrome: transformation and resistance*, edited by J. H. Mittelman. Princeton N.J.: Princeton University Press, 165–178.

Mulaudzi, C. 2006. *Occasional Paper No 51: The Politics of Regionalism in Southern Africa*. Johannesburg: IGD.

Muukkonen, M. 2009. Framing the Field: Civil Society and Related Concepts. *Nonprofit and Voluntary Sector Quarterly*, 4(38), 684–700.

Mwaniki, J. n.d. *The Impact of Informal Cross Border Trade on Regional Integration in SADC and Implications for Wealth Creation.* Unpublished paper. [Online]. Available at: http://www.sarpn.org/documents/d0001002/CFA-Mwaniki_CORN.pdf [accessed: 25 October 2012].

Nchito, W. S. and Tranberg Hansen, K. 2010. Passport, Please: The Cross-Border Traders Association in Zambia, in *Africa's Informal Workers*, edited by I. Lindell. London: Zed Books, 169–183.

Ndumbro, L. and Kiondo, A. 2007. *The Third Sector in Tanzania – Learning More about Civil Society Organisations, their Capabilities and Challenges*, Aga Khan Development Network. [Online]. Available at: http://www.akdn.org/publications/civil_society_tanzania_third_sector.pdf [accessed: 25 October 20112].

Neumann, I. 2003. A Region-Building Approach, in *Theories of New Regionalism. A Palgrave Reader*, edited by T. M. Shaw and F. Söderbaum. Basingstoke: Palgrave, 160–178.

Nwabueze, B. 2003. *Constitutional Democracy in Africa – Volume 2: Constitutionalism, Authoritarianism and Statism.* Ibadan: Spectrum Books Limited.

Nzewi, O. and Zakwe, L. 2009. *Democratising Regional Integration in Southern Africa: SADC National Committees as Platforms for Participatory Policymaking. Research Report 122.* Johannesburg: Centre for Policy Studies.

O'Brien, R. and Williams, M. 2010. *Global Political Economy.* Basingstoke: Palgrave.

Odén, B. 1999. New Regionalism in Southern Africa: Part of or Alternative to the Globalization of the World Economy?, in *Globalism and the New Regionalism*, edited by B. Hettne, A. Inotai and O. Sunkel. New York: Macmillan, 155–180.

———. 2001. Regionalization in Southern Africa, in *Regionalisation in a Globalizing World*, edited by M. Schultz, J. Öjendal and F. Söderbaum. London: Zed Books, 82–99.

Olivet, C. and Brennan, B. 2010. Regional Social Policy from Below: Reclaiming Regional Integration, in *World-Regional Social Policy and Global Governance*, edited by B. Deacon, M. C. Macovei, L. Van Langenhove and N. Yeates. London: Routledge, 63–81.

Oosthuizen, G. H. 2006. *The Southern African Development Community: The Organisation, Its Policies and Prospects.* Midrand: Institute for Global Dialogue.

Opoku-Mensah. P. 2008. The State of Civil Society in Sub-Saharan Africa, in *CIVICUS Global Survey of the State of Civil Society – Volume 2*, edited by V. F. Heinrich and L. Fioramonti. Bloomfield: Kumarian Press, 75–90.

Osei-Hwedie, B. Z. 2009. Interfaces Between Regional Civil Society Organisations and SADC Structures on Human Security, in *Furthering Southern African Regional Integration – Proceedings of the 2008 FOPRISA Annual Conference*, edited by J. M. Kaunda and F. Zizhou. Gaborone: BIDPA, 67–86.

Paasi, A. 2009. The Resurgence of the 'Region' and 'Regional Identity': Theoretical Perspectives and Empirical Observations on Regional Dynamics in Europe. *Review of International Studies*, 35, 121–146.

Paterson, B. 2009. Trasformismo at the World Trade Organization, in *Gramsci and Global Politics: Hegemony and Resistance*, edited by M. McNally and J. Schwarzmantel. London: Routledge, 42–57.

Perkin, E. and Court, J. 2005. *Networks and Policy Processes in International Development: A Literature Review*, Working Paper 252, London: ODI.

Peters, C. 2011. Is SADC Losing Track?, in *Monitoring Regional Integration in Southern Africa Yearbook. Vol. 10*, edited by Anton Bösl, A. du Pisani, G. Erasmus, T. Hartzenberg and R. Sandrey. Stellenbosch: Trade Law Centre for Southern Africa, 143–168.

Peters-Berries, C. 2010. *Regional Integration in Southern Africa – A Guidebook*. Bonn: InWEnt.

Pinfari, M. 2014. Transnational Civil Society and Regionalism in the Arab World: More of the Same?, in *Civil Society and World Regions*, edited by L. Fioramonti. Lanham, MD: Lexington, 161–176.

Pressend, M. 2010. *30 Years of the Southern African Development Community: What's to Celebrate?* [Online: The South African Civil Society Information Service]. Available at: http://sacsis.org.za/site/article/536.1 [accessed: 12 September 2012].

Radebe, Z. 2008. *State Sovereignty and Alternative Community in Southern Africa: Exploring the Zion Christian Church as the Building Block for Deeper Notions of Regional Community*, Master's Thesis, Grahamstown: Rhodes University. [Online]. Available at: http://eprints.ru.ac.za/1680/1/Radebe-MA-TR09–63.pdf [accessed: 25 October 2012].

Ranchod, K. 2007. State-Civil Society Relations in South Africa: Some Lessons from Engagement. *Policy: Issues & Actors*, 20(7), 1–23.

Reuter, M. 2007. *Networking a Region into Existence? Dynamics of Civil Society Regionalization in the Baltic Sea Area*. Berlin: Berliner wissenschafts-verlag.

Risse, T. 2002. Transnational Actors and World Politics, in *Handbook of International Relations*, edited by W. Carlsnaes et al. London: SAGE, 256–275.

———. 2010. *A Community of Europeans?* Ithaca and London: Cornell University Press.

Risse, T. and Sikkink, K. 1999. The Socialization of International Human Rights Norms, in *The Power of Human Rights – International Norms and Domestic Change*, edited by T. Risse and S. C. Ropp. Cambridge: Cambridge University Press, 1–38.

Ruiz, J. B. 2007. Strategic Regionalism and Regional Social Policy in the FTAA Process. *Global Social Policy*, 7(3), 294–315.

Rüland, J. 2014. Interregionalism and International Relations: Reanimating an Obsolescent Research Agenda?, in *Intersecting Interregionalism*, edited by F. Baert, T. Scaramagli and F. Söderbaum. Dordrecht: Springer, 24–46.

Saad-Filho, A. and Ayers, A. J. 2008. Production, Class, and Power in the Neoliberal Transition: A Critique of Coxian Eclecticism, in *Gramsci, Political Economy, and International Relations Theory: Modern Princes and Naked Emperors*, edited by A. J. Ayers. Basingstoke: Palgrave, 147–173.

Sachikonye, L. M. 2007. *Consolidating Democratic Governance in Southern Africa: Zimbabwe*, EISA Research Report No. 30. Johannesburg: EISA.

Saguier, M. 2007. The Hemispheric Social Alliance and the Free Trade Area of the Americas Process. *Globalizations*, 2(4), 251–265.

———. 2011. Transnational Labour Mobilization in the Americas, in *Civil Society and International Governance*, edited by Armstrong, V. Bello, J. Gilson and D. Spini. New York: Routledge, 181–197.

Santa Cruz, A. 2004. The Emergence of a Transnational Advocacy Network: International Election Monitoring in the Philippines, Chile, Nicaragua, and Mexico. *Portal*, 1(2), 1–31.

Saunders, C., Gwinyayi, A. D. and Nagar, D. 2012. *Region-building in Southern Africa: Progress, Problems and Prospects*. London: Zed Books.

Schmitz, H. P. 2012. *The Politics of Accountability: Rights-Based Approaches (RBA) and Poverty Eradication*, Paper Presented at the ISA Annual Conference, San Diego, 1–4 April.

Scholte, J. A. 1993. *International Relations of Social Change*. Buckingham: Open University Press.

———. 2000. Global Civil Society, in *The Political Economy of Globalization*, edited by N. Woods. New York: Palgrave, 173–201.

———. 2002. Civil Society and Governance, in *Towards a Global Polity*, edited by M. Ougaard and R. Higgott. London: Routledge, 145–165.

———. 2005. *Globalization – A Critical Introduction*. Basingstoke: Palgrave.

———. 2011. Conclusion, in *Building Global Democracy? Civil Society and Accountable Global Governance*, edited by J. A. Scholte. Cambridge: Cambridge University Press, 306–342.

———. 2012. More Inclusive Global Governance? The IMF and Civil Society in Africa. *Global Governance*, 18(2), 185–206.

Schoeman, M. 2001. The Limits of Regionalisation in Southern Africa, in *Security and Development in Southern Africa*, edited by N. Poku. London: Praeger.

Schulz, M. 2011. The Role of Civil Society in Regional Governance in the Middle East, in *Civil Society and International Governance*, edited by D. Armstrong, V. Bello, J. Gilson and D. Spini. New York: Routledge, 166–180.

Shaw, T. M., Söderbaum F., Nyang'oro, J. E. and Grant, J. A. 2003. The Future of New Regionalism in Africa: Regional Governance, Human Security/Development and Beyond, in The New Regionalism in Africa, edited by J. Grant and F. Söderbaum. Aldershot: Ashgate, 192–206.

Shilimela, R. 2008. *Overlapping Memberships of Regional Economic Arrangements and EPA Configurations in Southern Africa*, FOPRISA Report No. 5. Gaborone: Botswana Institute for Development Policy Analysis.

Shivji, I. G. 2007. *Silences in NGO Discourse: The Role and Future of NGOs in Africa*. Nairobi: Fahamu.

Sjögren, A. 1998. *Civil Society and Governance in Africa – an Outline of the Debates*, Working Paper n.1, Research Programme: Cities, Governance and Civil Society in Africa. Uppsala: NAI. [Online]. Available at: http://www.statsvet.su.se/publikationer/sjogren/anders_sjogren_csgov.pdf [accessed: 22 February 2010].

Slocum, N. and Van Langenhove, L. 2005. Identity and Regional Integration, in *Global Politics of Regionalism*, edited by M. Farrell, B. Hettne and L. Van Langenhove. London: Pluto Press, 137–151.

Söderbaum, F. 2004a. *The Political Economy of Regionalism: The Case of Southern Africa*, New York: Palgrave Macmillan.

———. 2004b. Modes of Regional Governance in Africa: Neo-liberalism, Sovereignty Boosting, and Shadow Networks. *Global Governance*, 10, 419–436.

———. 2005. Exploring the Links between Micro-Regionalism and Macro-Regionalism, in *Global Politics of Regionalism*, edited by M. Farrell, B. Hettne and L. Van Langenhove. London: Pluto Press, 87–103.

———. 2007. Regionalisation and Civil Society: The Case of Southern Africa. *New Political* Economy, 3(12), 319–337.

Söderbaum, F. and Shaw, T. M. (eds.) 2003. *Theories of New Regionalism: A Palgrave Reader*. New York: Palgrave.

Söderbaum, F. and Taylor, I. 2008. Considering Micro-regionalism in Africa in the Twenty-first Century, in *Afro-Regions: the Dynamics of Cross-border Micro-regionalism in Africa*, edited by F. Söderbaum and I. Taylor. Uppsala: the Nordic Africa Institute, 13–31.

Strange, S. 1994. *States and Markets*. London: Pinter.

Swilling, M., Russell, B., Sokolowski, S. W. and Salamon, L. M. 2004. South Africa, in Global Civil Society. Vol. 2 Dimensions of the Non-profit Sector, edited by Salamon et al. London: Kumarian Press. London: Kumarian Press, 110–125.

Tarrow, S. 1998. *Power in Movement: Social Movements and Contentious Politics*. Cambridge: Cambridge University Press.

Taylor, I. 2001. *Stuck in Middle GEAR. South Africa's Post-Apartheid Foreign Relations*. London: Praeger.

Taylor, V. and Whittier, N. 1995. Analytical Approaches to Social Movement Culture: The Culture of the Women's Movement, in *Social Movements and Culture*, edited by H. Johnston and B. Klandermans. Minneapolis: University of Minnesota Press, 163–187.

Thomson, A. 2010. *An Introduction to African Politics*. London: Routledge.

Thörn, Håkan. 2009. *Anti-Apartheid and the Emergence of a Global Civil Society*. Basingstoke: Palgrave.

Tickner, J. A. 2001. *Gendering World Politics: Issues and Approaches in the Post-Cold War Era*. New York: Columbia University Press.

TRALAC. 2012. *The Regional Indicative Strategic Development Plan: SADC's Trade-led Integration Agenda. How Is SADC Doing?* Stellenbosch: TRALAC.

Tsie, B. 2001. International Political Economy and Southern Africa, in *Theory, Change and Southern Africa's Future*, edited by P. Vale, L. A. Swatuk and B. Odén et al. Basingstoke: Palgrave, 110–147.

Tvedt, T. 2004. Development NGOs: Actors in a Global Civil Society or in a New International Social System?, in *Creating a Better World: Interpreting Global Civil Society*, edited by R. Taylor. Bloomfield: Kumarian Press, 133–146.

Vakil, A. C. 1997. Confronting the Classification Problem: Toward a Taxonomy of NGOs. *World Development*, 12(25), 2057–2070.

Vale, P. 2001. Dissenting Tale: Southern Africa's Search for Theory, in *Theory, Change and Southern Africa's Future*, edited by P. Vale, L. A. Swatuk and B. Odén. Basingstoke: Palgrave, 17–33.

———. 2003. *Security and Politics in South Africa: The Regional Dimension, Critical Security Studies*. Boulder: Lynne Rienner.

Van Langenhove, L. 2011. *Building Regions – The Regionalization of the World Order*. Farnham: Ashgate.

Van Rooy, A. 2004. *The Global Legitimacy Game: Civil Society, Globalization, and Protest*. Basingstoke: Palgrave.

Wallerstein, I. 2004a. The Dilemmas of Open Space: The Future of the WSF. *International Social Science Journal*, 56(4), 629–637.

———. 2004b. *World-systems Analysis: An Introduction*. Durham: Duke University Press.

Walz, K. 1988. The Origins of War in Neorealist Theory. *Journal of Interdisciplinary History*, 4(18), 615–628.

Wendt. A. 1994. Collective Identity Formation and the International State. *American Political Science Review*, 2(88), 384–396.

Williams, V. 2006. In Pursuit of Regional Citizenship and Identity: The Free Movement of Persons in the Southern Africa Development Community. *Policy: Issues & Actors*, 19(2), 1–15.

Withworth, S. 1994. *Feminist Theory and International Relations*. Basingstoke: Macmillan.

Woods, N. 2005. International political economy in an age of globalization, in *The Globalization of World Politics: An Introduction to International Relations*, edited by Baylis and S. Smith. Oxford: Oxford University Press, 325–347.

Yin, R. K. 2009. *Case Study Research: Design and Methods*. London: Sage.

Documents

ACA. 2009. *Strategic Plan 2009–2014*. Nairobi: ACA. [Online]. Available at: https://docs.google.com/file/d/0B1cqxeIPTijESX1VZ09qb21QT1k/edit [accessed: 14 September 2015].

ACA. 2011a. *Annual Report 2010/2011*. Nairobi: ACA. [Online]. Available at: https://docs.google.com/file/d/0B1cqxeIPTijEOTUwOUhpUXFHSEU/edit [accessed: 14 September 2015].

ACA. 2011b. *Summit Report*. HIV Capacity Building Partners Summit, 16th–18th March 2011, Hilton Hotel, Nairobi, Kenya. Nairobi: ACA.

ACA. 2013. *Annual Report 2012/2013*. Nairobi: ACA. [Online]. Available at: https://docs.google.com/file/d/0B1cqxeIPTijEN3Y5anluX0FtbHc/edit [accessed: 14 September 2015].

ACA. 2015. *About us*. Nairobi: ACA. [Online]. Available at: http://africacapacityalliance.org/about-us/#.VfbBbJfsTp0 [accessed: 14 September 2015].

ActionAid International. 2005. *Africa: Another Africa Is Imperative – Strategic Plan 2005–2010*. Johannesburg: ActionAid International. [Online]. Available at: http://www.docstoc.com/docs/5391870/ACTIONAID-INTERNATIONAL-AFRICA-ANOTHER-AFRICA-IS-IMPERATIVE-STRATEGIC-PLAN [accessed: 25 October 2012].

ARASA. 2007. *Aids and Rights Alliance for Southern Africa (ARASA) Strategic Plan 2008–2012*. Windhoek: ARASA. [Online]. Available at: http://www.docstoc.com/docs/124068589/pub-strategic-plan-May-2008 [assessed: 25 October 2012].

———. 2009. *HIV/AIDS & Human Rights in Southern Africa*. Windhoek: ARASA. [Online]. Available at: https://arasa.info/sites/default/files/ARASA%20Human%20Rights%20Report%202009.pdf [accessed: 25 October 2012].

———. 2010. *Annual Report 2010*. Windhoek: ARASA. [Online]. Available at: https://arasa.info/sites/default/files/ARASA_Annual_Report_2010.pdf [accessed: 25 October 2012].

———. 2012. *2011 Annual Partnership Forum: Biggest Convening of ARASA Partners Yet*. Cape Town: ARASA [Online]. Available at: http://www.arasa.info/index.php/about-us/news-letter/460-2011-annual-partnership-forum-biggest-convening-of-arasa-partners-yet [accessed: 31 July 2012].

———. n.d. *ARASA Declaration of Principles*. Windhoek: ARASA.

ARASA. 2013a. *ARASA Strategic Plan 2013–2017*. Windhoek: ARASA. [Online]. Available at: http://www.arasa.info/files/1914/0129/3072/ARASA_Strategic_Plan_1.pdf [accessed: 17 September 2015]

ARASA. 2013b. *ARASA Annual Report 2013*. Windhoek: ARASA. [Online]. Available at: http://www.arasa.info/files/9814/0059/9574/ARASA_2013_Annual_Report_Final_for_sharing.pdf [accessed: 17 September 2015].

ARASA. 2014. *2014 Annual Partnership Forum (APF)*. Windhoek: ARASA. [Online]. Available at: http://www.arasa.info/files/9614/0543/3825/ARASA_2014_APF_Report_Final_for_sharing.pdf [accessed: 17 September 2015].

ARASA. 2015. *About us*. Windhoek: ARASA. [Online]. Available at: http://www.arasa.info/about/ [accessed: 19 August 2015].

ASCCI. 2016. *About ASCCI*. Gaborone: ASCCI. [Online]. Available at: http://www.ascci.info/index.php/about-ascci [accessed: 8 February 2016].

———. 2012b. *ASCCI Strategic Plan 2012–2017*. Gaborone: ASCCI.

B2B Renewable Energies. 2012. *ASCCI Programmes*. Thessaloniki: B2B Renewable Energies. [Online]. Available at: http://www.renewablesb2b.com/ahk_south_africa/en/portal/geothermal/links/show/945196bed38dc40a [accessed: 13 July 2012].

CIDA. 2012. *Southern and Eastern Africa Regional Program*. Gatineau: CIDA [Online]. Available at: http://www.acdi-cida.gc.ca/acdi-cida/ACDI-CIDA.nsf/eng/NAD-41810435-K9Y [accessed: 30 July 2012].

COMESA. 2013. *About COMESA*. Lusaka: COMESA. [Online]. Available at: http://about.comesa.int/ [accessed: 30 January 2013].

DFID. 2006. *Southern Africa Regional Plan*. London: DFID.

Diakonia. 2011. *Programme on Social and Economic Justice (SEJ)*. Stockholm: Diakonia. [Online]. http://www.diakonia.se/SEJ [accessed: 20 November 2011].
EC. 2008. *SADC Regional Strategy Paper and Regional Indicative Programme 2008–2013*. Strasbourg: EC. [Online]. Available at: http://ec.europa.eu/development/icenter/repository/scanned_r7_rsp-2007-2013_en.pdf [accessed: 25 October 2012].
EJN. 2009. *Report of the Evaluation EJN Activities*. Cape Town: EJN. [Online]. Available at: http://www.norad.no/en/tools-and-publications/publications/publication?key=381003 [accessed: 30 August 2012].
———. 2010. *Memorandum of Understanding on General Cooperation – Pact of Regional Apex Organizations*. Cape Town: EJN.
———. 2011. *CSO Leaders Detained and Deported from SADC Summit*. Cape Town: EJN. [Online]. Available at: http://www.ejn.org.za/index.php/ejn-on-the-move/ejn-on-the-move-news/518-cso-leaders-detained-and-deported-from-sadc-summit [accessed: 25 October 2012].
———. 2016a. *Our Mission*. Cape Town: EJN. [Online]. Available at: http://www.ejn.org.za/index.php/our-mission [accessed: 8 February 2016].
———. 2016b. *Our Projects – SADC Advocacy*. Cape Town: EJN. [Online]. Available at: http://www.ejn.org.za/index.php/our-projects/sadc-advocacy [accessed: 8 February 2016].
Gender Links. 2009. *Roadmap to Equality. Lessons Learned in the Campaign for a SADC: Protocol on Gender and Development*. Johannesburg: Gender Links.
Gender Links. 2014. *Annual report 2013/2014*. Johannesburg: Gender Links. [Online]. Available at: http://www.genderlinks.org.za/page/annual-reports [accessed: 9 February 2016].
GIZ. 2011. *Afrika*. Bonn: GIZ. [Online]. Available at: http://www.gtz.de/en/weltweit/afrika/4569.htm [accessed: 21 February 2011].
———. 2012. *Identity*. Bonn: GIZ. [Online]. Available at: http://www.giz.de/en/aboutgiz/identity.html [accessed: 17 August 2012].
HIVOS. 2009. *Policy Update HIV/AIDS 2009*. The Hague: HIVOS.
Irish Aid. 2008. *Value for Money and Policy Review of Irish Aid Support to HIV/AIDS, 2000–2007*. Limerick: Irish Aid. [Online]. Available at: http://www.irishaid.gov.ie/Uploads/ValueforMoneyHIVFinalReportPrinter.pdf [accessed: 25 October 2012].
Kubatana Trust. 2013. *The Project*. Harare: Kubatana Trust. [Online]. Available at: http://www.kubatana.net/html/project/proj_cont.asp [accessed: 3 April 2013].
NAPSAR. 2011. *NAPSAR 2009–10 Annual Report*. Johannesburg: NAPSAR. [Online]. Available at: http://www.napsar.org/main/images/PDF/NAPSAR2009AnnualReport.pdf [accessed: 25 October 2012].
———. 2015. *Who We Are*. Johannesburg: NAPSAR. [Online]. Available at: http://napsar.org.za/index.php/about/who-are-we [accessed: 14 September 2015].

NCA. 2010. *Regional plan 2011–2015 Southern Africa*. Pretoria: NCA. [Online]. Available at: http://www.kirkensnodhjelp.no/PageFiles/837/Southern%20 Africa%20Regional%20Plan%20part%202011–2015.pdf [accessed: 25 October 2012].

Ncube, J. 2009. *The Role of the Private Sector and Civil Society in the Implementation of NEPAD, Presentation at the NEPAD Secretariat, AUC & UNECA Meeting*, Addis Abeba, Ethiopia, 28–29 May 2009. Gaborone: SADC.

Nkosi, Z. M. 2008. *Statement from the SADC Private Sector on Regional Economic Integration, Presentation Delivered at the SADC Summit, Sandton Convention Centre*, Johannesburg, South Africa, 17 August 2008. [Online]. Available at: http://www.sadc.int/english/regional-integration/tifi/sadc-free-trade-area/introduction/sadc-fta-launch/statement-by-the-private-sector/ [accessed: 25 October 2012].

OECD. 2005. *The Paris Declaration on Aid Effectiveness*. Paris: OECD.

OSISA. 2008. *Annual Report 2007*. Johannesburg: OSISA.

PAAR. 2011. *5th Southern Africa Social Forum in Maseru, Lesotho*. [Online]. Available at: http://www.alternative-regionalisms.org/?p=2232 [accessed: 24 May 2011].

Ramstedt, K. 2008. *SANASO Audit by More Stephens: Letter from Kristina Ramstedt, Embassy of Sweden to Maclean Sosono, Chairman of SANASO*, Lusaka, 25 November 2008. Lusaka: Embassy of Sweden.

RNE. 2009. *Review of Regional HIV/AIDS/SRHR Programme in Southern Africa Final Report, September 2009*. The Hague: RNE.

SACBTA. 2012. *Draft Strategic Work Plan for 2012–2014*. Gaborone: SACBTA.

SACU. 2013. About SACU. Windhoek: SACU. [Online]. Available at: http://www.sacu.int/about.php?id=395 [accessed: 16 March 2013].

SADC. 1992. *The SADC Treaty*. Gaborone: SADC. [Online]. Available at: http://www.sadc.int/index/browse/page/119 [accessed: 25 October 2012].

———. 1997. *Southern African Development Community (SADC) Code on HIV/AIDS and Employment*. Gaborone: SADC. [Online]. Available at: https://arasa.info/sites/default/files/SADC%20Code%20on%20HIV_AIDS%20and%20 Employment_sadc5.pdf [accessed: 25 October 2012].

———. 2001. *The Treaty of SADC – as Amended*. Gaborone: SADC. [Online]. Available at: http://www.sadc.int/english/key-documents/declaration-and-treaty-of-sadc/ [accessed: 25 October 2012].

———. 2003a. *Regional Indicative Strategic Development Plan*. Gaborone: SADC. [Online]. Available at: http://www.sadc.int/files/5412/9915/7922/SADC_RISDP_English.pdf [accessed: 25 October 2012.].

———. 2003b. *Charter of Fundamental Social Rights in SADC*. Gaborone: SADC. [Online]. Available at: http://www.sadc.int/index/browse/page/171 [accessed: 25 October 2013].

———. 2003c. *Declaration on HIV and AIDS*. Gaborone: SADC. [Online]. Available at: http://www.sadc.int/index/browse/page/175 [accessed: 25 October 2012].

———. 2008a. *Handbook SADC Free Trade Area*. Gaborone: SADC. [Online]. Available at: http://www.sadc.int/cms/uploads/SADC%20Free%20Trade%20Area%20Handbook%20-%20English.pdf [accessed: 25 October 2012].

———. 2008b. *SADC Declaration on Poverty Eradication and Sustainable Development*. Gaborone: SADC. [Online]. Available at: http://www.docstoc.com/docs/51615416/SADC-DECLARATION-ON [accessed: 25 October 2012].

———. 2008c. *The Approved Proposal for the Establishment of a SADC Regional Poverty Observatory (RPO)*. Gaborone: SADC. [Online]. Available at: http://www.ansaafrika.org/index.php?option=com_phocadownload&view=category&id=4:advocacy-lobbying-a-engagement&Itemid=99 [accessed: 25 October 2012].

———. 2008d. *SADC Protocol on Gender and Development*. Gaborone: SADC. [Online]. Available at: http://www.sadc.int/english/key-documents/protocols/protocol-on-gender-and-development/ [accessed: 25 October 2012].

———. 2009. *SADC HIV and AIDS Strategic Framework 2010–2015*. Gaborone: SADC.

———. 2011a. *Communiqué 2011 Meeting of SADC Ministers Responsible for Gender/Women's Affairs*. Gaborone: SADC. [Online]. Available at: http://www.sadc.int/index/browse/page/867 [accessed: 30 August 2012].

———. 2011b. *Meeting of SADC Ministers Responsible for Employment and Labour and Social Partners*. Gaborone: SADC.

———. 2011c. *SADC HIV and AIDS Work Plan 2012/13*. Gaborone: SADC. [Online]. Available at: http://www.hivsharespace.net/node/818 [accessed: 25 October 2012].

———. 2012a. *Record 1st Meeting of the RPO Steering Committee*, Gaborone, Botswana, 23–24 May 2012. Gaborone: SADC.

———. 2012b. *Background*. [Online]. Gaborone: SADC Available at: http://www.gov.mu/portal/sites/ncb/sadcsummit/intro.htm. [accessed: 18 July 2012].

———. 2013. *Activity Report of the SADC Secretariat 2011–2012*. Gaborone: SADC.

———. 2014. *Statement of the SADC Executive Secretary H.E. Dr Stergomena Tax at the Southern Africa Trust and Mail and Guardian Investing in Future and Drivers of Change Awards*. Gaborone: SADC. [Online]. Available at: http://www.sadc.int/files/5214/1456/4303/SADC_Executive_Secretary_Statement_at__Investing_in_Future_and_Drivers_of_Change_Awards_ceremony.pdf [accessed: 30 June 2015].

———. 2015a. *Health*. Gaborone: SADC. [Online]. Available at: http://www.sadc.int/themes/health/#HealthPolicyFramework [accessed: 21 May 2015]

———. 2015b. *Guidelines For Submitting Proposals to the SADC HIV and AIDS Special Fund (ROUND II)*. Gaborone: SADC. [Online]. Available at: http://www.sadc.int/opportunities/procurement/procurement-archive/guidelines-submitting-proposals-sadc-hiv-and-aids-special-fu/ [accessed: 20 May 2015].

———. 2015c. *HIV/AIDS*. Gaborone: SADC. [Online]. Available at: http://www.sadc.int/issues/hiv-aids/ [accessed: 21 May 2015].

———. 2016a. SADC Institutions. Gaborone: SADC. [Online]. Available at: http://www.sadc.int/about-sadc/sadc-institutions/ [accessed: 4 February 2016].

———. 2016b. SADC *Secretariat*. Gaborone: SADC. [Online]. Available at: http://www.sadc.int/sadc-secretariat/ [accessed: 4 February 2016].

SADC-CNGO. 2003. *Memorandum of Understanding on General Co-operation between SADC and SADC-CNGO*. Gaborone: SADC-CNGO.

———. 2005. *SADC-CNGO Strategic Plan 2005–2008*. Gaborone: SADC-CNGO.

———. 2009a. *SADC-CNGO Strategic Plan 2010–2014*. Gaborone: SADC-CNGO.

———. 2009b. *Civil Society Statement at the Occasion of 5th SADC Civil Society Forum held in Kinshasa, Democratic Republic of Congo*. Gaborone: SADC-CNGO. [Online]. Available at: http://www.sadccngo.org/forums.php?showid=15&lang=0&PHPSESSID=380augnek85vcfl6cti2u2sp51 [accessed: 13 July 2012].

———. 2010a. *Civil Statement on the Occasion of the 6th Southern Africa Civil Society Forum held on the 13–15th of August 2010*, Windhoek, Namibia. Gaborone: SADC-CNGO. [Online]. Available at: http://www.sadccngo.org/resources/report_stmnt.pdf [accessed: 13 July 2012].

———. 2010b. *Southern Africa Civil Society Poverty and Development Charter*. Gaborone: SADC-CNGO.

———. 2010c. *Report of the Post Forum Feedback Meeting for Civil Society in Namibia*, Safari Hotel, Windhoek Namibia, 5 October 2010. Gaborone: SADC-CNGO. [Online]. Available at: http://www.sadccngo.org/forums.php?showid=75&lang=0&PHPSESSID=5tqop74qpf1q9f1t4sasab8sg5 [accessed: 13 July 2012].

———. 2010d. *2010 Annual Report 1st January to 31st December*, Gaborone: SADC-CNGO.

———. 2010e. *Intensifying Regional Integration – Progress from 5th to 6th Southern Africa Civil Society Forum*. Gaborone: SADC-CNGO. [Online]. Available at: http://www.sadccngo.org/resources.php?showid=10&lang=0&PHPSESSID=r4dpmpdeb667sfbmcn0ff7r7r0 [accessed: 13 July 2012].

———. 2011a. *Outcome Report Southern Africa Regional Poverty Observatory Reference Group*, Gaborone, 8 April 2011. Gaborone: SADC-CNGO. [Online]. Available at: http://www.ansaafrika.org/index.php?option=com_phocadownload&view=category&id=4:advocacy-lobbying-a-engagement&Itemid=99 [accessed: 13 July 2012].

———. 2011b. *Civil Society Statement: 7th Southern Africa Civil Society Forum*. Gaborone: SADC-CNGO. [Online]. Available at: http://www.cso-effectiveness.org/IMG/pdf/7thcsfdeclaration_2_.pdf [accessed: 13 July 2012].

———. 2013. *9th Southern Africa Civil Society Forum*. Gaborone: SADC-CNGO. [Online]. Available at: http://www.sadccngo.org/wp-content/uploads/2013/09/9th-CSF-Statement-1489F56.pdf [accessed: 25 February 2015].

———. 2015. *11th Southern African Civil Society Forum Statement 11th-14th August 2015, Gaborone, Botswana*. Gaborone: SADC-CNGO. [Online]. Available at: http://www.southernafricatrust.org/wp-content/uploads/2015/09/11th-CSF-Declaration-August-2015.pdf [accessed 8 February 2016].

SADC PF. 2008. *Model Law on HIV in Southern Africa*. Windhoek: SADC-PF. [Online]. Available at: http://www.justice.gov.za/vg/hiv/docs/2008_Model-Law-on-HIV-in-Southern-Africa.pdf [accessed: 25 October 2012].

SAfAIDS. 2006. *SAfAIDS Annual Report July 2005–June 2006*. Harare: SAfAIDS. [Online]. Available at: http://www.safaids.net/files/2005%20%20 2006%20SAfAIDS_Annual_Report.pdf [accessed: 25 October 2012].

———. 2012. *SADC Best Practice Reports*. Harare: SAfAIDS [Online]. Available at: http://www.safaids.net/category/best-practices/sadc-best-practice-reports. [accessed: 3 August 2012].

———. 2015. *About Us*. Harare: SAfAIDS [Online]. Available at: http://www.safaids.net/content/about-us. [accessed 19 August 2015].

SAFCEI. 2009. *Religious Leaders for a Sustainable Future – Report, Declaration and Resolutions from the Summit of Religious Leaders of Southern Africa*, Midrand, South Africa, 10–12 February 2009. Cape Town: SAFCEI. [Online]. Available at: http://acen.anglicancommunion.org/resources/docs/Summit_2009A_Final_Report.pdf [accessed: 25 October 2012].

Salomao. 2008. *Statement by Tomaz Augusto Salomao, the Executive Secretary, SADC Secretariat, on the Occasion of the SADC FTA Launch, at Sandton Convention Center*, Johannesburg, South Africa, 17 August 2008. Gaborone: SADC [Online]. Available at: http://www.sadc.int/english/regional-integration/tifi/sadc-free-trade-area/introduction/sadc-fta-launch/speech-by-sadc-executive-secretary/ [accessed: 26 October 2012].

SANASO. 2011. *Organizational Background*. Windhoek: SANASO. [Online]. Available at: http://www.sanaso.org.zw/about.htm [accessed: 1 April 2011].

SAPSN. n.d.a. *SAPSN Introduction*. Lilongwe: SAPSN.

———. n.d.b. *Fact Sheet 4: Trade Injustices*. Lilongwe: SAPSN.

———. 2008. *The 2008 SADC People's Summit Report*. Lilongwe: SAPSN.

———. 2009. *SADC People's Summit Declaration (Kinshasa, the Democratic Republic of Congo, 6 September 2009)*. Lilongwe: SAPSN. [Online]. Available at: http://www.alternative-regionalisms.org/?p=3122. [accessed 22 April 2011].

———. 2010. *SADC People's Summit Declaration (Windhoek, Namibia, August 2010)*. Lilongwe: SAPSN. [Online]. Available at: http://www.alternative-regionalisms.org/?p=4521 [accessed: 30 August 2012].

———. 2014a. *SADC People's Summit*, 15–16 August 2014, The Bulawayo Communique. Lilongwe: SAPSN. [Online]. Available at: http://www.esaff.org/images/sadc_people_s_summit_2014___pdf.pdf [accessed: 25 February 2015].

———. 2014b. *SAPSN Rolls Mining Training and Meets SADC Secretariat*. Lilongwe: SAPSN. [Online]. Available at: http://sadcpeoplessummit.org/2014/05/21/sapsn-rolls-mining-training-and-meets-sadc-secretariat/#more-1548 [accessed: 25 February 2015].

———. 2014c. *More Positivity After SADC-SAPSN Secretariat's Meeting*. Lilongwe: SAPSN. [Online]. Available at: http://sadcpeoplessummit.org/2014/07/14/more-positivity-after-sadc-sapsn-secretariats-meeting [accessed: 25 February 2015].

SARDC. 2008. *Optimising Regional Integration in Southern Africa: Assessing Informal Cross Border Trade in SADC*. Harare: SARDC. [Online]. Available at: http://mail.sardc.net/books/ICBTReport/index.php [accessed: 30 August 2012].

———. 2012. *Regional Economic Development Institute*. Harare: SARDC. [Online]. Available at: http://www.sardc.net/redi/redi.asp?action=redi. [accessed: 9 May 2011].

———. 2016. *SARDC Profile*. [Online]. Available at: http://www.sardc.net/en/?page_id=10 [accessed 8 February 2016].

SASF. 2013. *About Us*. [Online]. Available at: http://southernafricasocialforum.wordpress.com/about-us/ [accessed: 30 January 2013].

SAT. 2008. *Strategic Framework 2008–2013*. Johannesburg: SAT. [Online]. Available at: http://www.satregional.org/sites/default/files/publications/strategic_framework_2008–2013.pdf [accessed: 1 August 2012].

———. 2011. *Annual Report April 2010 March 2011*. Johannesburg: SAT. [Online]. Available at: http://www.satregional.org/sites/default/files/publications/SAT%20annual%20Report%2020111%20%2027%20May%202011%20%284%29%20%282%29.pdf [accessed: 1 August 2012].

———. 2014a. *SAT Annual Report 2013/2014*. Johannesburg: SAT. [Online]. Available at: http://www.satregional.org/download/sat-annual-report-20132014-6/ [accessed: 15 September 2015].

———. 2014b. *SAT Strategy Overview 2014–2018*. Johannesburg: SAT. [Online]. Available at: http://www.satregional.org/download/sat-stratergy-overview-2014-2018-6/ [accessed 15 September 2015].

———. 2015. *About Us*. Johannesburg: SAT [Online]. Available at: http://www.satregional.org/about [accessed: 19 August 2015].

SATUCC. 2016. *About Us*. Gaborone: SATUCC [Online]. Available at: http://http://www.satucc.org/about-us-2/ [accessed: 8 February 2016].

———. 2015. *SADC Protocol on Employment & Labour*. Gaborone: SATUCC. [Online]. Available at: http://www.satucc.org/wp-content/uploads/2013/12/satucc-brochure-2015.pdf#page=1&zoom=auto,0,–14 [accessed: 8 February 2016].

———. n.d. *Southern African Trade Union Coordination Council: Engaging the New SADC*. Gaborone: SATUCC. [Online]. Available at: http://www.equinetafrica.org/bibl/docs/SOUtrade.pdf [accessed: 30 August 2012].

SEATINI. 2010. *Annual Report 2009*. Kampala: SEATINI. [Online]. Available at: http://www.seatiniuganda.org/downloads/Reports/SEATINI%20ANNUAL%20REPORT%202009.pdf [accessed: 25 October 2012].

———. 2011. *Annual Report 2010*. Kampala: SEATINI. [Online]. Available at: http://www.seatiniuganda.org/downloads/Reports/ANNUAL%20REPORT_2010_final_Aug24.pdf [accessed: 25 October 2012].

176 References

———. 2016. *About Us*. Harare: SEATINI. [Online]. Available at: http://www.seatini.org.zw/index.php/en/about-us [accessed: 8 February 2016].

SIDA. 2009. *Evaluation of the Swedish-Norwegian Regional HIV/AIDS Team for Africa*. Stockholm: SIDA. [Online]. Available at: http://sidapublications.citat.se/interface/stream/mabstream.asp?filetype=1&orderlistmainid=2817&printfileid=2817&filex=3769516387611 [accessed: 25 October 2012].

———. 2011. *Regional HIV&AIDS Team for Africa Support*. Stockholm: SIDA [Online]. Available at: http://www.swedenabroad.com/Page____103431.aspx. [accessed: 16 June 2011].

Singizi Consulting. 2012. *ARASA Programme Evaluation Final Draft*. Johannesburg: Singizi Consulting. [Online]. Available at: https://arasa.info/images/Reports2012/ARASA%20Evaluation%20Report%20final.pdf [accessed: 25 October 2012].

Southern Africa Trust. 2008. Workshop Report: Informal Cross-Border Trade in SADC. *Consultation and Planning Workshop*, 4–5 November 2008, Crossroad Hotel, Lilongwe, Malawi. Johannesburg: Southern Africa Trust. [Online]. Available at: http://www.southernafricatrust.org/docs/ICBT%20Workshop%20Report.pdf [accessed: 25 October 2012].

———. 2009. *Knowing Civil Society Organisations*. Johannesburg: Southern Africa Trust. [Online]. Available at: http://www.southernafricatrust.org/docs/Knowing_CSOs_September2009.pdf [accessed: 25 October 2012].

———. 2010a. *Making Regional Integration Work for the Poor: Interim Impact Assessment of the Southern Africa Trust 2006–2009*. Johannesburg: Southern Africa Trust. [Online]. Available at: http://www.southernafricatrust.org/docs/SATrust_ME_Report_200091028.pdf [accessed: 25 October 2012].

———. 2010b. *The Changing Landscape of Donor and Civil Society Relations in Southern Africa*. Johannesburg: Southern Africa Trust.

———. 2011. *Programme Areas*. Johannesburg: Southern Africa Trust. [Online]. Available at: http://www.southernafricatrust.org/programmes.html [accessed: 18 April 2011].

———. 2014a. Making sure the poor get SADC'S attention. *Mail & Guardian 20 June 2014*. [Online]. Available at: http://mg.co.za/article/2014-06-20-making-sure-the-poor-get-sadcs-attention [accessed: 9 February 2016].

———. 2014b. *Draft Proposal on SADC Mechanisms for Engagement with Non-State Actors*. Johannesburg: Southern Africa Trust. [Online]. Available at: http://www.southernafricatrust.org/docs/SADC-Mechanism-of-Engagement-with-NSAs.pdf [accessed: 30 June 2015].

SPSF. 2010. *Report 2008–2009. Presented to the SADC Meeting of Ministers of Labour and Employment and Social Partners*, Maputo, Mozambique, 26–30 April 2010. Johannesburg: SEG. [Online]. Available at: http://www.busa.org.za/docs/SEG%20report%20to%20ELS%202010.pdf [accessed: 30 August 2012].

———. 2016. *About Us*. Gaborone: SPSF. [Online]. Available at: http://www.spsf.org.bw/content/id/10/About-US/ [accessed: 4 February 2016].

Trades Centre. 2010. *Annual Narrative Report for the Period January–December 2009*. Harare: Trades Centre. [Online]. Available at: http://www.tradescentre.org.zw/index.php?option=com_docman&Itemid=5 [accessed: 25 October 2012].

———. 2011. *Annual Narrative Report for the Period January–December 2010*. Harare: Trades Centre. [Online]. Available at: http://www.tradescentre.org.zw/index.php?option=com_docman&Itemid=5 [accessed: 25 October2012].

———. 2012. *About Us*. Harare: Trades Center. [Online]. Available at: http://www.tradescentre.org.zw/index.php?option=com_content&view=article&id=2&Itemid=31 [accessed: 26 October 2012].

Trust Africa. 2008. *Survey of African Regional Organizations – Civil Society Organizations, Research Institutes and Think Tanks*. Dakar: Trust Africa.

Interviews and E-mail Communication

Ally, Russell, Ford Foundation, Johannesburg, 26 November 2009.

Anamela, Anne, Irish Aid, Pretoria, 26 November 2009.

Ashley, Brian, Alternative Information and Development Center (AIDC), Cape Town, 17 December 2009.

Barnard, David, Southern African NGO Network (SANGONET), Johannesburg, 26 November 2008.

Bond, Patrick, University of KwaZulu-Natal, Durban, 14 December 2008.

Castel-Branco, Carlos, Instituto de Estudos Sociais e Económicos (IESE), Maputo, 24 November 2008.

Chidaushe, Moreblessings, Norwegian Church Aid (NCA), Pretoria, 29 November 2009.

Chigwada, Tendai, Trades Centre, Harare, 3 December 2009.

Chiriga, Jennifer, African Forum and Network on Debt and Development (AFRODAD), Harare, 2 December 2009.

Chiriga, Jennifer and Mhlongo, Themba, Southern Africa Trust, Johannesburg, 2 December 2008.

Clayton, Michaela, AIDS and Rights Alliance for Southern Africa (ARASA), Oslo, 16 February 2012.

Clayton, Michaela, AIDS and Rights Alliance for Southern Africa (ARASA), e-mail communication, 3 August 2012.

Damon, Malcolm, Economic Justice Network (EJN), Cape Town, 15 December 2009.

Damon, Malcolm, Economic Justice Network (EJN), e-mail communication, 20 August 2012.

Davies, Geoff, South African Faith Communities' Environment Institute (SAFCEI), Cape Town, 17 December 2009.

Du Toit, Colleen and Sibanda, Mbizo, Charities Aid Foundation (CAF) Southern Africa, Johannesburg, 2 December 2008.

Gabriel, Neville, Southern Africa Trust, Johannesburg, 2 December 2008.
Guileugue, Fredson and Nemete, Nando, Mozambican Debt Group (MDG), Maputo, 20 November 2008.
Habib Adam, University of Johannesburg, Johannesburg, 25 November 2009.
Horn, Pat, Street Net International, Durban, 16 December 2008.
Horn, Pat, Street Net International, e-mail communication, 24 July 2012.
Kasiamhuru, Patricia, Southern African People's Solidarity Network (SAPSN), Harare, 2 December 2009.
Katchima, Moses, Southern Africa Trade Union Coordination Council (SATUCC), Gaborone, 8 December 2008.
Kujinga, Tapiwanashe, Pan African Treatment Access Movement (PATAM), Harare, 1 December 2009.
Law, Stephen, Environmental Monitoring Group (EMG), Cape Town, 15 December 2009.
Le Pere, Garth, Institute for Global Dialogue (IGD), Johannesburg, 27 November 2008.
Lewis, Jennifer, Gender Links, Johannesburg, 27 November 2009.
Machemedze, Rangarirai, Southern and Eastern African Trade Information and Negotiations Institute (SEATINI), Harare, 4 December 2009.
Matanga, Dakarayi, Zimbabwe Coalition on Debt and Development (ZIMCODD), Harare, 4 December 2009.
Mathiba-Madibela, Magdeline, SADC Gender Unit, Gaborone, 11 December 2009.
Mati, Jacob, CIVICUS World Alliance for Citizen Participation, Johannesburg, 27 November 2009.
McKinley, Dale, Anti-Privatization Forum (APF), Johannesburg, 1 December 2008.
Moiana, Alcino, Conselho Cristão de Moçambique (CCM), Maputo, 17 November 2008.
Msosa, Alan, International Institute for Democracy and Electoral Assistance (IDEA) Regional Office in Pretoria (formerly Southern African Network of AIDS Service Organizations (SANASO)), Stockholm, 23 April 2012.
Muchabaiwa, Bob, SADC Council of Non-Governmental Organizations (SADC-CNGO), Gaborone, 7 December 2009.
Muchena, Deprose, Open Society Initiative for Southern Africa (OSISA), Johannesburg, 1 December 2008.
Mussagy, Sabera, G20, Maputo, 21 November 2008.
Mxotshwa, Jefter, Network of African People Living with HIV for Southern African region (NAPSAR), telephone interview, 27 March 2012.
Ncube, Janah, SADC Directorate for Policy, Planning and Resource Mobilization, Gaborone, 8 December 2008.
Ngwane, Trevor, Soweto Electricity Crisis Committee (SECC), Johannesburg, 3 December 2008.
Nhampossa, Diamantino, União Nacional de Camponeses (UNAC), Maputo, 18 November 2008.
Osei-Hwedie, Bertha, University of Botswana, Gaborone, 5 December 2008.

Page, Sara, Southern Africa HIV and AIDS Information Dissemination Service (SAfAIDS), Pretoria, 24 November 2009.
Palmquist, Sofia, European Commission (EC)-Botswana, Gaborone, 10 December 2009.
Peak, Bobby, Groundwork, Durban, 12 December 2008.
Pressand, Michelle, Institute for Global Dialogue (IGD), Johannesburg, 27 November 2008.
Sandström, Anita, Southern African Aids Trust (SAT), Johannesburg, 27 November 2009.
Sandström, Anita and Thiis, Öyvind, SIDA/NORAD Regional HIV/AIDS Team, Lusaka, 7 March 2005.
Sanje, Doreen, SADC HIV/AIDS Unit, Gaborone, 11 December 2009.
Schoeman, Ria, Embassy of Sweden, Pretoria, 19 November 2009.
Simane, Mosweu, Botswana Council of Non-Governmental Organisations (BOCONGO), Gaborone, 5 December 2008.
Sucá, Amade, Action Aid, Maputo, 24 November 2008.
Tali, Maria, SADC Secretariat, e-mail communication, 22 May 2012.
Taylor, Tristen, Earthlife Africa, Johannesburg, 3 December 2008.
Tolmay, Susan, Gender Links, Johannesburg, 27 November 2009.
Uthui, Joao, Forum Nacional das Organizações Não Governamentais em Moçambique (TEIA), Maputo, 24 November 2008.
Vale, Peter, Rhodes University, Grahamstown, 2 March 2005.
Valy, Bayano, Southern African Research and Development Centre (SARDC), Maputo office, Maputo, 21 November 2008.
Van Tol, Isabelle, Royal Netherland Embassy (RNE), Pretoria, 30 November 2009.
Vilakazi, Simon, Economic Justice Network (EJN), Cape Town, 15 December 2009.
Yates, Samantha, Department for International Development (DFID), Pretoria, 4 December 2009.

Index

Action Aid (AA) 79, 82, 83
Africa: regionalism 1–4
Africa Capacity Alliance (ACA) 99, 108, 110–11, 115, 118, 121, 124–5, 135, 139, 142–3, 145–7
African Council of Aids Service Organizations (AFRICASO) 121
African Forum and network on Debt and Development (AFRODAD) 177
African Social Forum (ASF) 97
African Union (AU) 1, 80, 122
AIDS *see* HIV/AIDS
AIDS and Rights Alliance for Southern Africa (ARASA) 3, 100, 103, 107–9, 111–12, 115–22, 124–6, 134–7, 140, 145–6, 148
Alternative Information and Development Centre (AIDC) 84, 137
Alternatives to Neo-liberalism in Southern Africa (ANSA) 73, 75, 82, 135
Angola 17, 46, 67, 74, 137
Anti-Privatization Forum (APF) 84
Asia-Europe Meeting (ASEM) 59*n*11
Asian NGO Coalition for Agrarian Reform and Rural Development (ANGOC) 9–10
Association of SACD Chambers of Commerce and Industry (ASCCI) 61, 69, 73, 76–7, 82, 87, 89, 92, 133–5, 147
Association of South-East Asian Nations (ASEAN) 1, 7, 42*n*7, 129–31
authoritarian state 14, 20; Africa 43–5; Tanzania 46

Botswana 17, 46, 56, 61–3, 67, 92, 99
Botswana Council of Non-Governmental Organisations (BOCONGO) 92
Briefcase NGO (BRINGO) 15
Business Unity South Africa (BUSA) 61

Canadian International Development Agency (CIDA) 114
capitalism 8, 24, 29–30, 34; neo-liberal project 50–3; problem-solving civil society 53–6; SADC and neo-liberal regional governance 56–8; scientific 51; social structure 10, 20, 23, 28–9, 31–2, 35, 41*n*4, 50–8, 61, 78, 106, 133
Caribbean Community (CARICOM) 7, 130
Charities Aid Foundation (CAF) 177
Charter of Fundamental Social Rights 65, 72, 90
Christian: identity 94–5, 140, 141, 144, 145
civil society: Africa 59*n*9; concept 14–15; problem-solving 53–6; social structure and agency 23–8; state domination of 45–6
Civil Society Forum 67, 71–2, 74, 85, 87, 88, 90, 92, 132, 136, 141
civil society organizations (CSOs) 20, 21*n*1, 58*n*1; categorization of 135, 152*n*1–2; commercial CSOs 134–5; construction of regional target groups 38, 88–91, 122–4; critical reformist CSOs 134, 135–6, 137, 149; dependency on regional donor funds 34–5; donor influence on CSO agenda 35–6; exclusion in the SADC 73–7, 110–13; future research areas 150–2; global governance 31; HIV/AIDS 18–19; identity-making and 38–41, 42*n*8, 91–5, 124–6, 140–1; inclusion in SADC 69–72, 106–10; issue-framing and 36–8, 86–91, 119–24, 138–40; key regional CSO (RCSO) 61–3; Mozambique 54–5; partner CSOs 41*n*6, 99, 134, 135, 136;partnerships with 49–50; political elite 44; political opportunity approach 41*n*3; problematizing regionalization 144–50; regionalism 2–4, 6–17; regionalism of 141–4; regional issue-framing 36–7; relations between 36, 83–6, 119, 134–8; relations between donors and 34–6,

41n5, 78–83, 113–19, 132–4; relations between RIGOs and 31–4, 129–32; relations between SADC and 63–77, 100–13; research techniques 19–20; resistance CSOs 134, 135, 136, 137, 149 state domination of 45–6; structure and agency 23–9; Tanzania 54–5, 59n9; weakness of regional 152n13
civil society regionalization: case selection 17–19; dynamics of 129–41; identity-making 140–1; issue-framing 138–40; methodology 17–20; problematizing 144–50; relations between CSOs 134–8; relations between donors and CSOs 132–4; relations between RIGOs and CSOs 129–32; research techniques 19–20; studying 4–11
collective identity 16, 27, 39–40
Common Market for Eastern and Southern Africa (COMESA) 58n1, 70, 76, 89, 99, 108, 131, 135, 139, 143
community-based organization (CBO) 63, 67, 85, 146, 147
Congress of South African Trade Unions (COSATU) 137, 148
Conselho Crostão de Moçambique (CCM) 94, 137
Council of Ministers (COM) 46, 74
Cox, Robert 24
Coxian Critical Theory (CCT) 24–5, 27–30, 41n4, 43
Cross-Border Traders Association (CBTA) 63, 76, 135–6
CSO Directory (Tanzania) 19, 21n1
CSOs *see* civil society organizations (CSOs)

democracy 32, 43, 45, 48, 50, 87, 101, 126n1, 146, 152
Democratic Republic of Congo (DRC) 17, 46, 58n1, 67–8, 71
Department for International Development (DFID) 107, 113–15

East African Community (EAC) 1–2, 7, 70, 99, 108, 131
Eastern-Southern Africa (ESA) 70, 71, 121
Economic Community of West African States (ECOWAS) 1, 9
Economic Justice Network (EJN) 63, 67–8, 74, 76–7, 80, 83, 85, 86–7, 89, 91, 94–5, 131, 135–7, 141, 143–6

Economic Partnership Agreement (EPA) 57, 63, 70–1, 86, 88, 91, 94, 130–1, 135–6, 138, 143
Employment and Labour Sector (ELS) 72, 75
environmental governance 7, 131
European Commission (EC) 80, 82
European Union (EU) 1, 3, 42n7, 57

faith-based organizations (FBOs) 3, 15, 124
Fellowship of Christian Councils in Southern Africa (FOCCISA) 63
Food, Agriculture and Natural Resources (FANR) 47
Forum Nacional das Organizações Não Governamentais em Moçambique (TEIA) 71
framing 27; *see also* issue-framing
free trade area (FTA) 64, 70, 130
Free Trade Area of the Americas (FTAA) 7, 131

Gender Links 106, 109, 122–4
Gender Protocol Alliance 106, 109, 120, 143
German Agency for International Cooperation (GIZ) 80, 82
German Technical Cooperation (GTZ) 80
global social movements (GSMs) 31
governance: concept 14
governmental NGO (GONGO) 15
Growth, Employment and Redistribution Programme (GEAR) 51

Hemispheric Social Alliance (HSA) 9
Hettne, Björn 6, 12, 43
HIV/AIDS 37, 48, 57–8, 61, 72, 74, 80; categorization of regional CSOs 135; CSOs and identity-making 124–6, 140–1; CSOs and issue-framing 119–24, 138–40; CSOs dealing with 2, 17–20, 21n1, 141–5, 148–50; dependency on donor funds 114–17; donor influence on CSO agenda 117–19; donors and CSOs 113–19, 132–4; key RCSOs 99–100; regionalization in sector 99–126; relations between CSOs 119, 134–8; RIGOs and CSOs 129–32; SADC and CSOs 100–13
Humanist Institute for Development Cooperation (HIVOS) 114
human rights (HR) 3, 20, 21n1, 150–1; advocacy-based 117–18; African

Charter on Human Rights 123;
CSOs doing 119–20; HIV/AIDS
100, 102–4, 107–9, 111–12,
122, 130–1, 134; protection
and promotion 123–6; SADC-
CNGO 92, 136; SADC promoting
principles of 126*n*1; SADC
Treaty and RISDP 64, 90; SAPSN
movement 91; standards 32, 41*n*5;
Tanzania 46; Zimbabwe 140,
153*n*25

identity-making 9–11, 19–20, 26–9; CSOs
and 38–41, 91–5, 124–6, 140–1;
HIV/AIDS sector 124–6; national
identity 39, 40, 42*n*7–8, 44–5; non-
territorial 39–40, 42*n*8, 94–5, 144;
positive regional 124–6; regional
11, 91, 119, 124–6, 140, 142–4,
146, 151; supra-national identity
39, 40; trade sector 91–5
informal cross-border trade (ICBT) 53,
63–6, 72, 75–6, 87, 94, 130–1,
135–6, 143, 150
information and communications
technology (ICT) 150–1
infrastructure and services (IS) 47
Integrated Committee of Ministers (ICM)
65, 95*n*3
Inter-American Regional Labour
Organization (ORIT) 9
Inter-governmental organization (IGO) 20,
25, 29–31, 32–3, 36
International Conference on Poverty and
Development 66
international financial institution (IFI) 51
International Labour Organization (ILO)
42*n*8
International Labour Resource and
Information Group (ILRIG) 84
International Monetary Fund (IMF) 51, 93
international non-governmental
organization (INGO) 30, 79–83,
114, 146, 150
International Organization for Migration
(IOM) 53, 102
international relations (IR) 1, 9, 12, 24–5,
48
Irish Aid 105, 113–16, 118–19
issue-framing 9–10, 19, 20, 27–8; CSOs
and 36–8, 86–91, 119–24, 138–40;
HIV/AIDS sector 119–24; regional
10, 86–7, 120–2, 124, 133, 138–40,
148, 151; trade sector 86–91

Kubatana (Zimbabwe) 19, 21*n*1, 151,
153*n*25

lesbian, gay, bisexual and transgender
(LGBT) 112
Lesotho 17, 45–6, 58*n*1, 67, 109

Madagascar 17, 46, 58*n*1
Mail & Guardian (newspaper) 66, 151
Malawi 17, 46, 58*n*1, 63, 99
Malawi Economic Justice Network
(MEJN) 63
Maputo Corridor Logistics Initiative
(MCLI) 57
Maputo Development Corridor (MDC) 56
Mauritius 17, 46, 58*n*1, 66, 71
memorandum of understanding (MoU)
69–71, 73, 77, 85, 96*n*7
Mercado Común del Sur (MERCOSUR) 7,
129, 131
Mozambican Debt Group (MDG) 137, 147
Mozambique 17, 45, 46, 52, 54–6, 62, 67,
71, 94, 99, 109, 137–8, 147

Namibia 17, 46–7, 49, 58*n*1, 67–8, 94, 100
Namibian Economy Policy Research Unit
(NEPRU) 3
national identity 39, 40, 42*n*7–8, 44–5
nationalism 29, 39–40, 146–7
neoliberalism 20, 28, 30–1, 53, 56, 75, 93,
98*n*95; discourse 10, 25, 32, 34, 50,
53, 112, 133, 149; ideology 30–1,
38, 54
neo-patrimonialism 44
neo-realism 4, 24
network: definition 16
Network of African People Living with
HIV for Southern African Region
(NAPSAR) 100, 105, 107–8,
111–12, 118, 120, 122, 124–5, 132,
134–7, 140–1, 143–6
New Partnership for Africa's Development
(NEPAD) 2
New Regionalism Approach (NRA) 5–6
NGOs *see* non-governmental organizations
(NGOs)
non-governmental development
organization (NGDO) 15
non-governmental organizations (NGOs)
3, 6, 7, 9, 14–19, 30, 33–5, 37, 40,
58; civil society 50, 53–5, 59*n*9;
international NGO (INGO) 30,
79–83, 114, 146, 150; market-
oriented 35, 41*n*6; regional 61, 86,

99, 106, 113–14, 119, 139–40, 142, 148–51; Regional African AIDS NGOs (RAANGO) 99, 105, 107, 109, 113–14, 119; relationship with national governments 45–6; SADC Council of (SADC-CNGO) 3, 62–3, 66–9, 71–5, 82, 85–90, 92, 116, 132, 135–6, 139, 145–8
non-territorial identity 39–40, 42n8, 94–5, 144
North American Free Trade Agreement (NAFTA) 1, 3
Norwegian Church Aid (NCA) 79–80, 82, 94, 134

Open Society Initiative for Southern Africa (OSISA) 79, 82–3, 118, 134
Organisation for African Unity (OAU) 1–2
Organisation of the Islamic Conference (OIC) 59n11

Paris Declaration on Aid Effectiveness 78, 96n30
Partnership Forum (PF) 105–7, 109, 111–14, 132, 143, 149
people living with HIV and AIDS (PLWHA) 100, 108, 111–12, 114, 122, 125
People's Agenda for Alternative Regionalisms (PAAR) 98n97
People's Declaration 67, 77, 89
People's Summit 67, 77, 81, 83–5, 89–91, 93–4, 132–7, 140–1, 146–7
Policy Planning and Resource Mobilization Directorate 68
political opportunity approach 41n3
Poverty Reduction Strategy Paper (PRSP) 51
PRODDER database 19, 21n1
Protocol on Gender and Development 72, 102, 123, 143
Protocol on the Facilitation of the Movement of Persons 90
public-private partnership (PPP) 58

RCSO *see* regional civil society organization (RCSO)
Regional African AIDS NGOs (RAANGO) 99, 105, 107, 109, 113–14, 119
Regional AIDS Training Network (RATN) 99
Regional Audit of Sexual and Reproductive Rights 123

regional civil society organization (RCSO) 13, 16–17, 68, 73, 78, 86, 88, 92, 106–8, 119, 134, 138, 145, 149, 152; donor funds 78, 81; HIV/AIDS sector 120–2; key RCSOs in HIV/AIDS sector 99–100; key RCSOs in trade sector 61–3; relations between 83–6, 119; relations between donors and 78–83, 113–19; relations between SADC and 63–77; SADC-affiliated 80
Regional Economic Community (REC) 1, 110
regional governance: civil society organizations (CSOs) 2, 6–11, 13, 17–18, 32–4, 129–34, 136; frameworks 24, 29–30; market-oriented 82; neo-liberal 14, 20, 50–3, 56–8, 61, 64, 66, 69–70, 83, 111, 113, 139; SADC 100, 106, 109–11, 141, 144, 149; sovereignty-boosting 14, 20, 43, 46–50, 61, 113, 136, 149–50
regional identity 13, 27, 39, 42n7, 44–5, 94, 124, 129, 133, 139
Regional Indicative Strategic Development Plan (RISDP) 48, 56, 64–5, 67, 70, 72, 87, 90, 95n3, 101, 123
regional inter-governmental organization (RIGO) 1–2, 6–8, 10–11, 13, 17–19, 28, 99, 108–9, 113, 115, 133, 149, 150, 152; CSO inclusion and exclusion in 33–4; focal point creation for CSOs 33; issue preferences 32–3; relations between CSOs and 31–4, 129–32; SADC 46
regional issue-framing 10, 86–7, 120–2, 124, 133, 138–40, 148, 151
regional networks 8–10, 142–3, 147–8, 150; ARASA 145, 146; ASCCI 61, 133; coalition-building 132; consolidation 87, 91; donor money 81; EJN 63, 91, 145, 146; NAPSAR 100, 145, 146; ACA 139, 145, 146; SADC-CNGO 116, 132–3, 139, 145, 146; SANASO 116; SAPSN 91, 133, 141; SATUCC 62, 91, 133, 139, 145, 146
Regional Poverty Observatory (RPO) 66–8, 71, 77, 132, 135, 149
Regional Poverty Reduction Framework (RPRF) 66–8, 71

Regional Stakeholder Forum 68
regionalism: African 1–4; concept 11–14
regionalization: studying 4–11
resource mobilization theory (RMT) 26
Rights-Based Approach (RBA) 32, 41n5, 82, 124
RIGO *see* regional inter-governmental organization (RIGO)
Rosa Luxemburg Foundation 83
Royal Netherland Embassy (RNE) 105, 114–15, 118

SACD *see* Southern African Development Community (SADC)
SADC Council of Non-Governmental Organizations (SADC-CNGO) 3, 62–3, 66–9, 71–5, 82, 85–90, 92, 116, 132, 135–6, 139, 145–8
SADC Employers Group (SEG) 61
SADC Private Sector Forum (SPSF) 61–2, 69, 72, 76, 77, 89, 131, 135, 137, 139
SADC Today (newsletter) 70, 151
Seychelles 17, 46, 58n1
shaming 38, 90–1, 122–4
Social and Human Development and Special Programmes (SHDSP) 47–8
social movement: concept 16
social movement organization (SMO) 16
social structure 21n4; capitalist 10, 20, 23, 28, 29, 31, 32, 35, 41n4, 50–8, 61, 78, 106, 133; civil society 4, 8; deeper 8, 10; statist 10, 20, 23, 28, 29, 31, 34, 39, 41n4, 43–50, 61, 106, 133, 147–8; statist-capitalist world order 28–31; study of civil society 23–8
Solidarity for Asian People's Advocacy (SAPA) 9
South Africa 17, 19–20, 21n1, 43, 45–6, 49, 52–3, 56–7, 58n1, 59n9, 61, 67, 71–2, 74, 79, 84, 93, 99–100, 106, 109, 113–14, 117, 120, 137–8, 148
South African Cross-Border Traders Association (SACBTA) 63, 65, 76, 93, 135–6
South African Faith Communities' Environment Institute (SAFCEI) 95
Southern Africa Civil Society Reference Group 68
Southern Africa HIV and AIDS Information Dissemination Service (SAfAIDS) 3, 99, 106, 108–11, 115–16, 118, 120–5, 135, 137, 143
Southern African Aids Trust (SAT) 99, 105, 107–11, 115–16, 118–22, 124–6, 132, 135, 137, 139, 142–3
Southern African Cross Border Traders Association (SACBTA) 63, 65–6, 76, 93, 135, 136
Southern African Customs Union (SACU) 47, 58n1
Southern African Development Community (SADC) 2–4, 17, 19–20, 44–6, 52, 79, 80, 83–91, 94, 99, 140–4; Civil Society Forum 67, 71–2, 74, 85, 87, 88, 90, 92, 132, 136, 141; Common Poverty Matrix 68; CSO exclusion in 73–7, 110–13; CSO inclusion in 69–72, 106–10; Decent Work Programme 72; focal point creation 67–8, 104–6; HIV/AIDS Business Plan 108, 110, 114, 122; issue preferences 64–7, 100–4; neo-liberal regional governance and 56–8; Protocol on Gender and Development 72, 102, 123, 143; relations between, and CSOs 63–77, 100–13; RISDP 87; SADC-Parliamentary Forum (SADC-PF) 103, 109; SADC Secretariat 69–71, 74, 76–7, 80, 82, 87–8, 90, 101, 104–9, 112, 136, 142–3, 149–50; sovereignty-boosting regional governance and 46–50, 136, 149–50; Treaty 47–9, 47–50, 64–5, 72, 101, 123
Southern African Migration Project 45
Southern African Network of AIDS Service Organizations (SANASO) 116–17, 133, 149
Southern African NGO Network (SANGONET) 177
Southern African People's Solidarity Network (SAPSN) 3, 9, 63, 67, 73, 77, 81, 83–6, 89–94, 116, 123, 131–3, 135–7, 140–1, 144, 146–7
Southern African Power Pool (SAPP) 70
Southern African Research and Development Centre (SARDC) 53, 62, 64–5, 70, 73, 76, 82–4, 87, 135, 139, 151
Southern African Social Forum (SASF) 93, 94, 97, 98, 137

Southern Africa Trade Union Coordination Council (SATUCC) 62–3, 65, 67–9, 72–5, 81, 85–7, 89, 91, 93, 95, 132–3, 135–7, 139–41, 143–6, 148
Southern Africa Trust 3, 66, 71, 74, 77–83, 117, 145, 151
Southern and Eastern African Trade Information and Negotiations Institute (SEATINI) 3, 62, 70–1, 83–4, 89, 92, 131–2, 135, 139, 142–3
staging of culture 40
statism 8, 11, 28–9, 31, 39, 112; authoritarian state 43–5; SADC and sovereignty-boosting regional governance 46–50; social structure 10, 20, 23, 28–9, 31, 34, 39, 41n4, 43–50, 61, 106, 133, 147–8; Southern Africa 129–31, 150; state domination of civil society 45–6
statist-capitalist world order 20, 28–31, 32, 35, 43, 134, 139
Structural Adjustment Programme (SAP) 51, 53
Supra-national identity 39, 40
Swaziland 17, 46, 56, 58n1, 94, 99, 109
Swedish International Development Co-operation Agency (SIDA) 105–6, 111, 113–14, 116–18

Tanzania 17, 19–20, 21n1, 46, 51, 54–5, 59n9, 99, 138
Technical Advisory Committee (TAC) 105, 107–9, 112, 149

Trade, Industry, Finance, Mining and Investment (TIFI) 47, 65, 69, 74, 76, 106, 149
Trade and Development Studies Centre (Trades Centre) 62, 70, 82–4, 87, 89, 131, 132, 135, 142–3
Trade Protocol 47, 65, 72, 75–6, 90
trade sector: CSO relations 83–6; donors and CSOs 78–83; identity-making 91–5, 140–1; issue-framing 86–91, 138–40; key RCSOs 61–3; SADC and CSOs 63–77
Trade Union Confederation of the Americas (TUCA) 9
transnational advocacy network (TAN) 8, 26–7
Treatment Action Campaign (TAC) 117
Trust Africa 2, 78, 118, 145

UNAIDS's Regional Support Team 105

World Bank 51
world order: power structures in 41n1; statist-capitalist 20, 28–31, 32, 35, 43, 134, 139
World Social Forum (WSF) 97n95, 150
World Trade Organization (WTO) 41–2n6, 93

Zambia 17, 46, 58n1, 63, 67, 99, 113
Zimbabwe 2, 17, 19–20, 21n1, 45–6, 52, 55–6, 58n1, 62, 67, 84, 93–4, 99, 120, 140, 147, 151, 153n25
Zimbabwe Coalition on Debt and Development (ZIMCODD) 84, 9